Benjamin Franklin's Religion

Stephen J. Vicchio, Ph.D.

Minneapolis

Minneapolis
FIRST EDITION October 2023

Benjamin Franklin's Religion
Copyright © 2023 by Stephen J. Vicchio.
All rights reserved.

No part of this book may be used or reproduced in any manner whatsoever without written permission except in the case of brief quotations used in critical articles and reviews. For information, write to Calumet Editions, 6800 France Avenue South, Suite 370, Edina, MN 55435.

Printed in the United States of America

10 9 8 7 6 5 4 3 2 1

ISBN: 978-1-962834-01-8

Cover and interior design: Gary Lindberg

Contents

Introduction 1
Chapter One: Franklin's Early Religious Life 7
Chapter Two: Franklin on God and Jesus 29
Chapter Three: Franklin and the Bible 51
Chapter Four: Franklin on Deism and Other Intellectual Sources 73
Chapter Five: Franklin on Religious Freedom,
 Toleration, and Church and State. 95
Chapter Six: Franklin on Morality, Ethics and Virtue 117
Chapter Seven: Franklin on Other Religions. 141
Chapter Eight: Franklin on Immigration. 161
Chapter Nine: Franklin on Religious Tests 181
Chapter Ten: Major Conclusions of this Study
 on Franklin's Religion 201
Appendix A: Franklin on Happiness and Survival After Death 227
Appendix B: Foreign Words and Expressions. 235
Appendix C: Franklin as an Inventor and Scientist. 241
Appendix D: Franklin and George Whitefield 251
Appendix E: More on Deism and Franklin 257
Appendix F: Franklin and Diplomacy. 267
Appendix G: Franklin on Separation of Church and State 277
Appendix H: Franklin and Abortion 285
Bibliography. 293
Endnotes. 307
Index 339
Acknowledgments 349
About the Author 350

Also by Stephen J. Vicchio

Muslim Slaves in the Chesapeake: 1634 to 1865
Mala'ika: Angels in Islam
Evil and Suffering in the Bible
The Akedah or Sacrifice of Isaac
Evil in World Religions
Alexander Hamilton's Religion
The Idea of the Demonic
From Vladimir to Vladimir
Estevanico: The First Black Man in America

Benjamin Franklin's Religion

Introduction

Benjamin Franklin (1706–1790) was, without much argument, the first great statesman of the United States of America. He was also among the most knowledgeable leaders and more diverse in his interests and skills than any other American on record. He was a printer, publisher, husband, brother, father, son, inventor, businessman, friend, scientist, and diplomat in a time when such varied skills were highly regarded.

The overall purpose of this study is to describe and discuss the major religious beliefs and opinions of Franklin from his time on Milk Street in Boston to his death in Philadelphia on April 17, 1790. After this short introduction, this study will proceed in ten chapters, followed by four appendices and an extensive bibliography.

In the first chapter, we will set out three goals. First, to give a short summary of the life of Franklin. Second, to provide an analysis of what the statesman had to say about religion in his major works. And third, we will explore what we know of his earliest religious beliefs.

The two goals in Chapter Two are to identify and discuss what Franklin believed and wrote about God, as well as what he believed and wrote about Jesus Christ. As we shall see in this chapter, Franklin was a clear believer in monotheism but did not hold the theological view that Jesus Christ is, or was, God.

The third chapter of this study on Franklin's religion has four separate goals. First, to examine many very general comments about the Bible made by the statesman. Second, to examine several instances of peculiar circumstances where the Bible came up as a topic for discussion. Third, we will identify and discuss many of the Old Testament passages that he directly quotes from, or made some other uses of, these texts.

And finally, in Chapter Three, we will identify and discuss many of the New Testament passages that the statesman either makes some use of or quotes directly from them. Next to George Washington, Abraham Lincoln and Ronald Reagan, Benjamin Franklin knew the New Testament better than any other American leader.

The major focus of Chapter Four shall be the identification and discussion of the chief intellectual sources in the life of Franklin. More specifically, this chapter will be devoted to deism, Enlightenment ideas, the First Great Awakening, and other intellectual origins, including Franklin's father, Josiah's child-rearing practices, as well as the books that he borrowed and/or read over the course of his life.

We will find four distinct goals as the subject matter of Chapter Five. First, to identify and discuss what Franklin believed about the ideas of religious freedom in America. Second, to identify and discuss what the Founding documents of the United States contain and otherwise imply about those religious freedoms. Third, we will explore what many of the other Founding Fathers said and wrote about religious toleration. Among those Founding Fathers, we shall include the views of Washington, Jefferson, Madison, George Mason, Patrick Henry and many others.

In the sixth chapter of this study on Franklin's religion, the overall goal will be to explore his ethical and moral views, particularly what he said or wrote about the idea of virtue. In this chapter, we will begin with some eighteenth-century background information about ethics. This will be followed by his treatment of virtue.

Section three of Chapter Six will be devoted to what might be called "Benjamin Franklin's Moral Method" regarding his understanding of virtue. And in the final section of Chapter Six, we shall examine what he had to say and write about particular moral issues, such as slavery, religious intolerance, religious dissenters and a host of other moral questions, in both America and abroad.

The focus of Chapter Seven shall be on what Franklin has had to say and had written on religions other than his own childhood Presbyterianism and Congregationalism. More specifically, we will describe and discuss in separate sections of Chapter Seven what he thought about Judaism, Roman Catholicism, and the religion of Islam.

As we shall see in this chapter, he made several comments on each of these three traditions.

The subject matter of Chapter Eight of this study is an exploration of what the statesman had to say and write about the phenomenon of immigration in his colony/state of Pennsylvania, as well as the federal government. We will begin by analyzing and discussing the history of immigration in the United States. In the second section, we shall explore the phenomenon of immigration in America during Franklin's life, that is, 1706 until 1790.

In the third section of Chapter Eight, we will examine the process of immigration in America in the modern period, from 1920 until the present. And in the fourth and final section of Chapter Eight, we shall turn our attention more specifically to what Franklin believed, said and wrote about the idea of immigration in both Pennsylvania and in the United States. We shall see that he had a particular antipathy to German nationals who entered the city of Philadelphia. We will also see at the end of the chapter that the two most important sources for understanding the statesman's views on immigration were his 1751 essay, "Observations on the Increase of Mankind," and a May 9, 1753, letter to his friend, British statesman Peter Collinson.

The focus of Chapter Nine will be on the idea of religious tests in Great Britain and the United States, mostly in the seventeenth and eighteenth centuries. We will begin the chapter with an analysis of religious test laws that existed in Scotland and England from 1567 until the late seventeenth century. This will be followed in Chapter Nine by an introduction and an analysis of the only place in the US Constitution, besides its First Amendment, where the idea of religion appears. In Article VI, Clause 3 of the US Constitution, there is a provision that was put forth at the Constitutional Convention by South Carolina delegate Charles Pinckney that the following wording should be included:

> ...but no religious Test shall ever be required as a Qualification to any Office or public Trust under the United States.

As we shall see, Pinckney's proposal was passed in a vote at the convention, with the only dissent coming from Connecticut delegate Roger Sherman. We shall also see that among the delegates who voted for Pinckney's proposal was Franklin.

In the third section of Chapter Nine, we shall explore the views of ten other American Founding Fathers who commented upon the idea of religious tests in America. In that discussion, we find that men like John Adams, Thomas Jefferson and Alexander Hamilton, as well as many other early American Founding Fathers, decidedly favored Pinckney's point of view.

The fourth and final section of Chapter Nine shall be reserved for a discussion of what Franklin believed, said, and wrote about the phenomenon of religious tests in America. Not surprisingly, as we shall see, he was fully and consistently against the idea of any religious test for holding public office in America.

Finally, Chapter Ten is a summation chapter in which we shall review the major conclusions made in this study of Benjamin Franklin's religion. This will be followed by four appendices and an extensive bibliography.

Benjamin Franklin's birthplace.
Courtesy of the New York Public Library.

Chapter One
Franklin's Early Religious Life

In the words of Benjamin Franklin, "A republic if you can keep it."
—Nancy Pelosi, US Speaker of the House

I agree with Benjamin Franklin, who said no people should never give up their privacy or their freedoms in a promise of security.
—Martin O'Malley, Presidential Candidate
(This is, in fact, a misquote of Benjamin Franklin.)

He that lies down with dogs, shall rise up with fleas.
—Benjamin Franklin, Poor Richard's Almanack (1731)

Introduction

In this opening chapter on Benjamin Franklin's religion, we have the following goals: First, to give a short general summary of the life of Franklin. Second, we will examine the written works of Franklin that pertain to his views on religion. Third, we will concentrate on what can be garnered about Franklin's early religious life, primarily with his strict Calvinist parents.

We will dedicate separate sections regarding these three goals—the short biography, religion in Franklin's written works, and the idea of religion and religious practices in Franklin's early life. We move then to the short biography.

A Short Biography of Benjamin Franklin

In this short biography, we will divide the life of Franklin into the following nine parts:

Birth, early life and schooling
Apprentice printer
Escape to Philadelphia
The Pennsylvania Gazette
Early civic works
Inventions
The political scene
The new nation
Death and influence

Franklin was born on January 17, 1706, in Boston into what at the time was known as the Massachusetts Bay Colony. His birth was at his father's home at 17 Milk Street, across the street from the Old Meeting House in Southwest Boston. Franklin's father, Josiah Franklin, was a soap and candle maker. His mother was a stay-at-home wife and mother. Her name was Abiah Folger Franklin. Benjamin was Josiah's tenth son and seventeenth child, the youngest. By all early accounts, it seems that Josiah wished Benjamin to study for the clergy at the newly formed Harvard Divinity School, but the son did not follow the father's advice.

Benjamin, who did not have a middle name like Washington, Lincoln, and Grant, was sent to Boston's South Grammar School at the age of eight. Later on, the school was renamed the Boston Latin School that began one year before Harvard in April of 1635. In this sense, Boston Latin is most likely the oldest school, public or private, in America.[1]

With limited funds, Josiah could only afford the high fees at Boston Latin for a year, so Benjamin was only at the school for two semesters. The following year, in 1715, he matriculated at George Brownell's English School. The school curriculum concentrated on writing, grammar and penmanship, as well as arithmetic. In that year, Franklin showed great talent in writing and little interest in arithmetic. From very early on, he loved books and the process of reading. He would borrow books from friends and his father's private library and would save every penny he had to buy more books.[2]

These two years at the Boston Latin School and George Brownell's English School are the sum total of the formal education of Franklin. In his autobiography, he observed, "At ten years old, I was taken home to assist my father in his business."[3] So after the age of ten, Franklin had no more formal schooling.

When Franklin was fifteen, his older brother James started *The New-England Courant*, the first newspaper in Boston. In the earliest years, the paper featured news from abroad, articles, opinion pieces mostly written by James' friends, advertisements and the schedules of ships. When Benjamin Franklin was sixteen, he became a vegetarian mostly because he did not like to eat anything that had been alive but also partly because he wanted to save money to buy books.

The younger Franklin brother also wanted to write for the newspaper, but he knew that James would not let him. After all, Benjamin was only an "apprentice" to his older brother. So secretly, Benjamin began writing letters to the editor at night and signed them with the name of a fictitious widow named Silence Dogood. Most of the Dogood letters were filled with advice and criticisms of the government, the church and the society around her.[4]

Among the topics of Dogood's letters are advice for doing good, the rights of women, funeral elegies, freedom of speech, religious hypocrisy, the relief of poor widows, relief for spinsters, the vice of drunkenness, and what Franklin referred to as "Moonlighting," that is, sleeping with another man's wife while the moon is out.[5]

Many of the letters written by Silence Dogood offended the readers of *The Courant*, so much so that one letter from June of 1722 offended members of the Massachusetts Assembly, and James Franklin was jailed for two weeks for contempt. While James was in jail, the younger brother ran the newspaper. When James found out the true identity of Dogood, however, the two brothers had a falling out, and Benjamin decided to go to Philadelphia. Before Philadelphia, however, Franklin went to New York City to find employment but was unsuccessful in that endeavor.

Franklin left New York with no money in his pocket and proceeded to Philadelphia, where he found work in the printing establishment of Samuel Keimer. His lodges were at the house of John Read. In fact, Franklin eventually married Read's daughter, Deborah, in 1730 at the age of twenty-four.[6]

At the time, Philadelphia was a city of twenty-five thousand people. The city was founded in 1682, and by 1720, had become an important trading center in the New World, as well as a major port. The original immigrants to Philadelphia were Quakers, shortly followed by Mennonites, Jews, Catholics and Anglicans. This required a good amount of religious toleration in what came to be called the "City of Brotherly Love."[7]

Franklin met Sir William Keith, the governor of Pennsylvania, through connections with Deborah's family. Franklin and Keith became fast friends. Keith offered Franklin government work if he was willing to set up his own printing business. So, with a letter from the governor, Franklin returned to Boston to ask his father for a loan, but Josiah declined to give his youngest son the money he sought to begin his business.

Reportedly, Josiah thought that Benjamin was still too immature to run his own business but promised him that he would support his tenth and youngest son when he became a more seasoned and mature man.[8]

In 1728, Franklin fathered a son named William, but the mother of the boy was unknown. He also began his printing shop in Philadelphia in 1730, the year of Benjamin and Deborah's marriage. In 1729, Franklin bought a Philadelphia newspaper called *The Pennsylvania Gazette*.[9] It soon became one of the most successful publications in the colonies. Many of the articles were written by Franklin, most often using aliases.

Franklin's *Gazette* began publication in 1728 and was the second newspaper published in the Pennsylvania Colony. Franklin and his partner, Hugh Meredith, bought the paper and shortened its name from *The Universal Instructor in All the Arts and Sciences and the Pennsylvania Gazette* to simply *The Pennsylvania Gazette*.

Beginning in the late 1720s and early 1730s, we begin to see the aspect of Franklin's character that was devoted to the public good. In fact, he organized an organization known as the Junto Club, a young working man's group dedicated to self and civic improvement in Philadelphia in the mid-eighteenth century. The Junto Club was also known as the "Leather Apron Club," a reference to the attire of skilled workers of the day. The purpose of the club was to "debate questions of morals, politics, and natural philosophy, and to exchange knowledge of business affairs."[10]

Franklin also joined the Masons during this time. He was initiated into Masonry in 1731, most likely at the February meeting of the organization. According to Old Masonic and Franklin family traditions, the cornerstone of the statehouse in Philadelphia, later to be called "Independence Hall," was laid by Franklin and the Brethren of the Saint John's Masons Lodge. Franklin lived to be eighty-five years old and was a Mason for sixty of those years, which gave him many social and civic connections over the years.[11]

Franklin also helped launch many other civic projects, such as paving Philadelphia's roads as well as cleaning and lighting those streets. Franklin also participated in the opening of what was called the "Library Company" in 1731, the nation's first subscription library, by pooling resources and often buying books from Britain.[12]

The library, which is still in existence, is now known as the "Library Company of Philadelphia" or the LCP. The current collection contains approximately half a million books and seventy thousand other items, including twenty-two hundred that once belonged to Franklin. The LCP has also accumulated one of the most significant collections of historically valuable manuscripts and printed material in the United States.

In 1743, Franklin participated in the formation of the American Philosophical Society, the first learned society in America. The first proposal of this learned society was made by botanist John Bartram in 1739, but it was Franklin who issued a public call to found a society of "Virtuosi or ingenious men."[13] The organization is now known as the "American Philosophical Society," or APS. It is considered the first great "learned society" in America. It was founded on the principle of "Promoting useful knowledge."

In his "Proposals Relating to the Education of the Youth of Pennsylvania" in 1749, Franklin set out plans to open an academy, and he and his supporters did just that in 1751. Forty years later, in 1791, the academy changed its name to the University of Pennsylvania.

In 1751, Franklin also formed a group to establish the Pennsylvania Hospital.[14] The hospital established by Franklin and his partner,

Dr. Thomas Bond, established the nation's first hospital. The library, the Philosophical Society and the hospital are all still in existence today.

In 1752, Franklin assisted in forming the Philadelphia Contribution for Insurance Against Loss of Fire, an organization that insured property loss due to fire. This also led to the formation of the first fire department in Pennsylvania. After a visit to his native city of Boston, Franklin discovered that it was better prepared to fight fires than those in his adopted city of Philadelphia. So, in 1752, he established the first fire department in Pennsylvania.[15]

Franklin's printing business was thriving in the 1730s and 1740s. He also set up what amounted to franchise printing shops in other cities.[16] By 1750, Franklin retired from business and began to concentrate on his scientific experiments and inventions. Among these inventions were a more efficient stove, his well-known experiments on electricity, and the invention of swim fins for the hands to aid one in swimming.

During the 1740s and early 1750s, Franklin worked on several inventions and scientific projects. Among these were:

1. The invention of the Franklin Stove (1742)
2. The invention of the lightning rod (1753)
3. Swim fins for the hands
4. The urinary catheter (1752)
5. Bifocals
6. The glass armonica

In the late 1750s, Franklin became much more active in American and European politics. He traveled to England in 1757 to represent Pennsylvania in its fight against the descendants of the Penn family over who should represent the colony. Later, while still in England, he represented the interests of the colonies of Georgia, New Jersey and Massachusetts. Later, his son William would become the governor of New Jersey.

In 1765, Franklin was surprised by the American reaction to the Stamp Act, also known as the "Duties in American Colonies Act of 1765."[17] The act imposed a tax on the British colonies in America and required that many printed materials in the colonies be produced on stamped paper produced in London. This printed material included all legal documents, magazines, playing cards and newspapers. Another provision of the act was that the tax had to be paid in British currency.

The purpose of the Stamp Act was to pay for the British military stationed in North America after the French and Indian Wars. Most Americans were against the idea of the Stamp Act and thought that London should pay the expenses and salaries of all British officers. The Stamp Act was passed in Parliament a year after the 1764 Sugar Act, which was a modification of the Sugar and Molasses Act of 1733 that was about to expire in 1764.[18] The act required merchants in the American colonies to pay a sixpence per gallon tax on sugar and molasses.

Seeing the general American attitude toward the Stamp Act began to leave Franklin with the belief that perhaps America should break free from British control. For the remainder of his life, he worked diligently to bring about that goal of independence, mostly in the circles of American politics.

Franklin was elected to the Second Continental Congress and worked on a committee of five to draft what would be called "The Declaration of Independence." Although much of the language of the Declaration was supplied by Thomas Jefferson, many of the incorporated ideas were those of Franklin. He signed the Declaration in July 1776 and then promptly sailed to France to serve as the American ambassador there.[19] He was now a man in his late seventies. His wife Deborah had died several years before, in 1774, and Franklin tended to flirt with the ladies. His popularity in France undoubtedly was one of the reasons for the passing of the Treaty of Paris in 1783 after the Americans won the Revolutionary War.[20]

Franklin first went to France as the American Ambassador, sailing from Philadelphia on October 26, 1776. He worked for nine years in diplomatic matters, including the Treaty of Amity and Commerce, the Treaty of the Alliance on February 6, 1778, and the signing of the Treaty of Paris in 1783 and returning to the United States in 1785.

Back in America, Franklin became the president of the Supreme Executive Council of Pennsylvania. He also served as a delegate to the Constitutional Convention, as indicated earlier in this chapter. One of his final official acts was writing an anti-slavery treatise published in 1789.[21] This was one of the many pieces of evidence that established the moral and the ethical views of Franklin, about which we will say more in Chapter Six.

Franklin died on April 17, 1790, at the age of eighty-four. More than twenty thousand people attended his funeral. Franklin is interred at the Christ Church Burial Grounds in Philadelphia, an important colonial-era Church of England or Episcopal cemetery. He is buried alongside his wife, Deborah, and near the graves of his parents, Josiah and Abiah Franklin.[22]

We move now to the second section of the first chapter of this study on Franklin's religion, in which we will discuss several of his published writings where he references issues and questions related to religion and ethics.

Religion in Franklin's Written Works

Franklin made several observations about religion and ethics in his many published works. Among these published works were the following:

1. "Articles of Belief and Acts of Religion" (1726)
2. The Silence Dogood letters (1727)
3. "Doctrine to be Preached" (1731)
4. "On the Providence of God in the Government of the World" (1732)
5. "Self-Denial is Not the Essence of Virtue" (1735)
6. "Dialogue Between Two Presbyterians" (1735)
7. A letter to Madame Brillon (1781)
8. Benjamin Franklin's autobiography (1778 to 1790)

In this second section of Chapter One, we shall see that in each of the above-listed works, Franklin made many observations about religion and ethics. We will discuss these works one at a time and then make some general conclusions about them at the end of the section.

In the 1728 "Articles of Belief and Acts of Religion," Franklin sketched out in two parts many of his basic beliefs, such as the claim in part one that "I believe there is one Supreme most perfect Being,

Author and Father of the Gods Themselves."[23] In addressing this God, he adds, "O Creator, o Father, I believe that Thou art Good and that Thou art pleased with the pleasure of Thy children."[24]

There is also some indication that at least early on, Franklin was a believer in polytheism, for he thought there were many gods and that each one was in charge of its own stellar system. He goes on in the same essay to indicate that he also assents to the beliefs about God that He is powerful, wise and that He does not like "Treachery and Deceit, Malice, Revenge and intemperance, and every other hurtful Vice," while also being a "Lover of Justice, Sincerity, of Friendship, Benevolence, and every Virtue."[25]

In the second part of the "Articles of Belief," Franklin goes on to quote directly from John Milton's "Hymn to the Creator" from *Paradise Lost*.[26] He admired the poem that mostly speaks of God's control and ordering of nature. In the second part of the "Articles of Belief," he extolls what he sees as the most important virtues, including duty, thanksgiving, liberality, ambition, friendship, and many others.[27]

In the letters by Silence Dogood published in *The New-England Courant*, Franklin also made several observations about religion and ethics. In letter number nine, for example, he discusses at some length the idea of religious hypocrisy, including his view that "A little Religion, and a little Honesty, goes a great way in Courts."[28]

In the same letter, Franklin raises the question of, "Whether a Commonwealth suffers more by hypocritical Pretenders to Religion, or by the openly Profane?"[29] His conclusion is that the former, and not the latter, is true.

In letter seven, Franklin returned to religious themes where Silence Dogood spoke of funeral elegies and how poetry sometimes "ruins both Church and State." In the fourteenth and final Dogood letter, he addressed the question of religious zealotry. He related, "All I would endeavour to shew is, That an indiscreet Zeal for spreading an Opinion, hurts the Cause of the Zealot."[30]

In 1731, Franklin wrote an outline for an essay entitled "Doctrine to be Preached." This outline is a mere ten lines, but it is markedly different from some observations he made three years before in the "Articles." In the outline, Franklin appears to have abandoned the idea that God is only the Sovereign of our solar system, and there are other gods as well in other systems of the universe.[31] In the "Doctrine to be Preached," Franklin appears to have given up his earlier polytheistic view that there are many gods, each in charge of its own stellar system, in favor of the more traditional monotheism.

In the outline, Franklin suggests that God is omnipotent, omnibenevolent and omniscient, or All-Powerful, All-Good and All-Knowing. He also posits a belief in the immortality of the soul in the outline, something not found in the "Articles."

A year later, in 1732, in an article entitled, "On the Providence of God in the Government of the World," Franklin argues for the notion that God sometimes intervenes in the affairs of human beings, such as in his answering prayers as well as performing miracles in the world of men and women. In this same essay, he also affirms that God is "the Creator of the Universe and that He is infinitely Wise, Powerful, and Good."[32]

Two years later, in 1734, he completed an article he called "Self-Denial is Not the Essence of Virtue." In this essay, he directly contradicted the claim made in the "Articles" that men will be rewarded by God according to their virtues after death.[33]

Two months later, *The Gazette* published an article that many scholars attribute to Franklin entitled "Dialogue Between Two Presbyterians." In this piece, the character known only as "S" appears to hold the views of Franklin at the time. In that "Dialogue," among other things, he concludes, "Morality or Virtue is the End, and Faith is only a Means to obtain that End."[34]

Another important aspect of the "Dialogue" is that "S" quotes Holy Scripture nine times in the text supporting the theological positions he takes in the article. This is a significant change from earlier when he observed, "Revelation had indeed no weight with me."

Now fifty years later and much closer to the end of his life, in a letter to Madame Brillon dated April 10, 1781, one of his many French lady friends, Franklin again sketches out five principal metaphysical beliefs that are essential to religion in general. These five beliefs were the following:

1. That there is a God who made the world and who governs it by Providence.
2. That God should be adored and served.
3. That the best service to God is doing Good to Men.
4. That the human soul is immortal.
5. That in the future Life if not in the present one, vice will be punished, and virtue will be rewarded.

These five points made eight and a half years before his death give us a window into Franklin's final theological beliefs. The letter to Madame Brillon brings together in one place a general summary of the final views of Franklin's understanding of God, survival after death and ethics.

Finally, another place to find Franklin's beliefs concerning God, ethics and immortality is the printer-ambassador's autobiography, where he made many observations and opinions about these issues.

The Autobiography of Benjamin Franklin is the traditional title of his observations on his life, though he himself called the work a *Memoir*.[35] The statesman's account of his life is divided into five parts, reflecting the different periods at which he wrote them. The initial part is an introduction that he appears to have written at the end of his life after the other four parts had been completed.

The second part of the autobiography was written in 1771 when the statesman was sixty-five years old. It is addressed to his son William, who by that time was the governor of New Jersey. This part deals with Franklin's childhood, incidents in the lives of his parents, his fondness for reading, and his service as an apprentice to his brother James.

Part three of his autobiography was written in the early 1780s while he was in France. This volume was published in 1782 and was the final volume of this work. It discusses the French and American Revolutions and loyalty to the British Crown. It also gives a detailed plan for establishing the public library in Philadelphia.

The fourth portion of the autobiography is the period of *Poor Richard's Almanack*, the establishment of the Junto Club, the influences of the Rev. George Whitefield in Franklin's life, and what might be called the "Rise and Fall of Franklin's Philosophical Reputation." This period also includes an account of his experiments on electricity, among his other scientific work.

The fifth and final part of Franklin's autobiography was written between November 1789 and April 1790, the month of his death. This final part is the briefest of the five parts, and it speaks, for the most part, of his role in the area of politics and what today would be called Political Science.

Throughout all five portions of the autobiography, Franklin makes many observations about God, ethics and immortality. We will provide five examples here. Firstly, he observes in part two:

> I have been religiously educated as a Presbyterian...
> I was never without religious principles.[36]

In point of fact, he had been raised in both the environment of his mother's Nantucket Congregationalism and his father's Calvinist Presbyterianism, though he appears to have made no distinction between the two sects.

Secondly, in the same part of his autobiography, Franklin observes the following regarding different religions in America:

> These I esteem'd the essentials of every religion; and, being to be found in all the religions we had in our country, I respected them all, tho' with different degrees of respect, as I found them more or less mix'd with other articles, which, without any tendency to inspire, promote, or confirm morality, serv'd principally to divide us, and make us unfriendly to one another.[37]

This portion of the autobiography of Franklin confirms his views about religious toleration in America. However, at the same time, it points out the fact that religion in America has often divided Americans when it comes to religious dogma.

Thirdly, in part three of the autobiography, when Franklin was appointed to a committee charted to create a national seal for the new United States in July 1776, he turned his imagination to the Old Testament and the Book of Exodus, likening the chosen nation of Israel to the new North American Republic. He tells us:

> Moses lifting up his wand and dividing the Red Sea, and the
> Pharaoh in his chariot overwhelmed with the waters.
> This motto: "rebellion to tyrants is obedience to God."[38]

A few years later, in a letter to the French minister in March of 1778, Franklin observed, "Whoever shall introduce into public affairs the principles of primitive Christianity will change the face of the world." As we shall see in Chapter Six, he is most likely speaking here of the moral views of Jesus of Nazareth.

Fourthly, on June 28, 1787, in the fourth section of his autobiography, Franklin speaks again of the Providence of God and that the prayers of the colonies "were heard and they were graciously answered." He speaks of a "Superintending Providence in our favor."[39]

Fifthly, and finally, at the end of his life, Franklin made this theological pronouncement about the relationship of prayer to the new United States:

> I, therefore, beg leave to move—that henceforth prayers
> imploring the assistance of Heaven, and its blessings on our
> deliberations, be held in this Assembly every morning before we
> proceed to business, and that one or more of the clergy of this
> city be requested to officiate in that service.[40]

From these five comments of Franklin in his autobiography, we may make the following conclusions:

1. He believed in God.
2. He was in favor of religious toleration in America.
3. He believed that religion in America often inspired division and hatred among the different sects.
4. He was in favor of any nation that based itself on the moral teachings of Jesus Christ.
5. He believed that America was a chosen nation, much like the ancient Jewish state.
6. He believed in the efficacy of prayer even to the end of his life.

This brings us to the final section of this first chapter, in which we will discuss the earliest religious education of Benjamin Franklin in his childhood home in the city of Boston in the early eighteenth century.

Benjamin Franklin's Childhood Faith

Josiah Franklin (1657–1745) was an English-born businessman who fathered seventeen children with his two wives, Jane White and Abiah Folger, Benjamin Franklin's mother. Several sources for determining Franklin's earliest religious beliefs are extant. Those sources include the library of his father, Josiah, as well as the faiths of his parents and his uncle Benjamin and Franklin's relationship to Puritanism, Presbyterianism, the Quakers, and the Anglican Church in colonial America.

In his autobiography, Franklin tells us this about Josiah Franklin's library, "My father's little library consisted chiefly of books in polemic divinity." He goes on to speak about the differences in the creeds of the various churches when he wrote:

> That is why the Congregationalists are right, why the Quakers are right, why the Baptists are right, why the Methodists are right. Each denomination writing why it is right and everyone else is wrong.[41]

Nevertheless, Franklin goes on to describe some of Josiah's books in his small home library. These include Cotton Mather's 1710 tome *Bonifacius, or Essays to do Good*, and John Bunyan's 1678 work *The Pilgrim's Progress*, which may have been the first novel published in the English language.[42]

Benjamin's mother, Abiah Franklin, was from a Nantucket Congregationalist congregation. His mother, along with Josiah's Presbyterian roots, had Franklin telling us that, "I had been religiously educated as a Presbyterian and then some of the dogmas of that persuasion, such as the eternal decrees of God, election, reprobation, etc., appeared to me to be unintelligible, others doubtful, and I early absented myself from the public assemblies of the Sect."[43]

In the same portion of his autobiography, he says more about these doctrines of the church that he had some doubts about. Among these are the doctrine of Original Sin, the Divinity of Jesus, the Christian Trinity, and the idea of Providence in the Calvinist tradition that all that happens in history are the products of the Decrees of God, or what John Calvin called "The Providence of God."[44]

In his autobiography, Franklin claims to have been raised a "Presbyterian in Boston," but the Old South Church in which he was baptized was not Presbyterian. It was a Congregationalist church, his mother's denomination. He characteristically did not make a distinction between Calvinist Congregationalists and Calvinist Presbyterians.

Josiah Franklin's brother Benjamin, the man from whom the statesman was named, was another early religious influence on his nephew. Like his brother, Benjamin's Reform Christian inheritance came from the man that was to be known as "Benjamin, the Elder." He tutored his nephew in Biblical theology, as well as in the Franklin brother's dissent from the Church of England.

Uncle Benjamin wrote a poem for his nephew in 1710 when the boy was only four years old. It spoke of the uncle's devotion to God and the obligation of the nephew to be an "obedient son" to that God. In the poem, the uncle also spoke of the threats of "Satan, sin and the self." For Benjamin the Elder, "virtue, learning, and wisdom" would keep the nephew on the proper moral path.

Another way we can see Franklin's rejection of his father's Calvinism is in the subtitle of the "Articles of Belief and Acts of Religion," what he called "A Dissertation on Liberty and Necessity," in which he was decidedly against the "necessity" of Calvinism, while in favor of the "liberty" of human free will.[45]

By the time Franklin was fifteen years old, he had begun to read some of the Enlightenment thinkers in his father's library, as well as in other books he had borrowed from his friends. Again, in his autobiography, he comments on reading these works. He said:

> It happened that they wrought an effect on me quite contrary to what was intended by them. For the arguments of the deists, which were quoted to be refuted, appeared to me to be much stronger than the refutations. In short, I soon became a thorough Deist.[46]

Franklin goes on to speak of his struggles at an early age fully to accept either the doctrines of his mother's Congregationalist theology or his father's Calvinist Presbyterianism. What he replaced these points of view with was the Enlightenment's dictum that pertained to what they called the "Argument from Design," or what in Kantian terms was referred to as the "Teleological Argument" for God's existence.[47]

The Teleological Argument, or Argument from Design, was the philosophical foundation of Franklin's "On the Providence of God in the Government of the World."[48] The universe appears to exist in an Ordered fashion. If there is Order, then there must be Design. If there is Design, then a Designer must exist, or so the followers of the Argument, such as Franklin, have maintained. The Teleological Argument arose in the final section of Sir Isaac Newton's *Principia Mathematica*, where he suggests that the universe is like a watch and God is like a watchmaker. Franklin was very fond of this metaphor.

When Franklin arrived in Philadelphia in 1723, he attended a local Quaker meeting house. He was now seventeen and went to the same Quaker location for five weekly services in a row. Later he attended the First Presbyterian Church of Philadelphia, but he conflicted with the Rev. Jedediah Andrews when in 1735, the Synod of Philadelphia expelled the assistant minister, a man named Samuel Hemphill.[49]

Franklin defended Hemphill and left the Presbyterian church he had been attending, even though he continued to support the church financially. As editor and publisher of *The Pennsylvania Gazette*, Franklin used the tools at his disposal to critique what he disliked about the Presbytery. He produced two separate works—the "Dialogue Between Two Presbyterians," discussed earlier in the second section of this first chapter and in an essay that he entitled, "A Defence of the Reverend Hemphill's Observations; Or, an Answer to the Vindication of the Reverend Commission." In this latter work that was written and published on October 30, 1735, the statesman declared in no uncertain terms that:

> Christ, by his Death and Sufferings, has purchased for us those easy Terms and Conditions of our acceptance with God, proposed in the Gospel, to wit, Faith and Repentance.

Here in this 1735 essay, at the age of twenty-nine, Franklin appeared to have arrived at a belief in the most fundamental doctrine of the Christian church—that Christ died so that we may all be saved. In the same essay, he also related the following:

> I am conscious that I believe in Christ and I exert my best Endeavours to understand His Will aright, and strictly to follow it.[50]

Franklin's defense of the Rev. Hemphill marks a radical change in the way that he wrote about Christianity. Prior to "A Defence of the Reverend Hemphill's Observations," He said very little about the use of the Holy Scriptures. He gave very little consideration to the life of Jesus Christ, with the exception of his moral teachings, much like the view of Thomas Jefferson about the life of Jesus Christ.

From his writing of "A Defence" in the fall of 1735, the religious perspectives of Franklin began to evolve and to find much more value in the life, death and resurrection of Jesus Christ, as well as in the utility and value of the Old and the New Testaments.

This brings us to the major conclusions of this first chapter on the study of the religion of Benjamin Franklin. In Chapter Two of this study, we will examine what Franklin had to say and believe about God and the person of Jesus Christ.

Conclusions to Chapter One

We began this first chapter of the study of Franklin's religion stating that the chapter will consist of three essential parts. These were a short biography of the statesman, religious views found in his published works, and a close analysis of his earliest religious life with his parents, Josiah and Abiah Franklin.

In the first of these three sections, we provided and discussed a short biography of Franklin in nine separate parts, from his birth in 1706 until his death in April 1790. In the first of those parts, we pointed out that he only had two years of formal education when he was eight and nine years old.

We have also shown that at around the age of fifteen, Franklin began to have some serious doubts about many of the Christian doctrines he had learned from his mother's Congregationalism and his father's Calvinist Presbyterianism. In fact, we indicated that he often seemed to have made no distinction between the two Christian sects.

Among the traditional dogmas that he had doubts about were the ideas of Election and Reprobation, Original Sin, the Divinity of Jesus, the Christian Trinity and many other foundational Christian beliefs.

We also indicated in the first section that at the age of fifteen, Franklin began to have some affinity for the Enlightenment philosophical thinkers of the seventeenth and eighteenth centuries, particularly what is called the Argument from Design or the Teleological Argument for God's existence.

Also indicated in section one was that he worked for his brother James' printing firm when the younger boy was fifteen and sixteen and that Benjamin began clandestinely to author letters to his brother's paper that he left under the door of the printing establishment in Boston at night after the printing shop had closed.

After having a fallout with James Franklin, he left his apprenticeship and went to New York before finally settling in Philadelphia in the Pennsylvania Colony. As we have shown, he fathered a son named William in 1728 with an unnamed woman. He married his wife, Deborah, in 1730. At this time, in the late 1720s, Franklin also opened his own newspaper called *The Pennsylvania Gazette* with a partner named Hugh Meredith.

We have also shown in this period that Franklin began to be involved in a number of civic endeavors, such as the founding of the Junto Club, the establishment of Independence Hall in Philadelphia, the formation of the American Philosophical Society in 1743, the establishment of the Pennsylvania Hospital with Dr. Thomas Bond in 1751, and the establishment of the first subscription library in America that is still in existence and is now known as the Library Company of Philadelphia established in 1731.

Other civic works that Franklin was involved in included the establishment of a fire department in Philadelphia and the representation of the colony in London in a dispute with the Penn family over who owned and represented Pennsylvania while the great American statesman was still in London.

We also mentioned him being miffed about the general American attitude toward the British Stamp Act of 1765 and that he also represented the interests of Massachusetts, New Jersey, and the Georgia colonies while in London.

Franklin's political life in Europe and America was the focus of the next portion of the first section of Chapter One. This analysis included his participation in the writing of the Declaration of Independence, the signing of the Treaty of Paris, serving on the Continental Congress, the committee to develop the seal of the United States, as well as the writing of an anti-slavery treatise at the very end of his life.

We began section two of the first chapter with a catalog of eight different published works of Franklin, where he made several observations about religion, ethics and immortality. In our analysis of this section, we attempted to show how the metaphysical beliefs of Franklin evolved over time, from polytheism to monotheism, as well as rejecting Biblical revelation early in his adult life but then accepting the idea much later. In the third section of this opening chapter, we gave an account of the religious views during the earliest period of his life. We indicated that his parents came from two separate and distinct Christian sects—the Congregationalists and the Presbyterians—but he seems not to have made any distinction between the two sects.

In the third section of Chapter One, we indicated that around the ages of fifteen and sixteen, Franklin began to be persuaded by the philosophical arguments of the seventeenth- and early eighteenth-century Enlightenment thinkers and that the statesman was particularly enamored with the Argument from Design also known as the Teleological Argument for the existence of God. We will say more about these issues in Chapter Four of this study.

In the third and final section, we showed that he defended the Rev. Hemphill after being dismissed from the Presbytery in 1735. As a response to the dismissal, we indicated that the statesman Franklin wrote two separate tracts about Hemphill's dismissal—the "Dialogue Between Two Presbyterians," and his "A Defence of the Rev. Hemphill's Observations," published by Franklin's paper in 1735 after the sacking of the Rev. Hemphill.

Along the way in Chapter One, we have shown an evolution of beliefs about God, ethics and immortality that began with only cursory assent in the 1720s and 30s, and by the end of Franklin's life, in a 1781 letter to Madame Brillon, he assented to five fundamental Christian beliefs about the existence of God: that God made the Universe, the existence of the human soul, the soul's immortality, and rewards and punishments after death. We also showed that this evolution of his religious beliefs could clearly be seen in the four major parts of his autobiography, as well as his *Poor Richard's Almanack*, in which several observations about God, ethics and immortality can also be found.

During this first chapter on Franklin's religion, we indicated some of the earliest theological influences of the statesmen, including Enlightenment thinkers such as Voltaire and theologian George Whitefield, not to mention the influence of Franklin's sister, Jane Mecom (1712–1794), an Evangelical Christian in Boston.

Finally, we indicated that the earliest religious life of Franklin was, at times, quite ambiguous, sometimes looking like assent to certain dogmatic Christian ideas, and at other times, by the age of fifteen and sixteen, seemingly rejecting these same theological ideas.

This brings us to the second chapter, in which we will examine two goals. They are what Benjamin Franklin believed and wrote about God and what he wrote and believed about Jesus Christ at any given time in his life. Next, then, we move to God and Jesus.

Benjamin Franklin arriving in Philadelphia.
Courtesy of the New York Public Library.

Chapter Two
Franklin on God and Jesus

> The narrative was classic Franklin, witty and to the point. Religion was worthless unless it promoted virtuous behavior. Jesus was the greatest moral teacher who ever lived, but he was not God.
> —John Fea, "Religion and Early Politics"

> As a versatile, great man who grew up in the 18th century, Franklin had all of the characteristics of that era.
> —Zhang Duan, "Benjamin Franklin's Religious Views"

> He that spits in the wind also spits in his own face.
> —Benjamin Franklin, *The Autobiography of Benjamin Franklin*

Introduction

In this second chapter of this study on Benjamin Franklin's religion, we have two principal goals. The first of those is to describe and discuss the developmental progression of the statesman's views on God from his early childhood to the end of his life. As we shall see, we will maintain that he went through five successive stages in his life in regard to what he thought and wrote about God.

The second goal of this chapter is to describe and discuss what he wrote and believed about the person of Jesus Christ of Nazareth. Again, as we shall see Franklin's beliefs and writings, that pertain to Jesus Christ were, at times, subtle, as well as being quite complicated. We move first, then, to Benjamin Franklin on God.

Benjamin Franklin on God

In this first section of Chapter Two, we will make the argument that in the life of statesman Benjamin Franklin, he went through six separate and distinct phases regarding his beliefs about God. These phases may be summarized this way:

1. His earliest life (1706–1717)
2. His deistic period (1718–1720)
3. His polytheism (1721–1728)
4. His "On the Providence of God in the Government of the World" (1732)
5. His views on God in France (1776–1781)
6. His most mature view on God (1781–1790)

We will discuss each of these six phases of Franklin's beliefs about God, which, ironically, returns him in the final analysis to exactly where his religious life began in the city of Boston with his mother Abiah, his father Josiah, and his uncle, the elder Benjamin Franklin.

We suggested in Chapter One that Franklin grew up in a house dominated by the Puritanism of his parents and his uncle Benjamin. Until the age of fifteen, the young Ben Franklin attended the Old South Church in Boston, at the corner of Milk and Washington Streets, one block from the house where he was born at number 17 Milk Street.

The Old South Church community began in 1669 in the midst of twenty-eight members known as the "Schismatics," or the "Dissenting Brethren," who decided to break away from Boston's First Church. These dissenters were Pilgrims, Puritan Reformers and Bay Colony merchants. The original founders of the Old South Church included a butcher, a mason or bricklayer, a brewer, a fisherman, a bookseller, a shoemaker, two ship captains, a tailor, two felt-makers, a druggist, several farmers and a schoolmaster.[51]

Among the early members of the Old South Church in Boston were Samuel Adams; Samuel Sewall; Phillis Wheatley, the first known African American poet in America; as well as the elder Ben Franklin, the statesman's uncle; and his father, Josiah Franklin.[52]

As indicated earlier, the Old South Church was organized by Congregationalist dissenters from Boston's First Church. The Old South Church was also known as the "Third Church" to distinguish it from the First and Second Congregationalist Churches. The Third Church congregation began assembling in 1690 in what was known as the "Cedar Meeting House," at the corner of Washington and Milk Streets in Boston, a block from the Franklin home.[53]

We begin this second chapter with this material because, at least early on, Franklin appears to have attended services at the Old South Church with his parents. He had religious instructions from his parents, as well as from the elder Benjamin Franklin, his uncle, and he held a set of religious beliefs that were generally held by the Old South Church congregants.

The Congregationalist movement arose in England in the late sixteenth and early seventeenth centuries. By the time of Franklin, the Old South Church occupied a place of dogmatic beliefs between the Presbyterians of John Knox and the more radical Baptists.[54]

The early Congregationalists in America were distrustful of the establishment of a state religion and had worked tirelessly in favor of religious toleration and religious liberty. They also were dedicated to the reformation idea of "the Priesthood of all believers." The Congregationalists were originally called "Independents" in that the Old South Church, or Third Church, was separate from the First and Second Churches.[55]

Franklin's earliest religious beliefs likely included the existence of God, that God created the universe, that Jesus Christ was the Son of God, that the devil exists, and that human beings suffer from Original Sin.

The principles of John Calvin are sometimes described by the acronym TULIP. These letters stand for:

    T. Total Depravity
    U. Unconditional Election
    L. Limited Atonement
    I. Irresistible Grace
    P. Perseverance of the Saints[56]

What Calvin meant by these five beliefs is, first, that because of Original Sin, humans are totally depraved. Second, God freely chooses His Elect. Third, Jesus died only for God's Elect. Fourth, the Elect receives Irresistible Grace, the kind that cannot be given back nor tarnished. And finally, the Elected Saints of Christ will persevere.

In addition to the TULIP acronym, the Congregationalists and Presbyterians also assented to several other of John Calvin's theological principles, including the Providence of God, the Priesthood of All Believers, *Sola Scriptura*, or "By Scripture Alone" does God reveal Himself, and the ideas of Predestination and Election. In fact, in Calvin's case, he believed in "Double Predestination," in that both the Reprobate and the Saved are Predestined to their plights. This set of beliefs was a part of the theological system of Franklin's mother's Calvinist Congregationalism and his father's Presbyterianism. It is likely then that, even early on, Franklin was aware of Calvin's TULIP acronym.

In his *The Rise and Progress of Religion in the Soul*, completed in 1745, Philip Doddridge, an early Congregationalist minister, summarizes the collected beliefs of congregations like the Old South Church in Boston that pretty much looked like what we have suggested here.[57]

However, by the time Franklin was fifteen, his theological beliefs had begun to change, most likely because of the young Bostonian becoming enamored with the Enlightenment in general and with the movement known as deism in particular.[58]

To understand eighteenth-century deism, we must first return to the end of Sir Isaac Newton's *Principia Mathematica*, published in 1687. In that section, Newton suggested that the "Physical laws he had uncovered revealed a mechanical perfection of the workings of the universe." The English scientist said these laws were akin to the relationship of a watch to a watchmaker. In Newton's view, God is the Watch Maker and the universe is the Watch.[59]

This seventeenth-century analogy caused the development of three separate philosophical and theological views about the relation of God to the universe. These views looked like this:

Theism	Deism	Atheism
William Paley	Voltaire	Baron d'Holbach

Figure 2.1

The first theological response to Newton's analogy of the watch and Watch Maker is British philosopher William Paley (1743–1805), and other thinkers like him, in his 1802 book, *Natural Theology: Or, Evidences of the Existence and Attributes of the Deity*, took a theistic or monotheistic approach to Newton's analogy—that is, that God created the Universe and the laws by which it operates.[60]

At the other end of the spectrum in Figure 2.1 was the beliefs of eighteenth-century thinkers like the French Baron d'Holbach (1723–1789), who was an atheist and decidedly against the existence of God. Thus, the Baron d'Holback and other like-minded eighteenth-century European thinkers were not great believers in the analogy of the watch and the watchmaker because, in essence, there is no Watch Maker even though there is a Watch.[61]

There was a variety of other eighteenth-century atheists in Europe and America, including Benjamin Franklin's friend, who is only known as "J. H." in his *Papers*. J. H. sent an essay that outlined his atheist beliefs to the statesman, and Franklin responded to the essay, urging his friend not to publish it. We will say more about this friendship at the end of this section of Chapter Two.

Other eighteenth-century European atheists included Dutch philosopher Baruch Spinoza (1632–1677), though he may have been a pantheist; Denis Diderot (1713–1784); Pierre Bayle (1647–1706); and Scottish philosopher David Hume (1711–1776), who gave Franklin a tour of his city, Edinburgh.

It is between these two poles of Figure 2.1 that we find the eighteenth-century movement known as deism. We have chosen French philosopher and critic Voltaire (1694–1778) as the representative figure of this third perspective. In Voltaire's view, as well as others like him, God exists, and He made the natural laws by which the Universe operates, but then He has no relation to that Universe. Voltaire appears to have believed in what in his time was sometimes called a *"Deus Absconditis,"* or a God that absconds or "goes away" or "hides" after the creation.[62]

In his autobiography, Franklin refers to the fact that his father gave him some books from his private library that were supposed to defeat the claims of the deists. He claims, however, that these religious tracts had the exact opposite effect. Franklin thought the arguments for the deists were stronger than the Christian polemics that his father had preferred. Thus, the statesman says in his autobiography, "In short, I had become a thorough deist."[63]

It is not clear how long Franklin considered himself to be a deist. What is clear is that by the age of twenty, with the writing of his "Articles of Belief" in 1726, we begin to see a third phase of his personal belief about God, religion and immortality.[64]

In the first chapter of this study of Franklin's religion, we indicated that in this major work of his, he does not appear to have been a theist or monotheist, like William Paley, for example. Rather, the statesman seems to suggest something closer to the worldview of the polytheists, for in the "Articles," Franklin suggests that there are many other gods besides the God of the Judaic-Christian view and that each of these other gods is responsible for its own separate stellar system. He stated:

> I believe there is one Supreme most perfect Being, Author and Father of the Gods themselves. For I believe that Man is not the most perfect Being but One, rather that as there are many Degrees of Beings, his Inferiors, so there are many Degrees of Beings superior to him.[65]

Franklin goes on in the same work to describe these inferior deities, that each controls a different stellar system in the Universe and that the God of Judaism and Christianity made these inferior Gods.

Again, it is not at all clear how long Franklin held these polytheistic beliefs in his life. He does say in his autobiography that he arrived at the polytheistic view by combining the deist conception of God with the "God who is All-Good, All-Knowing, and All-Powerful." Franklin reasoned, He must have created these smaller gods "to rule over solar systems and to receive the worship of the beings on these other planets under their rule."[66]

It is interesting to note at this point, however, that there is no mention of Holy Scripture in any of the first three phases we have developed so far in this analysis in Chapter Two. In fact, as we have shown in the first chapter, by Franklin's 1731 outline for an essay to be entitled "Doctrine to be Preached," there is still no mention of either the Old or the New Testament.[67]

There is also nothing in these three early phases of the statesman's views on God and religion about God answering prayers, nor the idea of God performing or allowing miracles in the world. This was chiefly because the deists were not in favor of any of these ideas, as well.

Just a year later, however, in 1732, in his article called "On the Providence of God in the Government of the World," we begin to see Franklin arguing for the intervention of God into the affair of human beings, particularly in relation to prayer and the idea of miracles.[68]

It appears that in this fourth phase of his evolution of his religious views, we begin to see the statesman's earliest assenting to what might be called traditional theism. That is, a God who is All-Good, All-Knowing, All-Powerful, who performs miracles and who also answers prayers.

As we have shown in Chapter One, one other aspect of his 1732 essay is that the statesman is enamored with the Argument for Design, or the Teleological Argument for God's existence, such as figures like William Paley, who we saw earlier in this section of Chapter Two.

Franklin was convinced in his twenties that the Newton watch and Watch Maker analogy was the best way to prove the existence of God, and he read William Paley's book that does just that. He also read many of the other Enlightenment thinkers in this fourth phase, some assenting to the Paley view and some, like David Hume, for example, who decidedly argued against it, while others like Jean-Jacques Rousseau, Joseph Butler and Samuel Clarke all assented to the Argument for Design, or Teleological Argument for God's existence. Franklin was in this latter camp.[69]

On October 26, 1776, a month after being named an agent of a diplomatic commission by the Continental Congress, Franklin sailed from Philadelphia for France, where he was to negotiate and secure a formal alliance and treaty between the two nations. He was easily accepted into the French upper class, making many friends, including several French noblewomen.[70]

One of these women was Madame Brillon (1744–1824), with whom, though married, Franklin made a personal "Treaty." This "Treaty of Peace," written by Franklin, contained nine "Articles" pertaining to the requirements of the two parties of the alliance.

The friendship or alliance between the noble French lady and Franklin is important because, in one of his many love letters to Madam Brillon, he sketches out his views on religious matters, which apparently his French friend had asked for. In this April 13, 1781, correspondence, the American statesman sets forth a summary of five beliefs that he says are essential to religion in general and to Christianity in particular. He told Madame Brillon:

> First, there is a God Who made the World & Who Governs it by his Providence.
>
> Second, that He should be adored and served.
>
> Third, that the best service to God is doing good to Men.
>
> Fourth, that the human soul is immortal.
>
> And fifth, that in the future Life is not in the present one, Vice will be punished & Virtue rewarded.

At this point in Franklin's life, he will live another nine years until his death in April of 1790. In this fourth phase of his theological biography, he appears to assent to the following religious beliefs:

1. Theism/monotheism, or Belief in One God.
2. That God created the Universe.
3. That God is owed adoration and service from human beings.
4. That the best of that service is doing the moral Good to fellow people.
5. That the human soul exists and is immortal.
6. Vice will be punished and Virtue will be rewarded in the Afterlife.

It is important to point out that gone from this list are any hints of his earlier deism and polytheism in phases two and three of Franklin's beliefs on God, religion and immortality. However, we also see a new component in the Madame Brillon letter that we have not seen before, which is the connection that he makes between belief in God and moral principles.

We will say more about this moral component in his views in Chapter Six. It is enough to point out now, however, that for Franklin, there is an inextricable bond between belief in God and one's moral duties to other human beings.

This brings us to the sixth and final phase of the evolution of Franklin's beliefs and opinions about God, religion and immortality. On February 29, 1790, Ezra Stiles (1727–1795), President of Yale College, sent a letter to Franklin inquiring about the statesman's religious beliefs.

This request was significant for several reasons. One was that Franklin's letter back to Stiles, written on March 9, 1790, appears to be the statesman's final word on the issues at hand, for he died a month later on April 17, 1790. Another reason these two letters are significant is that his March 1790 response to Stiles is indicative of a final summary of his views. Thirdly, it is also significant to compare what he says in the letter to what he had said nine years earlier to Madame Brillon on exactly the same issues—God, ethics and immortality of the soul.

Franklin's response to President Ezra Stiles is a scant four paragraphs, three of theological content and a fourth, a postscript. In the first of these paragraphs, he turned his attention to God, Creation and the Children of God. In that initial paragraph, the statesman supplied the following:

> I believe in one God, Creator of the Universe. That He governs it by Providence. That He ought to be worshipped. That the most acceptable service we render to Him, is doing Good to His other children. That the soul of man is immortal and will be treated with Justice in another life respecting its conduct in this. These I take to be the fundamental principles of all sound religion, and I regard them, as you do, in whatever Sect I meet with them.

In this initial paragraph by Franklin to Ezra Stiles, he appears to do little more than repeat what he had said in his March 1781 letter to Madame Brillon nine years earlier. In the second paragraph to Stiles, however, we see some thoughts that cannot be found in the letter to the noble French lady.

In the second paragraph of the letter, the American statesman turns his attention to the figure of Jesus Christ. He told Stiles:

> As to Jesus of Nazareth, my opinion of whom you particularly desire, I think the system of morals, and his religion, as he left them to us, is the best the world has ever saw, or will ever see; but I apprehend it has received various corrupting changes, and I have with most of the present dissenters in England some doubts as to his divinity.

Later in this chapter, we will say more about what Franklin believed and said about Jesus Christ. It is enough now, however, to point out that the statesman had some doubts about his divinity. He continues in his second paragraph to President Stiles:

> Though it is a question that I do not dogmatize upon, having never studied it, and I think it is needless for me to busy myself with it now, when, I expect soon an opportunity of knowing the truth with less trouble I see no harm, however, in its being believed if that belief has the good consequent, as it probably has, of making his doctrine more respected and better observed; especially as I do not perceive that the Supreme takes it amiss, by distinguishing the unbelievers in this government of the world with any particular marks of his displeasure.

In the remainder of this second paragraph, Franklin makes several points about his faith. First, that he has doubts about the divinity of Jesus. Second, he has no trouble in seeing that others believe that Jesus is God. Third, the statesman holds that there may well be good consequences for that belief. And finally, those who do, as well as those who do not, believe that Jesus is God, would appear to have little consequence one way or the other for the Supreme Himself.

In the third paragraph of his return letter to Yale President Ezra Stiles, the statesman turns his attention to his beliefs about ethics and morality when he observed that:

> I shall only add, respecting myself, that, having experienced the goodness of that being in conducting me prosperously through a long life, I have no doubt of its continuance in the next, though without the smallest conceit of meriting such goodness.

Here, in this paragraph, Franklin appears to reaffirm his belief that the best aspect of the life of Jesus was his moral point of view and that the goodness reflected in that view can be seen throughout his life. He also indicates that this idea of goodness will continue in the next life, as well.

Franklin followed these three paragraphs to Stiles with the following postscript:

> I confide that you will not expose me to criticisms and censure by publishing any part of this communication to you. I have ever let others enjoy their religious sentiments, without reflecting on them, for those that appear to me unsupportable and even absurd.

He worries that the Calvinist Stiles will not criticize him for what he has written in his letter, and he makes the point that he has always respected the religious sentiments of others. The statesman finishes his letter to President Stiles this way:

> All sects here, and we have a great variety, have experienced my good will in assisting them in my subscriptions for building their new places of worship; and as I have never opposed any of their doctrines, I hope to go out of the world in peace with them all.

Franklin ends his letter to Ezra Stiles on a note of his philanthropy and generosity in regard to the building of churches and temples of various religions and denominations, followed by his commitment to the ideas of religious freedom and religious toleration that he demonstrated throughout his life.

Among the church-building projects that Franklin supported were the family pew in Philadelphia's Christ Church, the Episcopal Church where he and his wife are buried. Contributions were made to the fund to replace the steeple and the bell in 1752. The statesman contributed five pounds to the first project and three pounds for the bell.

The American statesman died a month after the letter to Ezra Stiles was composed. The letter stands as Franklin's final word on his thoughts and writings about God, Ethics and survival after death. In the end, Franklin appears to have assented to the following beliefs about God:

1. That He exists.
2. That He created the universe in an ordered way.
3. That human beings owe worship and fidelity to Him.
4. That Jesus Christ was not God.
5. That religious freedom and toleration were important gifts from God.
6. That the most important aspect of the life of Jesus was his moral point of view.
7. That God has provided the human with an immortal soul.
8. That God will use punishment and reward in the life to come.
9. That belief in God has good consequences for society.
10. That it is important financially to support religious institutions.

One final aspect of Franklin's views on God has to do with his approach to the opposite of theism, namely atheism. On December 2, 1757, the statesman received a letter from a friend only identified as "J. H." What is significant about that letter is that it was written by a non-believer, by an atheist.

On December 13, 1757, Franklin scolded his friend for preparing to publish the atheist tract. The American statesman wrote back to J. H.:

> I have read your manuscript with some attention. By the arguments it contains against the doctrine of a particular providence, though you allow a general providence, you strike at the foundation of all religion: For without the belief of a providence that takes cognizance of guards and guides and may favor particular persons, there is no motive to worship a deity, to fear its displeasure, or to pray for its protection. I will not enter into any discussion of your principles, though you would seem to desire it.

In Franklin's response to his anonymous atheist friend, the statesman makes pragmatic arguments against the publication of the theological tract. In the process, he was also true to his theism by suggesting that if God does not exist, then, as Dostoevsky once put it, "Then all is permitted."[71] Franklin ends the December 13, 1757, letter to J. H. this way:

> I would advise you, therefore, not to attempt to unchain the Tyger, but to burn this piece before it is seen by any other person, whereby you will save yourself a great deal of mortification from enemies it may raise against you and perhaps a good deal of regret and repentance. If men are so wicked as we now see them with religion, what will they be like without it? I intend this letter itself as a proof of my friendship and therefore add no professions of it, but subscribe simply yours.

What Franklin says here about atheism is perfectly consistent with what we have seen earlier in this section of Chapter Two on what he has said about God. But his arguments here are purely pragmatic—that religion is good for society, and without it, there would be no basis for morality and ethics. This theory is known as Divine Command Theory, as we shall see in Chapter Six of this study on Benjamin Franklin's religion.

One final view on God that the great American statesman had and shared with many of his fellow Founding Fathers of the United States is the view that the United States was to be understood as a new "Promised Land," and its citizens a new "Chosen People." In various ways in his life, he implied that he held this view, such as the work he did when choosing the national seal and his use of the Book of Exodus as the text for that seal. For Franklin, the ancient Jews wandered in the wilderness, only to be rewarded by the Promised Land of Israel. America was to be seen as a new Promised Land and Americans as the new "Chosen People."

This brings us to the second section of Chapter Two, where we will make several more observations about what the printer, publisher, and statesman Benjamin Franklin had to say and write about Jesus of Nazareth.

Franklin on Jesus of Nazareth

Earlier in this chapter, as well as in Chapter One, we indicated that Franklin had some serious doubts about whether Jesus Christ is/was God. He was not alone in this judgment. We stated elsewhere, for example, that Thomas Jefferson agreed with Franklin on two principal religious beliefs—that Jesus Christ was not God and that the greatest moral system of mankind that has ever existed was that of Jesus in the New Testament.

Franklin and Jefferson also shared a third belief about Jesus that his original, or "natural," message was corrupted in many ways, and we should endeavor to recover that original point of view, which included the belief that Jesus was not God.

Throughout Franklin's life, he also made several other observations about the person of Jesus Christ. Among these observations and beliefs of the statesman are the following:

1. Jesus was not fully human and fully divine.
2. That Jesus Christ was not God.
3. That Jesus died for all people, not just Christians.
4. That Jesus did not approve of dancing.
5. That Jesus came to restore natural religion.
6. That Jesus was committed to charity for the poor.
7. Franklin was skeptical of Jesus's temptation in the desert.
8. That the American statesman frequently discussed Jesus Christ with his friend, the Rev. George Whitefield.

Franklin spoke of Jesus with Preacher George Whitefield and was influenced by him. In this section, we will discuss these eight beliefs and observations about Jesus Christ of Nazareth made by Franklin one at a time, followed by our conclusions in this second chapter on Benjamin Franklin's religion.

First, it is clear that Franklin's parents believed that Jesus Christ was fully human and fully divine, as did his sister Jane and his close friend and preacher, George Whitefield. To these Puritans and evangelicals, Jesus was fully God and fully man. To doubt these truths, for these believers around Franklin, was to put one's soul in jeopardy.

Jesus had made the way for all sinners to be saved.⁷² Jane Franklin Mecom was Franklin's youngest sister and one of the statesman's most important confidants, particularly about religious matters. She was six years younger than her brother.

Second, in his autobiography, among other places, Franklin regularly expressed the view that Jesus Christ was human, but he was not God. Again, this was a view he shared with Thomas Jefferson, as well as many other Founding Fathers, such as Thomas Paine, for example.⁷³

For many of those in Franklin's life, honoring Jesus Christ required belief in doctrinal truths, like Jesus was fully human and fully divine. As Thomas Kidd, in his *Benjamin Franklin: The Religious Life of a Founding Father*, put the matter:

> Franklin was not so sure. Perhaps the Puritans and the Presbyterians of his youth had gotten it all wrong. Perhaps he was the one that was getting back to Jesus' core teaching. But he was sure that doing the Good was the grand point.⁷⁴

Professor Kidd seems to think that Franklin eschewed the idea that Jesus Christ was fully human, as well as being fully divine. Given the information available in Franklin's papers, as well as his autobiography, it seems that Professor Kidd is most likely correct about the statesman's skepticism about the matter of the identity of Jesus.

It is much clearer, however, that Franklin believed our third observation about Jesus Christ. Using Second Corinthians 5:14, that relates, "For Christ's love compels us, because we are convinced that one who died for all and therefore all died." He employed the scriptures of Jesus to show that the statesman was of the view that even those who did not know about Jesus could still be saved.

Fourthly, in 1740 Franklin was involved in a controversy regarding whether what were called "Dance Halls" would be allowed in the Massachusetts Bay Colony. George Whitefield and many of his followers were against the idea of the lascivious idea of a dance hall or dance school.⁷⁵

In the *Pennsylvania Gazette* from December 1740, however, Franklin was not sure about the matter. What he was sure about is that nowhere in the New Testament can it be found that Jesus Christ said anything about dancing or a dancing school, one way or the other.[76]

In point of fact, there are actually three references to the idea of dance and dancing to be found in the Gospels. Two are in the Gospel of Matthew and the third is in the Gospel of Luke. These passages come at Matthew 11:16–17 and 14:6, and Luke 15:21–29. The first of these speaks of music being played at a wedding, and "the guests did not dance."[77]

The second passage from Matthew, the one at 14:6, reveals that on "Herod's birthday, the daughter of Herodias danced for the guests and pleased Herod very much." Although the idea of dance is mentioned, Jesus made no comment about what he thought about that.

In the Gospel of Luke 15:21–29, verse 25, the evangelist used the Koine Greek word *chorus*, from which we get the English "chorus" and "choreography." Again, however, Jesus said nothing about what he believed the moral quality of that activity might be. Franklin's conclusion should be clear—Jesus said nothing about the idea of a dance hall.

A fifth observation that Franklin made many times about Jesus Christ for him is summed up in the Gospel of Mark 12:30–31. There we find the following words of Jesus:

> Love the Lord your God with all your heart and with all of your soul and with all your mind and with all your strength.
> The second is this: Love your neighbor as yourself. There is no commandment greater than these.

For Franklin, this is the essence of Christianity, and it is also consistent that Jesus's moral vision is the most important aspect of his ministry. In fact, in several places in his autobiography, the statesman refers to the Golden Rule, as Mark 12:30–31 is known in the history of Christianity.

Franklin was of the opinion, as his friend Thomas Jefferson was, that the teachings of Jesus, what they called the "Natural Teachings," or "Natural Religion," was the real reason for the appearance of Jesus on the Earth. Both men also believed that those natural teachings had been corrupted by organized churches. For the third president, as well as the first great American statesman, the goal of Christianity should now be to restore the churches to that Natural Religion in its pristine form.[78]

Jesus taught his followers about the poor and needy, particularly in the gospels. At Mark 14:7, Jesus commented, "The poor you will always have with you." He also makes similar remarks and concerns for the poor at the Gospels of Matthew 26:11 and John 12:8. Jesus was born to parents who were poor and needy, and he warned those who are wealthy that they have an important responsibility to give to the poor.

The best way to see Franklin's views on the poor is to examine his 1766 essay "On the Price of Corn and Management of the Poor." In this article, the statesman argued persuasively that welfare schemes do far more harm than good. If one argues against welfare programs, as Franklin did, one is immediately accused of not caring about the poor. But he takes this view head-on, making it clear that he is not opposed to helping the poor but differs in the means for achieving that goal. In the 1766 essay, he commented, "I think the best way to do good to the poor is not to make them easy in poverty but leaving them or driving them out of it."

Franklin's seventh observation about Jesus is related to the idea of him being tempted in the desert by Satan. In his "A Defence of The Reverend Hemphill's Observations," published on October 30, 1735, the American statesman speaks about his views regarding Jesus being tempted in the desert at the Gospel of Matthew 4:1–11.

In that essay, he made several observations about what he thought of the episode. Many of these comments of his are included in Thomas Kidd's book on Franklin's religious views in several conversations that he had with his friend, Polly Stevenson Hewson, many about Biblical topics, one of them being Jesus' temptation in the desert by Satan.[79]

Among the questions that Franklin asked Polly Hewson included the following in one of his letters to her. "Could the Devil really show Jesus all the kingdoms in the world in a single instant?" The statesman also asked, "How could the Devil perform miracles for the Son of God?" "Why would an omnipotent Jesus allow the Devil to carry him to the top of a mountain to see all of those Earthly kingdoms?"[80]

Hewson conceded that those who knew Greek would be able to interpret chapter four of the Gospel of Luke better than she could, but

Franklin had made his points about being skeptical about the idea of Jesus Christ being tempted in the desert by what has come to be called the "Evil One" in the Christian tradition.[81]

Finally, an eighth observation that Franklin makes concerning the person of Jesus Christ is related to his relationship and friendship with English minister and preacher George Whitefield. After he had been the statesman's guest at his home in Philadelphia, the Rev. Whitefield thanked him for "that kind offer for Christ's sake."[82] Franklin's response to his English friend is significant. He replied, "Don't let me be mistaken. It was not for Christ's sake, but for your sake."[83]

True to his principles regarding Jesus Christ, Franklin redirects the minister Whitefield's comment about Jesus so that we are back to the bottom line of Franklin on the figure. The reason that the statesman was so genial to his English friend had nothing to do with Jesus. It was because of their deep friendship and the statesman's dedication to his most fundamental moral dictum. That is, the Golden Rule.

One final point about Franklin on Jesus Christ is that he occasionally made very orthodox-sounding statements about Jesus as his Lord and Savior, as well as the limited powers of the unaided mind. But he bought into the Enlightenment dictum that Reason trumps Revelation and that God gave humans the ability to reason to distinguish them from the other animal species. As Franklin said in part two of his autobiography, "Reason must be our last judge and guide in everything," an observation he borrowed directly from John Locke's *An Essay Concerning Human Understanding*, which he read when he was an apprentice to his brother James.[84]

This brings us to the major conclusions we have made in this second chapter. In Chapter Three, we will introduce and discuss what Franklin had to say and write about the Holy Scriptures.

Conclusions to Chapter Two

We began this second chapter by indicating that it would have two primary goals. First, to say something about Franklin's beliefs and what he said in his written works about God. The second goal has been to explore what he believed and wrote about the person of Jesus of Nazareth. We dedicated one section each to these two issues.

Regarding the former question—Franklin's views on God—we have suggested that in his life, the American statesman went through a series of six separate phases about what he believed and what he said about God.

As we have seen, these six phases included Franklin's earliest religious life with his parents and his Uncle Ben, the Elder; Franklin's period of deism from the age of fifteen until about twenty; his brush with polytheism in his *Articles of Faith*, from approximately 1721 until 1728; his observations about God in his 1732 work "On the Providence of God in the Government of the World;" his beliefs about the Divine when in France (1776–1781), particularly in a 1781 letter he sent to Madame Brillon; and finally, his most mature views about God at the end of his life, like those communicated to the then President of Yale College, Ezra Stiles, in March 1790.[85]

Along the way, in the first section of Chapter Two, we also indicated the various churches that Franklin attended, including the Congregationalist Old South Church in Boston and Christ Church in Philadelphia, where he was active in the life of that religious community.[86]

We have shown that it is likely that his earliest religious beliefs about God were little more than a mirror of his parent's and uncle's religious faiths. We also indicated that early on in his life, he borrowed books from his father's library and from friends in developing those early perspectives on God. Among those books were John Bunyan's 1673 work *The Pilgrim's Progress* and Philip Doddridge's 1745 *The Rise and Progress of Religion in the Soul*.[87]

In the opening section of Chapter Two, we also introduced Isaac Newton's metaphor that God and the Universe are like a Watchmaker and His Watch, as well as the three major responses to that metaphor—theism, deism and atheism, indicating that William Paley, Voltaire and the Baron D'Holbach served as representative examples of those three theological points of view.

The nature and extent of the movement called deism was another subject of the first section of Chapter Two, as well as Franklin's brush with that view in his life. We also indicated that in his 1732 work "On the Providence of God in the Government of the World," he was enamored with the design argument for God's existence.

At the close of the first section of Chapter Two of this study of Franklin's religion, we have spent considerable time discussing two letters about God, religion and immortality, written by Franklin to his French friend, Madame Brillon, and to the president of Yale College, who had inquired of the statesman about his religious beliefs.[88]

In this material, we summarized the six beliefs that he sent to Madam Brillon in 1781, as well as a letter that he sent to President Stiles just a month before his death when he supplied some observations about the statesman's final word on God, ethics and immortality.

Indeed, at the very end of section one of Chapter Two, we have done two other things. First, we summarized ten theological beliefs held by Franklin the month before his death. Among these ideas and beliefs were that God exists, that He created the Universe out of nothing, that human beings owe God adoration and fidelity, and many other beliefs about God.

The final thing we have done in section one of Chapter Two of this study was to review what he had to do about the opposite of theism, that is atheism. There we introduced a letter written to a friend of Franklin's known only as "J. H.," an atheist who had sent the statesman a tract on his metaphysical view, asking for comment.[89]

Franklin's response to J. H. was critical of his friend's views, and the statesman raised several theological objections to them that were mostly pragmatic and moral in nature, including the idea that if there is no God, then there is no standard for morality and ethics. At the end of the first section of Chapter Two, we have also shown what he said to J. H. was perfectly consistent with the statesman's other observations about the divine and His existence.

In the second section of Chapter Two, we began by reiterating Franklin's skepticism about the divinity of Jesus Christ and that he was fully human and fully divine. We indicated that Thomas Jefferson also had doubts about these ideas relating to Jesus. We then went on in the same section to catalog eight differing beliefs that Franklin had about Jesus of Nazareth, as follows:

> That Jesus was not fully human and fully Divine; that Jesus was not God; that Jesus died for all people, not just Christians; that

Jesus did not comment about dance halls. That Jesus came to restore his natural religion, that Jesus was committed to the idea of charity to the poor, that Franklin was skeptical about Jesus's temptation by Satan in the desert and that he frequently discussed Jesus Christ with his friend, the Rev. George Whitefield.[90]

Most of the second section of Chapter Two was taken up with a discussion of these eight beliefs that Franklin appears to have held about Jesus. We also pointed out that he, in both his letters and in conversations with his friend, Polly Stevenson Hewson, often spoke about God, ethics, the Bible, and immortality of the soul, with each other.[91]

Included in those discussions and letters were doubts held by Franklin pertaining to the narrative of Jesus being tempted in the desert by the devil. He asked Polly, "Could the devil really show Jesus all the kingdoms of the Earth at the same time?" "How, and why, would Satan attempt to perform miracles before the Son of God?" "Why would an omnipotent Jesus allow the devil to carry him to the top of a mountain to see all of those earthly kingdoms?"[92]

It is clear that in these letters and discussions with Polly Hewson, as well as in Franklin's essay in which he defended the beliefs of the Rev. Samuel Hemphill, the American statesman had many observations about the person in Jesus Christ in regard to certain narratives found in the four Gospels. Finally, at the end of Chapter Two, we have shown that after George Whitefield visited the Philadelphia home of Franklin, the evangelist sent the statesman "His kind offer for Christ's sake." Franklin immediately responded by observing, "It was not for Christ's sake but yours."[93]

True to the principles that we have sketched out in these first two chapters, Franklin's response to the Rev. Whitefield spoke of the priority and the humanity of his views on the person of Jesus Christ—that his moral and ethical views were the most important element in the man From Nazareth's philosophical and religious views.

This brings us to Chapter Three, where we shall be dedicated to what the American statesman said, believed, and wrote about Holy Scripture. It is to the Bible, then, to which we turn next.

Benjamin Franklin opening the first subscription library in Philadelphia. Courtesy of the Library of Congress.

Chapter Three
Franklin and the Bible

> I am continually stunned by those who flatly assert that Benjamin Franklin was a deist. After all, he says in his autobiography, "I soon became a thorough deist."
> —Tom Van Dyke, "Ben Franklin and the Bible"

> Ben Franklin had a wonderful sense of humor, was a bit of a prankster, and particularly enjoyed playing on Christians, as he considered their religion to be fabricated.
> —Ed Darrell, Blog of Ed Darrell

> A Bible and a newspaper in every house, a good school in every district; all studied and appreciated as they merit; are the principal support of virtue, morality, and civil liberty.
> —Benjamin Franklin, *Poor Richard's Almanack*

Introduction

The main purpose of this third chapter is to describe and discuss the beliefs and thoughts of Benjamin Franklin on the Holy Scriptures or the Bible. This chapter consists of four sections. In section one, we will examine very general comments about the Bible that Franklin said or wrote.

In the second section of Chapter Three, we will describe and discuss several topics related to the Bible that came up in unique or peculiar circumstances. Passages, where the American statesman mentioned or wrote about the Old Testament, will be the focus of the third section. Finally, the fourth section of this chapter will pertain to passages in the New Testament that were quoted by, or spoken about, Benjamin Franklin.

Franklin's General Comments About the Bible

In his classic work the *Summa Theologica*, Thomas Aquinas makes an important theological distinction between what he called "Truths of Reason" and "Truths of Revelation."

The former, in his view, could be established by the use of reason alone, while the latter truths could not. For Thomas, God's existence, His attributes, the existence and the nature of the soul, as well as its immortality, all could be proven by using reason alone.[94]

On the other hand, the dual natures of Jesus Christ, the idea of transubstantiation, miracles, and the answering of prayers, Thomas believed, as well as the Trinity of three persons in one God, are all truths of Revelation. These truths cannot be established, according to Thomas, by reason alone. Rather, these Revealed Truths are gifts from God. This same distinction between Truths of Reason and Truths of Revelation has existed in philosophical discussions in the West since the middle of the thirteenth century and Thomas' time.[95]

We begin this first section of Chapter Three with this distinction because the first general comment of Franklin on the Bible is directly related to this Thomistic distinction. In a section of his autobiography about his early life, the American statesman made an observation about his early religious belief system when he wrote:

> My parents had early given me religious impressions and brought me through my Childhood piously in the Dissenting Way. But I was scarce 15 when, after doubting by turns of several Points as I found them disputed in the different Books I read, I began to doubt Revelation itself.[96]

The first general comment of Franklin's about the Bible, then, is that at the age of fifteen, he began to have doubts about the Truths of Revelation that may only come from the Holy Scriptures themselves in that they have been revealed to us by God Himself. A second general observation about the Bible can be seen in what was called Franklin's

"Appeal for the Hospital." In that essay, he relates that "The Bible teaches a future state of rewards and punishments" in an attempt to get people to contribute to a fund to help establish the Pennsylvania Hospital.[97] He appealed to the self-interests of the possible contributors to the hospital.

In another section of his autobiography, he outlines what he referred to as "Rules For Good Citizens," which had been assembled by the Presbyterian Churches Synod of Philadelphia in his day. This list included another general comment about Holy Scripture. The list included:

1. Keep Holy the Sabbath Day.
2. Be diligent in reading the Holy Scriptures.
3. Attend duly the Publick Worship.
4. Partake of the Sacrament.
5. Paying due respect to God at all times.[98]

Thus, Franklin assented to a general obligation to be diligent in reading the Holy Scriptures, again fairly early in his life, and it appears that he continued that practice in the remainder of his life, as we shall see later in this study of Franklin's religion.

Later in life, he also noted another general belief he had about the Bible. We have employed this observation as an epigram for this Chapter Three. To wit:

> A Bible and a newspaper in every house, a good school in every district; all studied and appreciated as they merit; are the principles and support of virtue, morality, and civil liberty.[99]

Another aspect of Franklin's views of the Bible has to do with what he believed about what he, Jefferson, and others called "Natural Religion." In order for a Biblical text to be truly with authority, in their view, it also had to pass the Enlightenment test of conforming to the standards of reason.

In September 1735, when Samuel Hemphill and Franklin were embroiled during the former's dismissal from the Philadelphia Presbyterian Synod, Franklin produced what is now a famous syllogism, that is:

> Asses are grave and dull Animals. Our Authors are grave and dull Animals. Therefore, Our Authors are grave, dull. Or, if you will, Rev. Asses.[100]

For Franklin, the response of the synod to the Rev. Hemphill was an irrational response, one that went against the laws of reason. And for Franklin, any theological comment about the authority of Scripture must also pass this test of rational authority. In his mind, the members of the Presbyterian Synod—the critics of Rev. Hemphill—had failed that test in spades.

Finally, while in London, Franklin wrote a newspaper piece criticizing the English practice of providing for the poor by taxing citizens (both directly taxing their incomes and also indirectly taxing commodities sold and bought by them). He rebuked the English authorities for these practices, and he appealed to Second Thessalonians 3:10 to support his rebuke.

This New Testament text simply relates, "For even when we were with you, we gave you this rule, 'The one who is unwilling to work shall not eat.'" In the larger context of the chapter, Paul is not saying that idle people should not eat. Rather, he addresses the overall Christian view of idleness and points to his own example of diligence, and that is precisely what Franklin did in his use of the passage.

This brings us to the second section of this third chapter on Franklin's views on the Bible, in which he primarily spoke or wrote about the Holy Scripture in certain peculiar situations, our next focus in Chapter Three.

Franklin on the Bible in Peculiar Situations

A second way in which Franklin makes observations about the Bible has often come in the context of unique or peculiar circumstances. For example, when he and Jefferson were tasked with the development of a national seal for the United States, this clearly was a set of unique circumstances.[101]

In this second section of Chapter Three, we will enumerate and then discuss seven separate places in the corpus of the American statesman where he speaks of or is involved in some aspect of the Holy

Scriptures related to peculiar circumstances.

These seven peculiar events or situations may be summarized this way:
1. Silence Dogood on the Bible (1774)
2. Franklin and Jefferson on the Great Seal of the US (1776)
3. Franklin's Proposed New Version of the Bible (1782)
4. The Bible in the Pennsylvania Constitution
5. Franklin as a Bible Merchant
6. Franklin's Bible Hoaxes
7. The Franklin Family Bible

We will describe each of these seven peculiar items about the Bible in the life of Franklin as well as the circumstances in his life in which these items or events occurred.

Among the fourteen letters to *The New-England Courant* in 1722, Mrs. Silence Dogood, one of Franklin's pseudonyms, makes several references to the Holy Scriptures of the Judeo-Christian tradition. In letter number nine, for example, Franklin observed,

> A man compounded of Law and Gospel is able to cheat a whole Country with his Religion, and then destroy them under colour of Law.[102]

In the same letter, he tells us,

> The most dangerous Hypocrite in a Common-Wealth is one who leaves the Gospel for the sake of the Law.[103]

In his fourteen letters of Mrs. Dogood, Franklin makes twelve references to the Bible, all of them to what she calls the "Gospel," or "Gospels." Most of these make a distinction between the "Gospel" and the "Law." Three of these Bible references are related to the moral teachings of Jesus, where Mrs. Dogood tells us:

> I intend to proceed bestowing now and then a few gentle Reproofs of those who deserve them, not forgetting at the same time to applaud those whose Actions merit Commendation.[104]

In August of 1776, Franklin and Thomas Jefferson were assigned the task by the Continental Congress to develop the idea of a national seal for the new nation. He did the "first draft," and Jefferson the editing of that draft. Franklin chose a dramatic historical scene from the Old Testament's Book of Exodus, where the Jews confronted a tyrant in order to gain their freedom.

The American statesman gave this description of the national seal, as well as a possible motto, "Rebellion to tyrants is obedience to God."[105] His description of the seal said this:

> Moses, in the dress of the High Priest, standing on the Shore, and extending his hand over the Sea, thereby causing the same to overwhelm Pharoah who is sitting in an open Chariot, a Crown on his head and a Sword in his hand. Rays from a Pillar of Fire in the Clouds reaching to Moses, expressing that he acts by the Command of the Deity.[106]

Franklin chose the Book of Exodus to express the burgeoning spirit of the emerging nation. In his edits, Jefferson struck "in the dress of a High Priest" in the first line of Franklin's text, and in the fourth line, he suggested "to express" instead of "expressing." Jefferson also suggested the context should be the "Children of Israel in the Wilderness, led by a Cloud during the day and a pillar of Fire at night," in the same way that the American settlers were in a "New Wilderness," as a "New Chosen People."[107]

Thirdly, in 1782, or shortly thereafter, Franklin proposed "A New Version of the Bible," in which he essentially rewrote many of the portions of the Old and New Testaments, including, for example, this version of the Book of Job 1:6 to 11:

> **Verse 6.** And it being *levee* day in Heaven, all God's nobility came to court to present themselves before him; and Satan also appeared in the circle, as one of the ministry.
>
> **Verse 7.** And God said to Satan, you have been some time absent; where was you? And Satan answered, I have been at my country-seat and in different places visiting my friends.

Verse 8. And God said, Well what think you of Lord Job? You see, he is my best friend, a perfectly honest man, full of respect for me, and avoiding everything that might offend me.

Verse 9. And Satan answered, Does your Majesty imagine that his good conduct is the effect of mere personal attachment and affection?

Verse 10. Have you not protected him, and heaped your benefits upon him, till he is grow enormously rich?

Verse 11. Try him; only withdraw your favor, turn him out of his places, and withhold his pensions; and you will soon find him in the opposition.[108]

In this "New Version" of Job 1:6–11, Franklin makes several subtle changes, mostly we suspect to bring this portion of Holy Writ up to date in the statesman's view. The *bene ha Elohim*, or "Sons of God," most likely angels, now become "Nobility." In the Hebrew text, when God asks Satan where he has been, he says, "roaming the Earth and going back and forth," while Franklin has Satan answer, "At my country-seat... and visiting my friends."

The Hebrew text uses the definite article *ha* and calls the figure "The Satan," while for the American statesman, it is simply "Satan." In verse eight, the God Yahweh calls Job His "Servant," and in Franklin's version, he says, "He is my best friend." Where the Hebrew text has God say that Job is *tam va yashar*, that is, "blameless and upright," as well as "fearing God and shunning evil, Franklin has God saying that Job is "a perfectly honest man, full of respect, and avoiding anything that might offend Me."

In his version of verse nine, he uses "personal attachment and affections."[109] In the Hebrew original, the text asked if "God has put a hedge around Job." In place of "You have blessed the work of his hands so that his flocks and herds are spread throughout the land," Franklin rewrote verse ten to say:

> Have you not protected him, and heaped your benefits
> upon him, till he is grown enormously rich?[110]

At the Book of Job's 1:11, the Hebrew Masoretic text gives us this in English translation:

> But stretch out your hand now and touch all that
> he has and he will surely curse you to your face.[111]

Franklin, on the other hand, chose to render the line this way,

> Try him; and only withdraw your favor, turn him out
> of his places, and withhold his pensions;
> and you will soon find him in the opposition.[112]

Presumably, Franklin's "New Version" of the Bible would include subtle changes and theological differences about the other books of the Old Testament. This one example, however, should serve as a reminder of how different, theologically and perhaps morally, he wished to present the Holy Scriptures.

When Franklin undertook this project to produce a "New Version" of the Bible, he may have had the Jefferson Bible in mind when he did so. Thomas Jefferson wrote to a Philadelphia publisher when he was a young man to get the Gospels in the original Hebrew, Greek, Latin, English, and French. He put the four texts in parallel columns, and then, using a razor, he cut out of each column what he did not believe in and pasted back together what remained.[113]

From the four parallel columns, Jefferson eliminated all references to the divinity of Jesus, to any metaphysical entities like angels, and anything that did not generally pertain to the moral precepts of Jesus. In developing his "New Version" of the Bible, Franklin may have had similar aims to Jefferson's in developing that project.

The American statesman, along with his friend, Francis Dashwood, also developed an abridged version of the Anglican Book of Common Prayer. Their version shortened the Sunday service. The pair ripped out large parts of the liturgy that excised half of the Apostle's Creed, including, interestingly enough, all references to Jesus Christ. The pair also removed many of the Psalms on the simple grounds that they were "too repetitive and only of interest to the Jews."[114]

They also removed all mentions of the Hebrew terms *alah* and *arar* that both imply a "curse," such as "Cursed is he that lieth with his neighbor's wife," at Proverbs 6:29, or Deuteronomy's 27:23, which warns that one is cursed if he "lieth with his own mother."[115] In his abridgment with Dashwood, Franklin wrote, "All cursing of mankind is best omitted from this abridgment."[116]

Franklin also penned a third fictional Biblical account that he said was "taken from an ancient Jewish tradition."[117] This text is variously called "The Chapter on the Ax" and "A Parable on Brotherly Love." It was written in a letter to Benjamin Vaughan on November 2, 1789. Like his many other Biblical hoaxes, this third attempt is a fictional story of Jacob's sons Reuben, Simeon, Levi, and Judah.[118]

The sons argue about an ax that Reuben purchased from an Ishmaelite merchants. Ultimately, the three younger brothers purchase axes of their own. Then, Reuben loses his ax, and Judah comforts him by offering to share his ax with him—thereby earning their father Jacob's approval and blessing. Franklin ends the narrative by saying, "The Heart of Judah is a princely Judah who hath the Soul of a King."[119]

This brings us to an analysis of the role that Franklin played in the forming of the Pennsylvania Colony-State Constitution and the place of the Bible in that document. On September 28, 1776, in section ten of that document, he, as president of the Pennsylvania Convention, signed Pennsylvania's Constitution. Section ten legislated a religious "Christian test" for all those who would occupy a seat in the Pennsylvania Assembly.[120] That religious test included the following words:

> And each member, before he takes his seat, shall make and subscribe the following declaration: I do believe in one God, the creator and governor of the Universe, the rewarder of good and the punisher of the wicked. And I do acknowledge the Scriptures of the Old and New Testaments to be given by Divine inspiration."[121]

This draft of the proposed Pennsylvania Constitution penned by Franklin goes on to tell us that "no religious test shall ever be required" of the members of the Pennsylvania Assembly.[122]

This brings us to the idea of "Benjamin Franklin as a Bible Merchant," the next set of peculiar circumstances on our list. In the October 2, 1729, edition of his *Pennsylvania Gazette*, we may find another aspect of his relationship with the Bible. That is, that, Franklin as a publisher, frequently published books of the Bible, as well as sold them in his Market Street bookshop.

In an advertisement from October 2, 1759, in *The New-England Courant,* Franklin advertises "Bibles, Testaments, Psalters, and Psalm-Books," among other items. From 1728 until 1748, he published sixteen books in his press. Most of these were reprints of small, inexpensive books previously published in Britain and whose popularity had already been proven.

Among the books published by Franklin in these years was a 1731 book on the "Great Awakening," which included "a small Quantity of David's Psalms."[123] He also published a travelogue of his friend George Whitefield in a 1740 edition.[124] And three books on the Psalms by Isaac Watts in 1729, 1740 and 1741.

In 1745, the American statesman also published a reprint of a New Testament, originally published in London by the T. Baskett Company, "Printer to the King's most excellent Majesty."[125] In 1748, he also produced on his Philadelphia press an "Inventory of Books in Stock," that included "fifty-one Testaments."[126] In 1766, Franklin's press produced a new version of *Poor Richard's Almanack* that the statesman entitled *Poor Richard Improved.*[127]

So, another important aspect of Franklin's relation to the Bible is that he often published books of the Bible, as well as books about the Bible, in his print shop on Market Street in Philadelphia.

Another aspect of the relation of the American statesman to the idea of Holy Writ is what has come to be known as "Benjamin Franklin's Bible Hoaxes." These were nothing more than making up Bible passages and quoting from them that do not really exist. Earlier, we have spoken in this chapter of the Bible hoaxes called the "Parable of Brotherly Love," in which he concocted a tale of Reuben and his brothers.

Two other examples of this phenomenon of Bible hoaxes are related to the fifty-first chapter of the Book of Genesis and what

Franklin referred to as "Hezekiah 6:1."[128]

In the former example, he also appended an additional fifty-first chapter to the fifty chapters that usually appear in the Book of Genesis. Franklin's creation includes fifteen verses that are introduced this way:

> Over one hundred years ago, the following so-called "Genesis 51" was used to puzzle Biblical scholars and today are read aloud in any mixed company. It is questionable if its fraudulent nature would be discovered, so beautiful is the spirit and language of the Old Testament imitated.[129]

The opening two verses of Franklin's Genesis 51 tell us this:

> And it came to pass after these things that Abraham sat at the door of his tent and about the going down of the Sun. And behold, a man bowed with age came from the way of the wilderness leaning on his staff.[130]

Franklin's version of Genesis 51 goes on, in verses six to twelve, to describe an encounter between God and Abraham about the stranger, followed by the patriarch being sent into the wilderness in verse thirteen. Franklin ended his Genesis 51 with this couplet:

> And God spoke again unto Abraham, saying, "For this thy sin shall thy seed be afflicted four hundred years in a strange land. But for thy repentance will I deliver them, and they shall come forth with power and with a gladness of Heaven and with much substance."[131]

In 1759, when in England as an agent of the colony of Pennsylvania, Franklin privately printed this "chapter," as he called it. He kept it in his Bible after the close of chapter fifty of Genesis. He sometimes appeared to have amused his friends by reading it aloud and hearing them express their surprise.[132]

The other example of a Benjamin Franklin "Bible hoax" was when he sometimes quoted a text he simply called "Hezekiah 6:1," which relates, "God helps those who help themselves."[133] Like Genesis 51, The Book of Hezekiah 6:1 was a phantom Scripture, a product of the imagination of Franklin.

Hezekiah was indeed a historical figure who flourished in the eighth century BCE. He was the son of King Ahaz and the thirteenth successor to King David of Judah in Jerusalem. There is, however, no evidence that King Hezekiah wrote any book of Hebrew Scripture.[134]

Our final example of peculiar circumstances related to Franklin and the Holy Scriptures is what we know of the Franklin family Bible and its history and family circumstances.

Franklin purchased his family Bible while in London. It is a King James Bible, published by Cambridge University Press in 1763.[135] The American statesman paid ten pounds for the Bible, which was called the "Baskerville Bible."[136] Later, this Bible was given to his daughter, Sarah, on the occasion of her marriage.[137] She, in turn, gave the Bible to her daughter, Deborah Franklin Bache.[138]

The Bible continued in its family descent until it was eventually inherited by Clare Duane Ellis and her husband, Wiley Ellis, of South Carolina. Mrs. Ellis was the great-great-granddaughter of Benjamin Franklin. She inherited the Bible from her father, William Duane. The Ellises donated it to the Independence National Historical Park Museum in Philadelphia.

This brings us to the third section of Chapter Three of this study on Franklin's religion, in which we will enumerate, describe and discuss many passages from the Old Testament that had been spoken of or written about by him. It is to the Old Testament, then, to which we turn next.

Franklin and the Old Testament

Already in this third chapter, we have indicated that American statesman Benjamin Franklin employed passages from the Books of Genesis, Exodus and the first chapter of the Book of Job that he had rewritten. In the overall *corpus* of Franklin, particularly in his autobiography, as well as in his religious works mentioned in Chapters One and Two, we can find direct quotations from—or the mention of—nine books in the Old Testament.

These Old Testament books were the following:

Genesis

Proverbs
Exodus
Ecclesiastes
Leviticus
Deuteronomy
Samuel
Psalms
Book of Job

Of these Old Testament books, the one that he quoted from the most often was the Book of Psalms. Among the Psalms that Franklin mentioned or quoted from directly included Psalms 8, 82, 94, 106, and 127. Regarding Psalm 8, the relevant verses for him were 3 to 5. Concerning a conversation about man's relationship to God, he asks why the Divine "would regard such an inconsiderable nothing as man?"[139] The American statesman's response came directly from the King James Version of Psalm 8:3 to 5, which tells us:

> When I consider Thy Heavens, the works of Thy fingers, the moon and the stars which Thou hast ordained. What is man that Thou art mindful of him? And the Son of Man, that Thou visitest him? For Thou hast made him a little lower than the Angels and hast crowned him with glory and honour.[140]

In his phase of deism, Franklin, at times, seemed torn between his monotheistic upbringing and his Newtonian deism. We have suggested in Chapters One and Two that he appeared to have had periodic musings towards polytheism. As Thomas Kidd suggests, "Maybe one also remembered the Bible's occasional references to the 'gods,' such as Psalm 82."[141]

In the opening verse of Psalm 82 in the King James Version, the version read by the Franklin family, the Psalmist tells us, "God standeth in the congregation of the mighty; he judgeth among the gods."

Franklin was also fond of quoting Psalm 94:7 to 9, mostly because of the statesman's adage, "Any fool can criticize, condemn and complain—and most fools do." This adage may well have been from Psalm 94:8, which states, "Understand, ye brutish among the people, and ye fools, when will ye be wise?"[142] He also appears to be quoting Psalm 106:34 to 36 in his autobiography when he relates, "Tell me and I forget. Teach me and I remember. Involve me and I learn."[143]

During the American Revolution, Franklin repeatedly quoted the opening verse from Psalm 127:

> Unless the Lord builds the house,
> the builders labor in vain.
> Unless the Lord watches over the city,
> the guards stand watch in vain.[144]

Franklin and other Founding Fathers employed this image of the Jews building the ancient city of Jerusalem to parallel the American colonies building their great cities in the New World.

As we shall discover in Chapter Six, a chapter on the statesman's views on Virtue and Ethics, he used Psalm 3 as one of the main sources of his moral perspectives. The psalm in question mentions eight separate virtues in its thirty-four verses. These include trust, honor, peace, discipline, judgment, the Good, and understanding and wisdom. The latter two virtues are employed three times each.

The American statesman also regularly quoted directly from the ancient books of the Torah, the first part of the Hebrew Scriptures, and generally the oldest portions of the Biblical texts. In addition to quoting Genesis and Exodus mentioned earlier in this third chapter, Franklin was also very fond of the Book of Deuteronomy, particularly passages like 27:23 that use the word *arar*, or "curse," that he despised, as well as several other passages that support the idea of the golden rule in the Old Testament, as well portions that suggest that help should be given to the poor.

Among the passages of the Torah about the poor that Franklin was most fond of were Leviticus 19:9 to 10, which directs us to "Make provisions for the poor;" Leviticus 25:35 and 36, which tells us to "help the poor among you;" and Deuteronomy 15:7 and 8, that says to "Help the poor among your fellow Israelites."[145]

He understood Deuteronomy 15:10 and 11 that "The poor will always be among you," but he also knew and quoted Psalm 82:3 and 4, as we have indicated earlier in this chapter, that one should "uphold the cause of the poor."[146]

Franklin was also aware of the fourteenth chapter of the Book of Proverbs, which says much about the state and plight of the poor such as verse 21 that relates, we ought to "be kind to the needy" and verse 31 that "If one oppresses the poor, it shows contempt for one's Maker."[147] Proverbs 22:22 to 23 also warns against exploiting the poor, and Proverbs 29:7 informs us that "The righteous should surely care about the poor."[148]

In her essay "A Little Black Mark," contemporary Jewish writer, Behar Behuukkotai, quotes Franklin's autobiography regarding his views on virtue. Then she likens a section in the 1784 version of the work to the idea of *Tzedek* and *Middot* or "Justice" and "Virtue" in classical Hebrew. She is particularly cognizant that Leviticus 25:14 and 17 are much like Franklin's dedication to the Golden Rule.

Franklin was also very fond of the adage, "God helps those who help themselves," which can originally be found in Aesop's *Fables*. A similar sentiment is found in Euripides' *Hippolytus Veiled*.[149] Al-Qur'an, the Muslim's Holy Book, at Surah 13:11, also contains a similar sentiment that can be found in the 1736 version of *Poor Richard's Almanack*. It is Franklin's version, of course, that is most widely quoted in America.[150]

Franklin was also very fond of and employed several other Old Testament passages, including Ecclesiastes 9:7, First Samuel 28, Proverbs 6:29, and several other sections mentioned in his autobiography, as well as his many religious works. He recommended Solomon's advice from Ecclesiastes 9:7 to "Eat bread with joy and drink thy wine with a merry heart."

Franklin employed First Samuel 28 to argue against witchcraft in Old Testament places like the narrative of the "Witch of Endor," and the statesman regularly quoted passages like Proverbs 6:29 to argue against the sin of adultery.

One final Old Testament text that Franklin mentions in his letters is an episode in the fourth and fifth chapters of the Book of Judges in which Jael, the wife of Heber the Kenite, murders the Canaanite general Sisera with one of the wooden pins that served as tent posts. She waited for the Canaanite to fall asleep in her tent, and then with one terrible blow from a mallet, she drove the pin into his skull at the temple.[151]

This brings us to the final section of Chapter Three on Franklin and the Bible, in which we will describe and discuss many of the sections of the New Testament that he directly quoted or made some use of one way or another.

Franklin and the New Testament

Regarding the New Testament, four different kinds of passages have been quoted by or employed by Franklin. These may be summarized this way:

1. General comments about the New Testament by Franklin.
2. Comments about the poor and their plight by Franklin.
3. Adages where Franklin reflects New Testament values.
4. Passages used by Franklin to respond to the Rev. Hemphill's accusers.

In this section, we will end Chapter Three by speaking of several examples of these four "uses" of the New Testament by Franklin. In the first category of general comments, we will provide three examples: Hebrews 11:1, Second Corinthians 5:14, and the Gospel of John 10:34. In the first of these, while Franklin was on a diplomatic mission in France with John Adams during the American Revolution, he told Adams that he still had "two of the Christian graces, faith and hope, but my faith is only that of which the Apostle speaks, the evidence of things not seen."[152] Here he speaks of the opening verse of chapter eleven of the letter to the Hebrews.

Franklin made another general comment about the New Testament in the context of whether non-Christians will be saved. For this question, the statesman turned to Second Corinthians 5:14, which tells us, "For the love of Christ urges us on, because we are convinced that one has died for all; therefore, all have died." Franklin used this verse, of course, to combat the erroneous view that only Christians can receive salvation in the life to come.

In a third general comment of Franklin's on the New Testament, he speaks of the moral character of human beings being above the animals when he quotes Jesus in the Gospel of John at 10:34, "Is it not written in your Law, I said, 'You are gods.'"[153] Here it is clear that he believed that humans were far more like gods than the other animals.

Our second category of Franklin on the New Testament involves the many places in his adages where he appears to be reflecting the values of the New Testament. Again, we will cite three examples of this phenomenon.

In one of his many adages, he observed, "Fear not death; for the sooner we die, the longer shall we be immortal."[154] Here the American statesman supports the two New Testament values that one ought not to fear death and his belief in the eternal duration of immortality of the soul.

Franklin also tells us, "The end of passion is the beginning of repentance," indicating his view of the relative values of passion and repentance. He also relates, "Love your neighbor but do not pull down his hedge," another example of the relative values in the New Testament of brotherly love and fighting with one's enemies or neighbors.[155]

Various other adages, some of which the American statesman has become famous for, and reflect New Testament values, include:

- Silence is not always a sign of wisdom, but babbling is always folly.
- People who are wrapped up in themselves make small packages.
- Do not sell virtue to purchase wealth.
- We must all hang together or we will hang separately.
- It is common for men to give pretending reasons instead of one real one.
- There is never a good war or a bad peace.[156]

This brings us to our fourth category of Franklin on the New Testament—the statesman's defense of the Rev. Samuel Hemphill when the latter had been accused of heresy by the Presbyterian Church in 1735. Franklin entitled his essay "A Defence of the Reverend Hemphill's Observations." The essay was printed and sold by Franklin at his new printing office on Market Street in Philadelphia.[157]

The American statesman's essay was important for two purposes in regard to our concerns in this section of Chapter Three. First, the subtitle of the essay was this: "Or, An Answer to the Vindication of the

Reverend Commission."[158] In other words, he had intended his essay to be a response to the commission that had called Samuel Hemphill a heretic.

The other reason the 1735 essay on the Rev. Samuel Hemphill is significant is that Franklin quotes the New Testament six times during Hemphill's defense. These six passages are the following: II Corinthians 5:15; I Peter 2:24; I Timothy 1:5; Titus 2:14; and two passages from the Gospel of Matthew, 9:13 and 22:37–40.

In addition to these six uses of Franklin's defense of the Rev. Samuel Hemphill, emblazoned on the title page of the essay, he also included three New Testament quotes. These were Titus 1:13, and First Timothy 1:4 and 4:7. The verse from Titus tells us, "This testimony is true, for this reason rebuke them sharply, so that they may become sound in the faith."[159] This verse comes immediately after the old Greek syllogism, "Cretans are always liars, vicious brutes and lazy gluttons," said the Cretan, implying that Hemphill's accusers should be numbered among the Cretans in the view of Franklin.

At First Timothy 1:4, Paul tells us, "Not to occupy themselves with myths and endless genealogies that promote speculation rather than the divine training."[160] Again, Franklin seems to imply that Saint Paul had the Rev. Samuel Hemphill's accusers in mind when the evangelist wrote this verse to Timothy.

At First Timothy 4:7, which was also emblazoned on the title page of Franklin's essay written in defense of Samuel Hemphill, the text in question advises us to "Have nothing to do with profane myths and old wives' tales."[161] The American statesman again makes the implication that this is precisely what the members of the synod who had accused the Rev. Hemphill of heresy were now doing—making profane myths and old wives' tales about the Rev. Samuel Hemphill.

This brings us to the major conclusions we have made in this third chapter. In Chapter Four to follow, we will return to the idea of deism, as well as several other intellectual foundations that went into the making of the religion of Benjamin Franklin.

Conclusions to Chapter Three

In the introduction to this third chapter on Franklin and the Bible, we suggested that the chapter would have four main sections. The first of these would be general comments he made about the Holy Scriptures. The introduction also told us that the second section would be about several peculiar situations where the Bible can be found or discussed in the life of Franklin. In the remaining two sections of Chapter Three, we indicated that they would be taken up with separate sections on Franklin regarding the Old Testament and the New Testament.

In section one of this chapter, we made several general comments that Franklin made about the Bible, including that at the age of fifteen, he began to doubt the idea of Revelation itself, that he was in favor of diligent reading of the Holy Scriptures, and that he also was in favor of a Bible to be found in every home in Pennsylvania and America.

We also have shown in the first section of Chapter Three that Franklin was against the idea of the British government's practice of taxing the poor and that he appealed to II Thessalonians 3:10 in support of his rebuke.

In section two of Chapter Three, we enumerated and discussed seven peculiar sets of circumstances in which Franklin's views on the Bible can most easily be seen. These included: Silence Dogood on the Bible, Franklin and the Great Seal of the United States, Franklin's New Version of the Bible, the Bible in the Pennsylvania Constitution, the American statesman as a Bible merchant, Franklin's Bible hoaxes, and a discussion of the Franklin family Bible.

In each of these seven instances, we also showed the circumstances under which the Bible had come to the fore in the life of Franklin, the first great American statesman and one of the first great authors.

Passages from the Old Testament quoted or discussed by Franklin were the subject matter of the third section of Chapter Three. In this section, we have shown that Franklin utilized verses from ten different books of the Old Testament. These were: Genesis, Exodus, Leviticus, Deuteronomy, Samuel, Psalms, the Book of Job, Proverbs, the Book of Daniel, and Ecclesiastes.

We also indicated that Franklin was much more comfortable with the books of the Torah and the *Kethuvim*, or Writings, than he was with the *Nabiim*, or Prophets in Classical Hebrew, and this was mostly because of his overall interests in justice and virtue.

In the fourth and final section of Chapter Three, we turned our attention to Franklin and the New Testament. In that section, we made the claim that he had four separate kinds of New Testament passages that he quoted directly or commented upon.

These included very general comments about the New Testament; comments about the poor; adages where Franklin appears to be mirroring New Testament Values; and finally, passages of the New Testament where he was responding to the criticisms of his friend, the Rev. Samuel Hemphill. Among the general comments of Franklin's on the New Testament, we discussed the statesman's belief in what the Book of Hebrews calls "evidence for things unseen." And that he believed that human beings have a moral status closer to God than to animals. We also have shown that he believed in the possibility of salvation for those people who do not know about Jesus Christ.

In the material about the poor in section three, we introduced and discussed ten Franklin adages where he appears to reflect the values of the New Testament. Among these adages were: Do not fear death for the sooner we die, we will be immortal; that the end of passion is the beginning of repentance; that one should love his neighbor but not pull down his hedge, as well as many other adages of the first American statesman.

Finally, we showed that Franklin employed his knowledge of the Bible to respond to the Presbyterian Synod of Philadelphia when it had branded the Rev. Samuel Hemphill a heretic of the church. We have also shown that he very adeptly employed many passages from the New Testament in his effort to vindicate the character and beliefs of his friend, Samuel Hemphill. Indeed, in his "A Defence of the Reverend Hemphill's Observations; Or, an Answer to the Vindication of the Reverend Commission," we have shown that Franklin responded to the synod in defense of his friend by implying that his accusers were makers of myths and old wives' tales and that the accusers "may not have been sound in their faiths."[162]

Indeed, we have shown that he very slyly suggests that the Rev. Hemphill's Presbyterian accusers, at least for Franklin, were very much akin to the old Greek adage, "all Cretans are liars," said the Cretan and in the statesman's mind the accusers too were Cretans.[163]

This brings us to the fourth chapter, where we will say more about the movement of deism and the other intellectual influences in the life and works of Franklin.

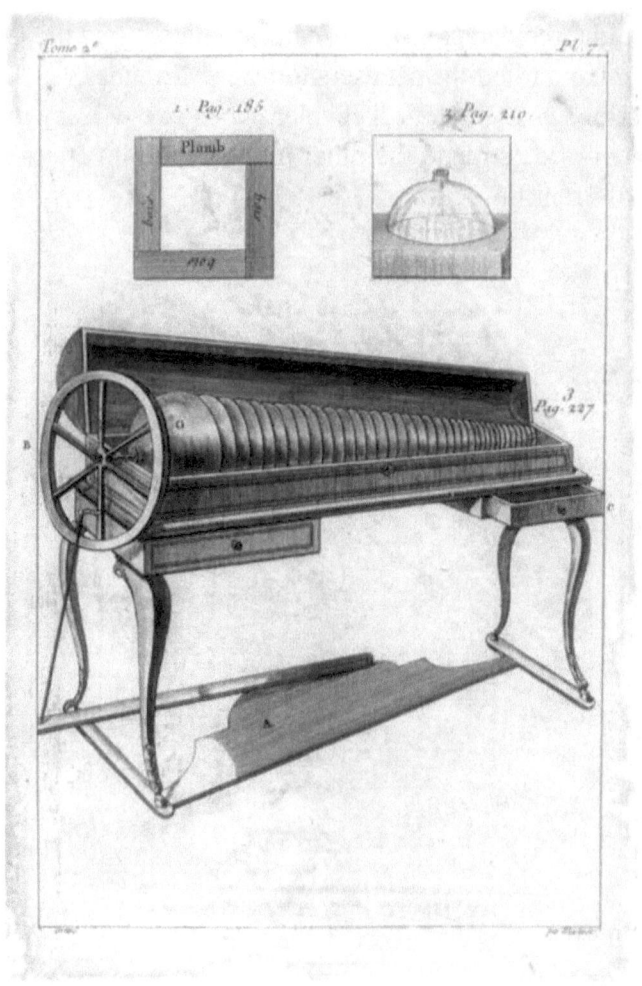

By fitting a series of graduated glass discs on a spindle laid horizontally in a case and revolving the spindle by a foot treadle, Franklin created bell-like tones by touching his wet fingers to the revolving glasses. The glass armonica became popular in Europe, and both Mozart and Beethoven composed music for it. Courtesy of the Library of Congress.

Chapter Four
Franklin on Deism and Other Intellectual Sources

> Benjamin Franklin was a real tomcat, no woman was safe from his lightning bolt.
> —Samuel Smiles, *Mrs. Isabella Beeton and Benjamin Franklin*

> Deism believes in God and there it rests.
> —Thomas Paine, "Of the Religion of Deism Compared with the Christian Religion"

> Write to Please Yourself.
> When You write to please others,
> You end up Pleasing No one.
> —Benjamin Franklin, *The Autobiography of Benjamin Franklin*

Introduction

The purpose of this chapter is to give a summary and analysis of the intellectual influences of Benjamin Franklin, the first great American statesman. We will divide Chapter Four into four separate sections in which we will say more about his relation to deism in the first section.

This will be followed by an introduction and discussion of Franklin's relation to the movement known as the Enlightenment. In the third section, we will examine and discuss the intellectual influence that the movement, known as the Great Awakening, might have had on Franklin, particularly in relation to British preacher George Whitefield.

Finally, in the fourth section of Chapter Four on the intellectual influences on him, we will enumerate and discuss several other intellectual influences on the life and times of Franklin, including his father Josiah's child-rearing practices and his reading regiment over the years. We return next, then, to Franklin and deism.

Franklin and Deism

We will begin this first section of Chapter Four by saying more about the theological movement known as deism and how Franklin understood that movement and what he thought and wrote about it. We already have spoken in Chapter One on his claim at the age of fifteen that he was "an avowed deist."[164]

In this section, we will say more about what deism is and was, as well as answer the question about how long the American statesman remained a deist. In fact, we shall see that the evidence available for answering that question is rather ambiguous.

Deism was a theological movement that began in the English-speaking world with the publication of Lord Herbert of Cherbury's tome, *De Veritate*, published in London in 1624. As far as we know, this was the first time the word "deism" appeared in the English language.[165]

The appearance of English philosopher John Locke's *An Essay Concerning Human Understanding* in 1690 marked the beginning of a new phase of English deism. Locke criticized the work of Lord Herbert because he appears to have argued for the idea of innate ideas, which Locke was decidedly against.[166]

A few years later, in 1696, John Toland published his popular tract known as *Christianity Not Mysterious*. This work renewed the debate about the deist movement and caused theological responses from several prominent British thinkers, including Thomas Chubb and Thomas Woolston, as well as Anthony, the Third Earl of Shaftesbury.[167] The latter figure never said or wrote outright that he was a deist, but he shared many of the ideas that tended to be held by the deists in Britain.

Meanwhile, the first hint of deism in the French-speaking world is found in the sixteenth-century French city of Lyon. In 1563, Pierre Viret, a close colleague of Protestant reformer Jean Calvin, wrote *Instruction Chretienne*, describing various freethinkers who needed to be combated. Among these were what Viret called those *"qui s'appelent deistes,"* or "Those who call themselves deists."[168]

A century later, in 1654, the French Catholic Church and a barrister named Jean Filleau claimed that the Catholic reformer Cornelius Jansen, Saint Cyran and five others met in Bourgfontaine in order to plan the destruction of French Catholicism and to supplant it with a form of deism.[169] Subsequent French deists included Simon Tyssot de Patot (1655–1738); Jean Meslier (1664–1729); Julien Offray de La Mettrie (1709–1751); and, of course, Francois Arouet, also called Voltaire (1694–1778), whom we discussed earlier in this study of Franklin's religion.

Other historians have suggested that philosopher Jean Jacques Rousseau (1712–1778) was another French thinker who tended to share many of the deist's beliefs. Rousseau was Swiss, however, and spoke Swiss French like those in Geneva.

The two major ideas to which all deists, those in England as well as among eighteenth-century French speakers, assented were first, that Reason, along with features of the natural world, is a valid source for religious knowledge. And secondly, Revelation is not a valid source of religious knowledge.

Earlier in this study, in the first section of Chapter Three, we distinguished between the ideas of Truths of Reason and Truths of Revelation made famous by the thirteenth-century Italian philosopher Thomas Aquinas. For the most part, the English deists eschewed the idea of Revelation in favor of the notion of Natural Truths, or Truths of Reason. By the publication of Matthew Tindal's *Christianity as Old as the Creation* in 1730, this book came to be known as the "deist's Bible."[170] Tindal's book was soon the object of severe criticism from a host of British and European thinkers, such as Scottish philosopher David Hume and his *Natural History of Religion*, published in 1757.[171]

Among other things, Hume suggested that the Argument from Design, also called the Teleological Argument for God's existence, used by thinkers like Tindal and William Paley, was no more probable than the belief that the universe was designed by several gods, or a form of polytheism. In fact, Hume goes on to observe that it was polytheism, not monotheism, that was "the first and most ancient religion of mankind."[172] Hume also suggested in the same work that the basis of religion is not reason but rather "ignorance and fear of the unknown."[173]

Thus, Hume, in his *Natural History of Religion*, as well as in his later work, *The Dialogues Concerning Natural Religion*, in 1776, dealt a severe blow to the deist's rosy picture of a prelapsarian Creation and early humans basking in the wonders of a designed universe.[174]

Meanwhile, in France, religious skepticism of "Natural Theology" also became popular with thinkers such as Pierre Bayle, Charles-Louis Montesquieu, and Voltaire, who claimed to be a deist. The French deists also included Maximilien Robespierre. In fact, the deists proposed replacing the Roman Catholic Church with belief in deism as the national faith.[175]

Before 1776, the Unites States were colonies of the British Empire, and Americans were British subjects. Nevertheless, English deism was an important influence in the thinking of several American Founding Fathers, including Thomas Jefferson and Benjamin Franklin.

The most prominent American deist, in addition to Jefferson and Franklin, was Thomas Paine. In his *Of the Religion of Deism Compared with the Christian Religion*, Paine sketched out six "distinguishing elements of deism." These propositions were the following:

1. Belief in God.
2. Belief that God created the Universe.
3. The Ability to Reason was given to Humans by God.
4. A Rejection of Literary Texts and Revelation.
5. A Rejection of Demagogy.
6. A Rejection of Miracles and Holy Mysteries.[176]

By number five above, Paine means the "rejection of religious manipulation," which means something like not assenting to the view that religion does not drastically change over time. The rejection of miracles is related to another essay by David Hume, "Of Miracles," which is part ten of his work, *An Enquiry Concerning Human Understanding*, published in 1748.[177] Paine's views on mystery and miracles are based on Hume's essay.

Franklin admits in his autobiography, as we have shown a few times in this study, to be a "thorough deist." We also have shown that after coming across some Christian books "against the deists" in his father's library, Franklin wrote, "It happened that they wrought an effect on me quite contrary to what was intended by them, for the arguments of the deists, which were quoted to be refuted, appeared to me to be much stronger than the refutations."[178] By the age of fifteen, then, we see Franklin struggling with his parent's brand of Christianity, and he had begun to reject a number of major beliefs about that faith, and consequently, he started to identify with the deists.

It is clear that in some of his early religious works described in Chapter One, including the 1728 "Articles of Belief and Acts of Religion" and "A Dissertation on Liberty and Necessity," Franklin was enamored by the deist's Argument from Design. In the latter work, he made it very clear when he wrote:

> By God's Wisdom hast Thou formed all things, Thou hast created Man, bestowed Life and Reason and played him in dignity superior to Thy other earthly Creatures. Praised be Thy name forever.[179]

Franklin alludes here to his Enlightenment belief of Reason over Revelation, as he also did at the age of fifteen, as well as to his dedication and belief in the deist idea of the Argument from Design, or the teleological argument for God's existence.

In Franklin's "On the Providence of God in the Government of the World," he also assented to many of the basic beliefs of deism as sketched out by Thomas Paine. In fact, in that work, he tells us in the introduction that he intends to offer the reader "nothing but plain Reasoning devoid of Art and Ornament, unsupported by the Authority of any Books or Men."[180] Franklin adds to this passage:

> ...because I know that no Authority is more convincing to Men of Reason than the Authority of Reason itself.[181]

Again, in this passage, he reveals his preference for Reason in the eighteenth-century debate of Reason versus Revelation, and he also, perhaps, alludes to the design that the "Authority" uses to convince men of his design.

In these two short passages, Franklin gives his assent to all of the first four of Thomas Paine's propositions on the nature of deism. That still leaves the question, however, about how long he continued to think of himself as a deist. Certainly, he appears to be leaning in that direction in his defense of Hemphill. Franklin also seems to be assenting to propositions in several places in the *Poor Richard's Almanack,* many from the later 1750s.[182]

We have argued, however, in the first chapter of this study, that by the writing of a letter to Madame Brillon in 1781, in which Franklin sketches out for his friend his religious beliefs, it appears that he no longer considers himself to be numbered among the believers in a *Deus Absconditis.*[183] That is, a God who made the world and the rules by which it operates but has no further commerce with it. This same conclusion can be seen in the letter he sent to President Ezra Stiles, who inquired about the statesman's religious beliefs around the time that Franklin died in April of 1790.[184]

This brings us to the second section of Chapter Four, in which we will analyze and discuss the influence that the movement known as the Enlightenment had on the life and times of Benjamin Franklin.

Franklin and the Enlightenment

The idea of belief in deism, of course, was part of a larger movement from the late seventeenth century to the early nineteenth century known as the Enlightenment. The Enlightenment became a political movement at that time, first in Europe and then later in America. In the seventeenth century, scientific discoveries influenced the thinkers of the Enlightenment, including Galileo, Robert Boyle, and, of course, Sir Isaac Newton, discussed earlier in Chapter Two of this study.[185]

As we have shown, Newton provided a model for looking rationally at human institutions and at nature itself. Jean Jacques Rousseau first raised the time-honored idea of the Divine Right of Kings, suggesting that no human monarch received the sanction for his rule from God. In his work, *The Social Contract*, the French philosopher argued that it is the "Consent of the People" that sanctions any political rule and not on the Divine for political authority.[186]

The thinkers of the Enlightenment also began to support other political ideas that became the foundation of Enlightened governments, like the use of Reason and the idea of Equality. The European Enlightenment followers of the seventeenth and eighteenth centuries heralded the idea of individuals reasoning for themselves under the auspices of the elimination of social standing.

This tended to make the European followers of the Enlightenment anti-clerical. The movement, for the most part, rejected traditional Roman Catholicism and instead developed a way of understanding the relation of God to the universe and human beings in a deistic fashion with a belief in a *Deus Absconditis*.

Other ideas that became popular in European Enlightenment thinking in the seventeenth and eighteenth centuries were rationalism, empiricism, progressivism and cosmopolitanism. Rationalism was the idea that human beings are capable of using their God-given faculty of reason to gain knowledge of man and the world. Empiricism promoted the idea that knowledge comes from the use of sense experience and observations of the world.187

Progressivism was the belief that through their powers of reason and observation, human beings could make unlimited, linear progress in history over time. This belief became particularly important as a response to the carnage and upheaval in the wake of the English civil wars in the seventeenth century.

Finally, the idea of cosmopolitanism reflected the Enlightenment thinker's view of himself as being an actively engaged citizen of the world, as opposed to being a more provincial and closed-minded individual. The Enlightenment thinker endeavored to be ruled by reason and not by prejudice.

Meanwhile, during the same period in America, we also begin to see the development of an American Enlightenment movement, and Franklin was part of it, as we have seen in our discussion of him on deism.

The American brand of the Enlightenment was characterized by six key ideas to which Franklin, in one way or another, assented. These six ideas were the following: deism, liberalism, republicanism, conservatism, toleration and scientific progress. Already, we have said enough about deism and its relation to Franklin. That leads us to a discussion of the other five ideas that characterizes the American form of the Enlightenment movement, which we will discuss next.

Liberalism in the late eighteenth century was the notion that human beings had been given a set of natural rights, either by God or the government, and that this government is not absolute but rather based on the will and the consent of the governed. Merchants embraced liberalism in America, and we began to see the development in the British colonies of a new middle class. This new mercantile spirit made no distinction between a consumer, a producer or a citizen.

One way that Franklin was involved in the idea of liberalism was his joining the "Leather Apron Club," which supported middle-class issues, including discussions of liberal and civil causes.[188]

The idea of "classical republicanism" was the notion that the new American nation ought to be ruled by a republic in which the government's highest offices are to be determined by a vote of its citizens rather than a claim to a hereditary right. Classical republican values included: patriotism, virtuous citizenship and property rights. In classical republicanism, a citizen exercises his freedoms within the context of existing social relations, historical associations and traditional communities, not as autonomous individuals set apart from the political and the social order.[189]

George Washington's forming of a militia and eventually the Continental Army from regular citizens is a fine example of republicanism at work. Likewise, Franklin's many civic projects in Philadelphia, such as the forming of the fire department, the building of the public library, and the establishment of a hospital, are all fine examples of American republicanism.[190]

The idea of conservatism in the American brand of the Enlightenment suggested that living in a society is the product of living in what Edmund Burke called a "Political Society." Conservatives in America attacked the idea of a social contract in thinkers like Thomas Hobbes, John Locke and Jean-Jacques Rousseau as a mythical construction that overlooked the plurality of groups.

Conservatism figured prominently in the American Enlightenment experience. This can be seen in the pitting of Thomas Jefferson's liberalism against James Madison's conservative views that a Constitutional Convention should be held every twenty years. As Madison wrote, "For the Earth belongs to the living generation," so each new generation should be empowered to reconsider its constitutional norms.[191]

Franklin also showed his commitment to the Enlightenment idea of conservatism. Liberalism in his day meant being open to change. Conservatism meant being in the conservative middle of the present public political spectrum. Franklin knew the work of Edmund Burke and admired his brand of what was called conservatism.[192]

The American Enlightenment movement was dedicated to the idea of toleration or what was also called "tolerant liberalism" at the time. American thinkers inherited this principle of tolerant pluralism from the European Enlightenment, mostly inspired by Scottish Enlightenment thinkers like John Knox, David Hume and George Buchanan.[193] The American statesman met David Hume on one of his trips to Britain. In fact, the Scot gave him a personal tour of Edinburgh.[194]

These Scottish Enlightenment thinkers based their views on toleration in a writing by John Locke entitled *A Letter Concerning Toleration*, which Franklin also admired. He saw toleration as a way for human beings to develop moral virtue. This led him, among other things, to donate funds to many churches and Christian denominations in Philadelphia.[195]

Finally, the American Enlightenment's enthusiasm for scientific discoveries can be seen no better in any other example than in the work of Franklin. Some might even say that, more than anything else, he was an "Enlightened Scientist."

Franklin's work on electricity, the development of the idea of the cardiac catheter, his lightning rod, and his many other practical inventions like the glass armonica, bifocals, swim fins for the hands, and the Franklin stove, for example, were all scientific developments that he brought to Western and American society.

Franklin was an Enlightenment scientist who was intrigued by the basic operations of nature, not just as a tinkerer and inventor. He carried out experiments and frequently quoted the scientific pamphlets of famous scientific thinkers who were enthusiastic about his work. He was well acquainted, for example, with the work of Sir Isaac Newton and employed Newton's theories when he observed that a conductor of electricity could experience change from a greater distance than a blunt conductor. This led to his invention of the lightning rod. He also discovered the basic principle of the conservation of electrical charge, another important principle in Enlightenment thought. Noble prize winner in physics for his work on electrons points to the fact that "Benjamin Franklin is often too much underestimated as an Enlightenment Scientist."[196]

So as part of his intellectual predecessors, it is important to remember great scientists like Isaac Newton. Franklin was indeed an "Enlightenment Scientist." His study of philosophy, ethics, the natural sciences, the matter of health in society, as well as his activities in civil affairs and politics, demonstrated the versatility of his skills and competencies and the vast nature of his intellectual curiosity, which made him a great thinker and scientist of the American Enlightenment.

Franklin had a mind for many different subjects, and in all of these endeavors, he demonstrated skill, discipline and responsibility to his fellow citizens of Philadelphia, Pennsylvania, and the United States. Regarding public education, he founded a reading and writing club called the Junto, as well as the American Philosophical Society, in his adopted city.

He also drew up a plan of what was to become the University of Pennsylvania, originally known as the "Academy of Pennsylvania."[197] Franklin also advocated, from very early on, for a Bible to be in every home and a good school in every community.

It is worth pointing out that, in all the other colonies, colleges and universities were primarily established by religious institutions. Harvard, for example, was first established to train Puritan ministers. Yale College, as well, was founded by Calvinist clergymen. The College of William & Mary, founded in 1693, was originally run by Virginia Anglicans. Evangelical Presbyterians founded the College of New Jersey, later to be called Princeton University, in 1746.

Franklin wanted his academy to be different. Instead of primarily training the clergy, his institution would educate young men of all classes and colors to be successful businessmen, public servants, and, above all, moral citizens.

By the time he died in his adopted city on April 17, 1790, he had become famous nearly worldwide as a journalist, inventor, businessman, statesman, diplomat, civic leader, musician, and scientist, not to mention being something of a humorist and a traveler. If there was such a thing as an American Enlightenment, then he was one of its leaders and chief proponents.

Another big difference between Franklin's academy and the other colleges in the colonies had to do with the curriculum. Instead of the traditional curriculum and the study of ancient languages and Greek and Roman classics, the academy would instruct its students about contemporary arts and sciences. Franklin, the Scientist, argued that the academy should teach what he called "practical knowledge." Interestingly enough, however, the academy's original board of trustees did not agree with his educational vision, and they chose a more traditional curriculum like at Harvard and Yale.

In 1750, Franklin published an essay suggesting that lightning is a form of electricity and could prove it by flying a kite in a lightning storm. Two years later, he stepped out into the streets of Philadelphia, and as thunder and lightning crashed around him and across the sky, he released a kite into the air with a metal key tied to its string.

Franklin watched as the loose threads of the string began to repel each other, and as he moved his hands closer to the key, he saw a spark. He proved that lightning is a form of electricity. The statesman won international acclaim throughout the American colonies and in Europe.

Franklin was truly what today would be called a "Renaissance Man." But in his own time—the eighteenth century—he was known as the best example of what can be called the "American Enlightenment."

This brings us to the third section of this fourth chapter on the intellectual influences of Franklin, in which we will introduce and discuss what was called the "Great Awakening" in British and American theology in the eighteenth century.

Franklin and the Great Awakening

A third major intellectual movement that influenced the life of Franklin was what was known as the "Great Awakening." In her essay "The First Great Awakening," Christine Leigh Heyman summarizes the phenomenon this way:

> What historians call "the first Great Awakening" can best be described as a revitalization of religious piety that swept through

the American colonies between the 1730s and the 1770s. That revival was part of a much broader movement, an evangelical upsurge taking place simultaneously on the other side of the Atlantic, most notably in England, Scotland, and Germany. In all these Protestant cultures during the middle decades of the eighteenth century, a new Age of Faith rose to counter the currents of the Age of Enlightenment, to reaffirm the view that being truly religious meant trusting the heart rather than the head, prizing feeling more than thinking, and relying on biblical revelation rather than human reason.[198]

Heyman tells us that the earliest evidence for the First Great Awakening in America came among Presbyterians in Pennsylvania and New Jersey, led by the Tennent family—the Rev. William Tennent and his four sons, all of whom "were trained ministers."[199] In fact, the Tennent family established a seminary to train ministers that were initially known as the "Log College," but today it is referred to as the Princeton Theological Seminary.

The First Great Awakening quickly spread to the New England Congregationalists, mostly Puritans and Baptists. By the 1740s, these churches were conducting what was known as "revivals" throughout the colonies. The greatest of these New England preachers was Jonathan Edwards, who is sometimes called "the Father of the First Great Awakening," at least according to Diane Severance in her essay, "What was the Great Awakening?"[200]

Dr. Severance describes preaching style of the Rev. Jonathan Edwards this way:

> The preacher's monotone voice filled the church in Northampton, Massachusetts. As the brilliant Jonathan Edwards spoke, he kept his eyes focused on the back wall of the church. Gently, Edwards' words began to sink into the hearts of the assembly, and although his method of speaking lacked enthusiasm, his words were powerful. Revival followed.[201]

Jonathan Edwards was born on October 10, 1703. At the tender age of thirteen, he entered Yale University and graduated in 1723. Four years later, he married Sarah, and in 1727 he became the assistant minister at his grandfather's church in Northampton. When his grandfather died, Edwards became the head minister. He served in that capacity for twenty-four years until 1751.

Another important figure of the First Great Awakening—particularly for our purposes—was British preacher the Rev. George Whitefield. Even though Whitefield was ordained in the Church of England, he eventually became a Calvinist, his sermons often akin to those of the Swiss Reformer John Calvin.

George Whitefield made several trips to America, preaching up and down the eastern seaboard. He often preached in outdoor venues, and the crowds were so large that they sometimes reached twenty-five thousand people or more. Whitefield spread the message of the First Great Awakening, which helped consolidate the colonies prior to the American Revolution.

Franklin went to hear the Rev. Whitefield speak in 1739 in Philadelphia. The American statesman tells us in his autobiography that,

> He preached one evening from the top of the Courthouse steps... The streets were filled with his hearers... I had the curiosity to learn how far he could be heard by retiring backwards down the street... and found his voice distinct until I came near Front Street.[202]

Franklin continued his critique of Whitefield's preaching:

> Multitudes of all denominations attended his sermons... It was wonderful to see the change soon made in the manners of our inhabitants. From being thoughtless or indifferent about religion, it seemed as if the world were growing religious, so that one could not walk through the town in the evening without hearing psalms sung in different families of every street.[203]

Franklin alludes here to his long-held belief that one of the most important aspects of the idea of religion and religious practices is their "Utility" in regard to society as a whole. In his view, they are entirely good for the state.

When George Whitefield spoke in Philadelphia in 1739, Franklin helped to finance the building and the auditorium where

Whitefield preached. The same building was later donated to become the first structure of the University of Pennsylvania. In fact, a bronze statue of the Rev. Whitefield can still be seen on the university's campus.[204] The Great Awakening Revival also resulted in the founding of Princeton, Brown, Dartmouth, Columbia, and Rutgers universities.

In his printing press, Franklin published the Rev. Whitefield's *Travel Journal*, as well as his *Sermons* that helped to spread the popularity of the English preacher in America.[205] There is also a lengthy correspondence between Franklin and the Rev. Whitefield.[206]

Franklin wrote about Whitefield's November 1739 oration from the courthouse steps in Philadelphia. He was a "young, blue-eyed evangelist, just shy of twenty-five years of age. He had scarcely set foot in the colonies before he went to work on one of his first projects in the new world—an orphanage for the colony of Georgia."[207] Franklin had doubts about the success of the orphanage and told Whitefield so, mostly because the Pennsylvanian wished for the orphanage to be built in Philadelphia.[208]

For Franklin, much of his relationship with the Rev. Whitefield was strictly a business relationship. He disliked the minister's brand of Calvinism, but he thought that the Englishman's books might be profitable, particularly since Franklin was in competition with a rival printer. Whitefield wanted the notoriety of the American press, just as he had effectively exploited the British press by advertising his services in London's newspapers in the mid-1730s.[209] George Whitefield died on September 30, 1770. As he was dying, his final words were reported to have been, "How willing I would ever live to preach Christ! But I die to be with Him."[210]

The friendship between Franklin and Whitefield lasted for more than thirty years. Some suggest it was a friendship of two odd partners, but there can be little doubt that George Whitefield was one of the great intellectual influences in the life of Benjamin Franklin. Although we have listed George Whitefield as a major intellectual influence on Franklin, it is clear that he was at times ambiguous about his friend. He disliked Whitefield's Calvinism while, at the same time, he admired "the extraordinary influence of his oratory on his hearers and how much they admired and respected him." In fact, Franklin once described Whitefield's followers as "Half Beasts and half Devils."[211]

This brings us to the fourth and final section of Chapter Four, in which we will explore other intellectual sources for the religious views of Franklin. The major conclusions of the chapter will follow this section.

Other Intellectual Sources for the Religious Views of Franklin

In addition to the three major intellectual sources already mentioned for the life of Benjamin Franklin, in this final section of Chapter Four, we will mention two other sources in forming the religious views of his. These two sources are his father Josiah's child-rearing practices and the many books in his four-thousand-volume personal library.

In his autobiography, Franklin spoke of his father's child-rearing practice, which the statesman found helpful in his life. According to him, his father was a man of "solid judgment" whose advice was regularly sought. But rather than secluding himself from those who sought his advice, Josiah Franklin had these people join his family at the dinner table. Thus, providing instant learning opportunities for his children.[212]

The American statesman tells us this about the Franklin family dinner table:

> At his table he liked to have, as often as he could, some sensible friend or neighbor to converse with, and always took care to start some in genius or useful topic for discourse, which might intend to improve the minds of his children. By this means, he turned our attention to what was good, just, and prudent in the conduct of life.[213]

Franklin continues in his autobiography by revealing three other aspects of his father's child-rearing practices at the Franklin family dinner table. The statesman called these: introduced possibilities, observed interests, and practiced kind correction.[214] By "introduced possibilities," Josiah Franklin meant the idea of introducing to his children many of the ways that Josiah's friends made a living. The father did this in the context of paying careful attention to the many books read by his son.

For example, this led to Benjamin's apprenticeship with his brother James' printing firm. It gave the younger brother his first opportunity to engage his interests in writing the Mrs. Silence Dogood letters, for instance, an occupation that launched him toward a career of fame and influence at home as well as abroad.

Finally, the notion of "practiced kind correction," as described in his autobiography, Josiah took gentle opportunities to point out to his son spelling and grammar errors, as well as ways in which Benjamin's writings, for example, might be improved.[215] Thus, Josiah Franklin had a profound influence on the intellectual life of his most famous son.

Another intellectual influence from his life is to peruse the "Library of Benjamin Franklin" holdings at the American Philosophical Society in Philadelphia. This list includes 3,747 books that were owned by Franklin and provide another avenue for determining his intellectual formation.

Earlier in this study of the religion of Franklin, we mentioned Cotton Mather's *Essays to do Good*.[216] Franklin saw this work, like he saw the Gospels and the life of Jesus Christ, as two of the foundations of his ethics and morality, as we shall see in Chapter Six of this study. Walter Isaacson's "Citizen Ben's Seven Great Virtues," an article written for *Time* magazine on June 7, 2003, also sketches out some of Ben Franklin's principal readings on virtue. Franklin first read Mather's book in 1717, when he was eleven years old. He had found the Mather volume in his father's private library.

Other volumes from his personal library that Franklin admired included:

> Cotton Mather's *Bonifacius, or Essays to do Good* (1663)
>
> Plutarch's *Life of Pericles*
>
> John Locke's *A Letter Concerning Toleration* (1689)
>
> Samuel Sewall's *The Selling of Joseph* (1700)
>
> Joseph Addison's *Cato: A Tragedy*
>
> John Trenchard and Thomas Gordon, "Cato's Letters"[217]

We will end Chapter Four by analyzing how each of these five works is a representative example of how Franklin's library and reading may have affected his intellectual and political life.

Cotton Mather (1663–1728) was a Boston-born 1678 Harvard College graduate and one of only two American colonists who were admitted to the Royal Society of London, the other being Benjamin Franklin. Mather entered Harvard at age twelve, graduated at sixteen, and received his Masters of Divinity from Harvard Divinity School in 1681 at the age of nineteen. Later Mather became a Calvinist minister.[218]

Cotton Mather is important for our purposes for three main reasons. First, in his autobiography, Franklin tells us that he first read Mather's *Bonafacius*, or *Essays to do Good*, at the age of eleven. The book had a lasting effect on him, particularly in regard to his views on ethics, as we shall see later in this study in Chapter Six.[219]

A second book in Franklin's library that he says had an effect on him is Plutarch's *Life of Pericles*, the fifth-century BCE statesman. He mostly admired Pericles because of his views on democracy and virtue. In regard to the former, Franklin speaks of Pericles' idea of a commonwealth and the role of the marketplace in politics. Regarding the latter, he admired Pericles on the Mean, as well as what he had to say about "Waste."[220]

We have spoken of John Locke's *A Letter Concerning Toleration* earlier in this chapter and will say much more about it in Chapter Five to follow. The "Letter" was originally published anonymously in Latin in 1689 and was part of the philosopher's *An Essay Concerning Human Understanding*.[221] Franklin greatly admired the Englishman's "Letter" and always referred to it whenever he spoke or wrote about religious toleration.

A fourth book from his library mentioned in his religious writings is the 1700 publication of Samuel Sewall's *The Selling of Joseph*.[222] Sewall's work was a strong refutation of the arguments made for slavery in America. Sewall was a Massachusetts judge best known for his involvement in the Salem witch trials, for which Sewall later admitted that he was wrong about them.[223]

Franklin was influenced by Samuel Sewall primarily on his views about slavery, the final issue that the first American statesman wrote about in his political career. Like Sewall, Franklin, as well as Thomas Jefferson for that matter, was diametrically opposed to the idea of slavery and believed it should have been abolished in America.[224]

A fifth book of Franklin's, which he had inherited from his father upon the death of the latter, was Joseph Addison's *Cato: A Tragedy*, written in 1712 and first performed on April 14, 1713, in London.[225] Addison's drama is based on the events of the final days of the life of Cato, the Younger (95–46 BCE) and his resistance to the tyranny of Julius Caesar. Addison's play was admired by many Colonists in America primarily for the parallels to Caesar and George the Second of Britain. Patrick Henry's famous quote, "Give me liberty or give me death," was taken right out of the mouth of Cato in Joseph Addison's drama. Benjamin Franklin tells us that he admired Addison mostly because of his "literary style."[226]

Again, he discovered the work of Joseph Addison in his father's library at home. He found a volume of Addison's essays from *The Spectator*. Addison was the son of an Anglican minister and a brilliant essayist. The young Franklin was entranced. In *The Spectator*, he discovered the latest English philosophical trends. Addison also denounced religious intolerance, something that Franklin found to his liking, as well.[227]

A final book in Franklin's reading that influenced his political career is a collection of letters written between November of 1720 and December of 1723 that has come to be known as the *Cato's Letters*.[228] This collection was written by two British journalists named John Trenchard and Thomas Gordon and published in the *London Journal*.[229] The two writers used the pseudonym Cato, who commented on various aspects of British society and politics.

In letter number 15, for example, Cato observed:

> In those wretched countries where a man cannot call his tongue his own, we can scarcely call anything else his own. Whoever would overthrow the Liberty of the nation, must begin by subduing, a thing terrible to publick traitors.[230]

This is very good advice for those in contemporary America who wish to prohibit what is sometimes called "hate speech."

In another of the letters, the two writers seem to be quoting directly from John Locke's essay on toleration, when Cato remarked:

> Every man's Religion is his own... which actions utterly exclude all force, power, or government... It is a relation between God

and our own soul only... Religion, therefore which can never be subject to the jurisdiction of another, can never be alienated to another, or put in his power.[231]

Franklin so greatly admired the Cato *Letters* that he published a volume of them. He was particularly indebted to Trenchard and Gordon for their views on what will become the First Amendment of the US Constitution. The Cato *Letters*, however, did not advocate a complete separation between church and state. In fact, Cato defended the Anglican Church's establishment that barred dissenters from holding public offices.

This brings us to the major conclusions of Chapter Four. In Chapter Five to follow, our main focus will be on what Franklin had to say and wrote about religious toleration.

Conclusions to Chapter Four

We began this fourth chapter of this study of Benjamin Franklin's religion by suggesting that the chapter will include four kinds of sources or materials about the intellectual influences of Franklin.

In the first of those sections, we have examined and said more about the philosophical movement of deism than what we had outlined earlier in this study. We also examined the origin of English-speaking deism to be in the work of Lord Herbert of Cherbury, and we indicated other English-speaking deists in the seventeenth and eighteenth centuries, such as Matthew Tindal and David Hume.

We also indicated that the most prominent American deist in the eighteenth century was Thomas Paine and his book *Of the Religion of Deism Compared with the Christian Religion*. In fact, we have shown that Paine set out six distinguishing aspects of his version of deism. There were: that God exists; that He created the Universe; that He endowed humans with reason; that the deist rejects written texts; as well as demagogy and miracle and mystery. In the second section of Chapter Four, we turned our attention to the eighteenth-century philosophical movement known as the Enlightenment.

We began this section by sketching out several of the major beliefs in the Enlightenment movement, including the rejection of

Roman Catholicism, the emphasis on reason, the rejection of Scripture and Revelation, and the eschewing of what the deists called "Miracle and Mystery."

In the second section of Chapter Four, we introduced and discussed the ideas of rationalism, empiricism, progressivism and cosmopolitanism, as well as how Franklin was an advocate of all four of these ideas.

Rationalism and empiricism, as we have shown, were the two most prominent European philosophical systems in the seventeenth and eighteenth centuries. The former movement believed that all knowledge came from the use of the mind and was championed by René Descartes. The latter philosophical view, empiricism, was advocated mostly in Britain by figures like John Locke and Thomas Hobbes.

Next, in the third section of Chapter Four, we turned our attention to the phenomenon of the First Great Awakening, its nature, and some of the major figures in the movement, including Jonathan Edwards and English preacher George Whitefield. Indeed, we wrote extensively about the relationship and friendship between the Rev. Whitefield and Benjamin Franklin, pointing out that, at times, it seemed to be characterized by ambivalence. In the fourth section, we examined two other intellectual sources in the life of Franklin. These were his father Josiah's child-rearing practices as set forth by the American statesman in his autobiography. Indeed, in this final section of Chapter Four, we have identified and discussed instant learning possibilities, introduced possibilities, observant interests, and practiced kind correction. After sketching out the nature of these four child-rearing practices by Josiah Franklin, we also indicated how these practices might have borne fruit in the life of Ben Franklin.

At the close of Chapter Four, we suggested that a final intellectual influence on the religious life of Franklin was many of the books in his personal library or in his readings that were mentioned by him. More particularly, we have indicated six books that he spoke of, or wrote of, as intellectual influences.

These six, in particular, were the Rev. Cotton Mather's *Bonifacius, or Essays to do Good*; Plutarch's *Life of Pericles*, popular in Colonial America for its republicanism; John Locke's 1689 anonymous *A Letter*

Concerning Toleration, greatly admired by Franklin; Samuel Sewall's 1700 work, *The Selling of Joseph*; Joseph Addison's 1712 drama, *Cato: A Tragedy*, that Franklin admired for Cato's response to the tyranny of Julius Caesar in that it reminded him of America's plight with King George II; and John Trenchard and Thomas Gordon, *Cato's Letters*.

Each of these six books are mention by Franklin as playing a role in the formation of his intellectual life going all the way back to the age of eleven when the statesman first read Mather's *Essays to do Good* and *Cato's Letters*, produced between 1720 and 1723.

Along the way, we also mentioned Franklin's admiration for fifth-century BCE Athenian, Pericles; Samuel Sewall's views on slavery and witch burning; John Locke on religious toleration; and Cotton Mather, both as a man and as a Colonial author.

This brings us to Chapter Five, where we will explore the idea of toleration to be found, particularly in regard to religious toleration, in the thinking of the first great American statesman.

It is to the ideas of religious freedom and religious toleration, then, to which we turn next in this study of the religion of Benjamin Franklin.

The reception for Franklin at the court of France in 1778. He received a laurel wreath upon his head. From left to right, some of the members of the French court, including Duchesse Jules de Polignac, Princesse Lamballe (holding flowers), Diana Polignac (holding wreath), Comte de Vergennes, Mme Campan, Countesse de Neuilly, Marie-Antoinette (seated), Louis XVI, Princess Elizabeth.
Courtesy of the Library of Congress.

Chapter Five
Franklin on Religious Freedom, Toleration and Church and State

> Mr. Franklin, who was renowned for his religious tolerance and liberal theology, would not have advocated the Jews be expelled from this country, or that their rights be abrogated by an emerging constitution of a new nation.
> —Kate Ohno, "Ben Franklin on Toleration"

> Franklin's motion for prayers in the Constitutional Convention has been used as the basis for another clerical falsehood that has been presented to the eyes or ears of nearly every man, woman, and child in the United States.
> —John E. Remsburg, "Six Historic Americans"

> The modesty in a sect is perhaps a singular instance in the history of mankind, every other sect imagining itself in possession of the truth and that those who differ are far in the wrong.
> —Benjamin Franklin, *The Autobiography of Benjamin Franklin*

Introduction

The purpose of this chapter is to examine Benjamin Franklin's views on the issues of religious freedom and religious toleration. As we shall discover, the first great American statesman had a good deal to say and write regarding these political and philosophical issues. We will open with some general observations about him on the notion of religious freedom. This will be followed by a much lengthier section on the idea of religious freedom, the separation of church and state, and religious tolerance to be found in the founding documents of the new nation, the United States.

In the third section, we will examine the phenomenon of religious toleration and how it was discussed by the other Founding Fathers, including George Washington, Thomas Jefferson, James Madison, and many other later eighteenth-century American thinkers.

Finally, in the fourth section, we shall explore what Franklin had to say and wrote about the phenomenon of religious toleration from the intolerance he saw among the Puritans in his youth until his views on the notion of religious toleration at the close of his life.

Franklin on Religious Freedom

To summarize the views of Franklin on religious freedom, we must first provide some background material on the issue in the early American colonies/states. Historians tell us that, at the time of independence, approximately 98 percent of all Americans identified themselves as "Protestant Christians."[232] About 75 percent of Americans at that time would say they were affiliated with the Reform Christian tradition.[233]

For the most part, the founders of the United States, those who were intimately involved in the political affairs that led to independence, reflected these demographics, including Franklin, whose parents were a Calvinist Congregationalist and a Calvinist Presbyterian, as we have shown in Chapter One of this study.

There was also, however, a wide range of religious beliefs among the American founders, from those who were quite orthodox in the faith to those like Franklin, who were quite skeptical at the time. Thomas Jefferson and Thomas Paine, the famous author of *Common Sense*, also were not orthodox in their beliefs, as indicated earlier in this study.[234]

On the other hand, men like John Witherspoon, a signer of the Declaration of Independence, held more to a traditional, or orthodox, view of the Christian religion. So, there was a wide range of beliefs among the Founding Fathers.

From as early as Silence Dogood's letter number eight to *The New-England Courant* on July 9, 1722, Franklin expressed his deep belief in the guarantees of the First Amendment of the US Constitution. Mrs. Dogood related,

> Without Freedom of Thought, there can be no such Thing as Wisdom; and no such Thing as publick Liberty, without Freedom of Speech; which is the Right of every Man, as far as by it, he does not hurt or controul the Right of another.

Later, in the same letter, written when the statesman was a mere sixteen years old, Franklin, as Mrs. Dogood, also related:

> Freedom of Speech is ever the Symptom, as well as the Effect of a good Government. In old Rome, all was left to the Judgment and Pleasure of the People, who examined the publick Proceedings with such Discretion, and censured those who administred them with such Equity and Mildness, that in the space of Three Hundred Years, not five publick Ministers suffered unjustly. Indeed whenever the Commons proceeded to Violence, the great Ones had been the Agressors.

Mrs. Dogood goes on in letter number eight, as well as letter number nine, to endorse the idea of the right to practice one's faith "in any way a man wishes to do so." Even as late as June 28, 1787, three years before Franklin's death, the statesman proposed the saying of a "Prayer" at the opening of the Continental Congress.[235] In his notes from that day, James Madison tells us that several members of the Congress objected to Franklin's motion.[236]

So the motion was tabled until the following day when there was a vote on Franklin's suggestion and where the proposal was defeated. He recorded his reaction to the vote in his notes, saying, "The Convention, except for three or four persons, thought Prayer unnecessary."

What is significant about this event, however, is not the issue of the separation of church and state as some have maintained. Rather, the issue is that even late in his life, Franklin was still dedicated to the idea of a prayer to be said by a "Minister: expressing his deeply held religious preferences to ask for blessing on the activities of the Continental Congress."

Two other events at the end of Franklin's life also point to his belief in religious liberty. He contributed to the building funds of each and every religious sect in Philadelphia, including a five-pound contribution to the Mikveh Israel congregation for its new synagogue in April of 1788, two years before Franklin's death.[237]

At the time, there was some debate in the Massachusetts Bay Colony about whether Jews should be expelled from the colony. Similar questions were raised in the seventeenth century in the Pennsylvania Colony, as well as the Maryland Colony. Even in Franklin's day, these concerns were still sometimes raised, but he was entirely against the idea and said so many times.[238]

Another way that Franklin's dedication to religious freedom can be seen is in a collection of facts related to his funeral. When he was carried to his grave in April of 1790, he had left instructions that his casket was to be carried by "All the Clergymen, one of them from every faith."[239]

Two other events in the life of Franklin also point to his dedication to the idea of religious freedom. The first of these is an essay that he wrote entitled "A Witch Trial at Mount Holly." It is a parody of sorts of the seventeenth-century witch trials in Massachusetts. In Franklin's account, a couple of accused witches were subjected to two tests: weighed on a scale against a Bible and tossed in the river with hands and legs tied to see if they would float.[240] The witches agreed to the two tests, but only if their accusers were subjected to the same tests. Both of the accusers, as well as one of the accused, failed to sink in the river, thus indicating that they were witches. The skeptics present concluded that most people float, but the others were not so sure, so they put off the conclusion until the following spring when the experiment could be repeated.[241] Beneath these two witch experiments, of course, were two more fundamental metaphysical beliefs. That is, witches are very heavy, and they are too heavy to float.

The aspect of Franklin's tale, in addition to the parody of the Massachusetts witch trials, is the discussion that if the women were, in fact, witches, then they should be able to express their religious convictions in the same way as everybody else. The right to free worship, in Franklin's view, should be preserved for witches as much as for everyone else.[242]

A similar set of circumstances arose regarding another religious issue in 1763 when some frontier settlers murdered a band of Native Americans who were living peacefully in Lancaster County, Pennsylvania. Among the reasons that they were killed was because of their "bizarre religion."[243]

Franklin also had in his possession the narrative of a Swedish missionary telling the Native Americans of the Susquehanna Tribe that only Christians would inherit the Kingdom of God. Franklin concluded that the "palming off of such tenets on Christianity most likely would obscure the propagation of the faith."[244] The chief told Franklin he could not accept the missionary's message because the Swede wanted the Native Americans to give up their traditional faith in favor of Christianity.[245]

The description of the faith of the Susquehanna Tribe impressed Franklin very much, so much so that it reminded the statesman of his own beliefs. The chief recounted that their ancestors had taught them that good deeds performed in this life would be rewarded in the next life "according to the person's virtue." As we have seen in Chapters One and Two of this study, Franklin had a similar view.[246]

On the other hand, the chief related, "The wicked will suffer punishment in the great beyond according to the severity of their crimes."[247] In regard to the nature of religious truths, the chief and his tribe regarded it as "sacred, inviolable, and the natural right of every person to examine and judge for himself," or so we learn from Franklin.[248]

Franklin also tells us that the chief asked tough questions of the Swedish missionary. Did he believe that all of their forefathers are now suffering in hellfire? Why did God reveal Himself to the Natives through nature rather than giving them the revelation necessary in order to be saved through Jesus Christ?[249]

The great American statesman did not oppose the missionary's message, mainly because he believed it would "civilize" the Native people, and he was decidedly against that. Nevertheless, this is another example in which he was a clear believer that the Susquehanna Indians should exercise their right to practice their faith in whatever way they preferred and that the Swedish missionary was engaged in the practice of religious intolerance when it came to the faith of the Native Americans.[250] Franklin penned a narrative he entitled, "A Narrative of the Late Massacres." He went so far as to petition the Royal Government for stronger authority in enforcing the law. Even though Franklin knew this stance could well hurt him politically and put him at odds with the Penn family. Nevertheless, he said in his narrative that the settlers "had no right" to take away the religious rights of the Native Americans. Thus, we have another example of his life-long commitment to the idea of religious freedom.

In Philadelphia, Franklin was surrounded by Lutherans, Moravians, Quakers and Jews, as well as Calvinists, like his parents. They were all living side by side in the "City of Brotherly Love." It is very clear that throughout his life, he was dedicated to the idea of all of these religions and Christian denominations to exercise their right to practice their religions anyway they saw fit.

Another way that Franklin was clearly dedicated to the idea of religious freedom is how many religions and denominations tried to claim him as one of their own. Among these, of course, were the Congregationalists, the Presbyterians and the Anglicans.

But it was also true of the Quakers. The Catholics thought him almost a Catholic. In fact, John Adams, who was somewhat jealous because of Franklin's popularity, called Franklin "almost a Catholic."[251] His biographer, Stacy Schiff wrote that he "was held in high esteem by the Catholics, by the Church of England, by every religious denomination, each of whom happily claimed him as one of their own: a monochromatic blur amid the brilliant plumage of Paris."[252]

Franklin wrote in one letter that,

> If Christian Preachers had continued to teach as Christ and his Apostles did, without salaries, and as the Quakers now do, I would imagine that Tests would never have existed.[253]

Here he appears to be making three separate points. First, that the most primitive form of Christianity is no longer being taught. Secondly, that the Quakers appear to be closer than any other sect of the statesman's time. And thirdly, that Franklin seems to be identifying with those Quaker beliefs and practices, and that is why the Society of Friends, like many other sects, have claimed Franklin as one of their followers.[254]

Another way to see the ecumenism of Franklin and also his regard for religious freedom is to look at the many different ministers in many different denominations and religions whose books he published over the years. We have already mentioned George Whitefield, but Franklin also published tomes by Ralph Erskine, Josiah Smith, Samuel Finley, Gilbert Tennent, Samuel Davies, Samuel Jacob Blair, and Henry Scougal.[255] He also published the Rev. Alexander Craighead's three theological works, *The Renewal of the Scottish National Covenant* (1743); *Solemn League* of 1744; and the *Covenant*, published by the Franklin Press in 1748. The Rev. Craighead had also anonymously written the first treatise in America denouncing King George III of England in 1743.[256]

Craighead reportedly left Pennsylvania for North Carolina to pastor a Presbyterian church on Sugar Creek in Mecklenburg County, where his teachings inspired the 1775 Mecklenburg Declaration of Independence.

Another way to see Franklin's devotion to religious freedom and religious toleration is that among the books that the statesman published in 1722 includes the Roman historian Cato's "Essay on Free Speech."

One final aspect of Franklin's advocacy of religious freedom is that he marveled at how, despite being the object of persecutions themselves, many Christian denominations were perfectly willing to become the oppressors of others themselves. This was despite the fact that many denominations had escaped Britain precisely so they could exercise their religious rights. The religious wars of the seventeenth century left a bad taste in the mouths of many Protestants, particularly those who came to North America to escape religious persecution in Europe.

This brings us to the second section of Chapter Five, in which we will discuss the idea of religious toleration as guaranteed by the Founding documents of the United States.

The Founding Documents on Religious Freedom and Toleration

In this study on Franklin's religion, we already have said a great deal about the phenomenon of religious toleration in the life and times of the first great American statesman in two important contexts. The first of these was his defense of the Rev. Samuel Hemphill against the onslaughts of the Presbyterian Synod of Philadelphia that wished to remove Hemphill from the pulpit. The other context of Franklin's views on religious toleration is his admiration for John Locke's *A Letter Concerning Toleration* published in 1689.

We will begin this second section of Chapter Five with a short summary of early American attitudes toward religious toleration. The first item to recall about that phenomenon is that many of the people of British North America that eventually formed the United States of America were settlers in North America who, often in the face of religious persecution, refused to compromise their passionately held religious views back in Europe, and so they fled. The religious persecutions that drove settlers from Europe to British North America sprang from the convictions held by Protestants and Roman Catholics alike that uniformity in religion must exist in any given society. This conviction was based on the view that there is one true religion, and the civil authorities may have the duty to impose that system of beliefs in the interest of saving their souls.

Roger Williams, the eventual head of the Rhode Island Colony after leaving Massachusetts, called the Massachusetts requirement "an enforced uniformity of religion."[257] In some areas, Catholics persecuted Protestants. In others, Protestants persecuted Catholics. Although Britain renounced religious persecution in 1689, it persisted for many decades in much of Europe.

From the Colonial era to the present, religious freedom and religious tolerance have played significant roles in the political life of the United States. Religion has been at the heart of some of the best, as well as some of the worst, movements in American history. The guiding principles that the framers of the Constitution intended to govern the relationship between religion and politics are set out in Article VI of the Constitution and in the opening sixteen words of the First Amendment of the Bill of Rights. Those sixteen words were/are the following, "Congress shall make no law respecting an establishment of religion, or prohibiting the free exercise thereof." The philosophical foundations for these ideas on religion were the thoughts and the writings of people like Roger Williams, mentioned earlier, as well as William Penn, John Leland, Thomas Jefferson, James Madison and many other political leaders who were decisive in the struggle for what was called the struggle for "freedom of conscience."[258]

The framers of the US Constitution took great pains to preserve several aspects of religion in the new United States. Those aspects included:

1. The central place of faith in America.
2. The centrality of religion in the lives of Americans.
3. The protection of religious beliefs in its broadest sense.
4. Religious liberty as the first liberty.
5. The guarantee of religious liberty in the Constitution.
6. Religion in public life and politics.

Regarding numbers one and two above, it is clear that God and religion are central places in the lives of most Americans. It may be argued that the United States is the most religious nation of all industrialized nations, and religious beliefs are at the center of life for millions of Americans. These beliefs, however, are not confined to worship and family life. They also shape the political and social views of a vast number of citizens.

The First Amendment's religious Liberty Clause states that "Congress shall make no law respecting an establishment of religion, or prohibiting the free exercise thereof." Taken together, these two clauses safeguard religious liberty by protecting religions and religious convictions from government interference or control and ensure that religious belief, or non-belief, remains voluntary, free from government coercion.

These two clauses equally apply to actions of local, state and national governments because the US Supreme Court has ruled that the Fourteenth Amendment ensures that "States are not to deprive any person of liberty," and thus the First Amendment applies to States.

The "no establishment" clause means, then, that neither the state nor the national government can establish a particular religion, or religion in general, of its citizens. The "Free Exercise Clause" is the freedom of every citizen to reach, hold, practice, and/or change one's religious beliefs.

The Supreme Court has argued that the federal government must maintain what it called "benevolent neutrality" that permits religious exercise to exist but denies it government sponsorship. The "no establishment" clause serves to prevent both religious control over government, as well as political control over religion. The Supreme Court has interpreted "free exercise" to mean that any individual may believe anything he or she wants, but there may be times when the state may limit or may interfere with practices that follow from those beliefs.[259]

The court also required that the state must demonstrate a compelling interest of the "highest order" before it can burden or interfere with religious conduct. Even then, the government has to demonstrate that it has no alternative means of achieving its interests that would be less restrictive of religious conduct.[260]

In 1990, in its decision of *Employment Division v. Smith*, the Supreme Court stated, "The government no longer has to demonstrate a compelling government interest unless a law is specifically targeted at a religious practice or infringes upon an additional constitutional right, such as free speech."

Regarding number four in the above list, that is, "Religious liberty as the first liberty," is based on the long-held American belief that religious liberty and religious toleration should be considered as our "First Liberties" because freedom of the mind is logically, as well as philosophically, prior to all other freedoms protected by the Constitution. The idea of first liberties has traditionally been thought to have at least five elements.

These elements of first liberties generally include the following notions:

1. A definition of religious liberty.
2. The freedom of conscience.
3. Religious liberty.
4. The right to practice.
5. Religious toleration of others.

The idea of religious freedom, or item number one on our list, is sketched out in the Founding documents we have been discussing in this third section of this Chapter Five of this study of Franklin's religion.

That there shall be freedom of conscience for people of all faiths or no faith at all is what is meant by number two. That religious liberty is an "inalienable right," one that cannot be taken away, is the meaning of number three. Number four on the above list is the right to freely practice any religion or no religion at all without government coercion or control. And finally, religious toleration is the view that every individual citizen in America has the duty not to interfere in the exercise of the rights of other citizens to practice their religions anyway that they see fit.[261]

Finally, in the last thirty years in the United States, the idea of religious liberty has, at times, seemed to be in peril. In several US court cases, the issue of how far religious liberties extend in the Unites States has developed in this country, beginning with the 1995 *Rosenberg v. Rectors and Visitors of the University of Virginia* (1995), the Supreme Court ruled that Catholic and Evangelical student organizations on campus had a right to receive university funds like other student clubs and organizations.

Another four or five important cases also arose from that time until the *Masterpiece Cakeshop v. Colorado Civil Rights Commission* in December of 2017, when a Denver bakery owner refused to make a wedding cake for a gay couple. The owner cited his religious belief that marriage "can only be between a man and a woman." The couple sued, and a Denver court ruled that the baker had violated Colorado's public accommodations law. The statute forbids discrimination by businesses serving the public, including on the basis of sexual orientation.

In another 2017 case, the Trump Administration invoked freedom of religion when it allowed employers of a religious exemption to the use of contraceptives required by the Affordable Care Act. The issue was whether contraceptives must also be made available to women who are studying to become Roman Catholic nuns.[262] Thus, from 1990 until the present time, many more religiously conservative Americans are concerned that the government is limiting the extent of religious freedom too far.

This brings us to the idea of religious toleration in many of the other Founding Fathers of the United States, the topic of the third section of this Chapter Five. This will be followed by a fourth section, where we will speak more specifically about Benjamin Franklin's views of the idea of religious toleration.

Religious Toleration of the Other Founding Fathers

In this chapter, we have already spoken of the role of religious toleration in the philosophical and ethical views of Roger Williams in both the Massachusetts Bay Colony and Rhode Island.

The idea of religious toleration in the early United States was an important notion for many of the other American Founding Fathers besides Benjamin Franklin and Roger Williams. In 1777, for example, Thomas Jefferson drafted the "Virginia Statute for Religious Freedom." Among other things, Jefferson's draft advocated the separation of church and state and suggested that citizens must be left alone to find their own ways to God and to religious truth.

Jefferson also maintained that one's civil rights should not depend on one's religious beliefs. He also maintained that all citizens of Virginia had the moral duty to not infringe upon nor impede, in any way, the practice of religion by any other citizen. In other words, Jefferson advocated the idea of religious toleration, as explained in the previous section of this chapter.

Another Virginia Founding Father, James Madison, also co-authored Jefferson's 1777 draft. Like Jefferson, Madison advocated for the 1777 bill throughout the Revolutionary War, but it only became law in 1786. Nevertheless, the Virginia bill became the foundation for future documents about the separation of church and state, including the First Amendment to the US Constitution. One of the ways that James Madison referred to religious toleration was in a speech he delivered in 1785 when he referred to the United States as an "Asylum to the persecuted and the oppressed of every nation and every Religion."[263] It was unusual, nor surprising according to Madison, that intolerance was sometimes evident in the very earliest days of the United States of America. One of the main sources that Jefferson and Madison relied upon in the formulation of the 1777 "Bill for Establishing Religious Freedom," was John Locke's 1689 essay, "Letter on Toleration."[264] It is also likely that Jefferson read other Enlightenment thinkers like

Voltaire on what the French philosopher called "Intolerance."

The same sources of Jefferson and Madison's views on toleration can also be seen in the views of George Washington. His personal library holdings in his home at Mount Vernon included both John Locke's 1689 essay and Voltaire's *Toleration and Other Essays*.[265]

In his biography called *Washington: A Life*, Ron Chernow tells us this about our first president:

> One thing that has not aroused dispute is the exemplary nature of Washington's religious tolerance. He shuddered at the notion of exploiting religion for partisan purposes or showing favoritism for certain denominations.[266]

This is also a proper description of the views of Franklin, as well, as we shall see in the final section of this chapter.

Chernow goes on in his biography to discuss letters that George Washington wrote to various religious congregations in early America regarding the issue of religious toleration. Again, Chernow wrote:

> As President, when writing to Jewish, Baptist, Presbyterian, and other Congregations—he officially saluted twenty-two major religious groups—he issued eloquent statements on religious toleration. He was so devoid of spiritual bias that his tolerance even embraced atheism.

Again, what Chernow says of George Washington was also true of Thomas Jefferson, James Madison, and, of course, Benjamin Franklin. This is also true of other of the Founding Fathers, as we shall see later in this chapter.

When George Washington dispatched Benedict Arnold on a mission to court the French Canadians' support for the American Revolution in 1755, he told Arnold "not to let their religion get in the way. Operate on a policy of Prudence and a true Christian Spirit." General Washington added, "Prudence will lead us to look upon their errors with compassion, without insulting them."[267]

In addition to the views of Jefferson, Madison, and Washington on the issue of religious toleration, another Virginian Founding Father, George Mason, also proposed a Virginia bill with the following clause,

"All men should enjoy the fullest toleration in the exercise of Religion, according to the dictates of Conscience."[268]

Mason also suggested an alternative formulation pertaining to the same bill:

> That Religion out of the duty that we owe our Creator, and the manner of discharging it, being under the direction of reason and conviction only, not of violence and compulsion, all men are equal to the full and free exercise of it according to the dictates of Conscience.[269]

The phrase "the dictates of Conscience" refers to what one's moral intuitions tell you is the right moral action to pursue in a given moral situation. It was employed by George Mason and used by other American Founding Fathers, as well, as we shall see later in this chapter.

In 1784, patriot Patrick Henry introduced a bill calling for the support of "teachers of the Christian Religion." By this, Henry meant teachers in his Anglican-Episcopal faith, but this was a bill to which both Washington and Jefferson were opposed.[270] In 1786, after Henry's bill was defeated, the Virginia Bill for Establishing Religious Freedom was passed. Interestingly enough, of all of his accomplishments that Jefferson chose to be on his tombstone, his authoring of this bill, along with his writing of the Declaration of Independence and the establishment of the University of Virginia, are the only three things that appear on his grave at Monticello, in Virginia.

This brings us to the fourth and final section of Chapter Five, in which we will discuss the views of the first great American statesman Benjamin Franklin on the idea of religious toleration. We end, then, with Franklin's views on the matter at hand.

Franklin on Religious Toleration

One aspect of Benjamin Franklin's views on religious toleration is that the colony he chose in which to live after he left his childhood home in Boston and the Massachusetts Colony was the city of Philadelphia and the Pennsylvania Colony. What is significant about that fact is that the colony of Pennsylvania was created by its Founders as a "Holy Experiment in Religious Freedom and Tolerance."[271]

The Quakers, who dared to exchange the persecution and tyranny of the Old World for freedom in the New World, had greatly distrusted earthly authority. Franklin, as their elected representative, most assuredly did not advocate intolerance against any group of people, as he put it, "whether by Law or by Cabal."[272]

Although Franklin did not write an essay or narrative explicitly referring to "Religious Tolerance" or "Religious Toleration," he did speak and write about the idea on many occasions. Perhaps the best summary of his views on the matter is a newspaper article published on June 3, 1772, in the *London Packet*, a London newspaper. The article was entitled "Toleration in Old and New England."[273]

The subject matter of the article is revealed in the opening of the essay in which he related:

> I understand from the public papers that in the debates on the bill for relieving the Dissenters in the point of subscription of the Church Articles, sundry reflections were thrown out against that people, importing that they themselves are of a persecuting intolerant spirit, for that when they had here the superiority they persecuted the Church and still persecute it in America.[274]

Franklin goes on in this same essay to point out that in England and America, since the religious wars in the seventeenth century, intolerance has been a far more widely phenomenon than we choose to remember. Every sect, he points out, has believed that only they possess the truth. And "because they are the possessors of that Truth, they were in their right to persecute Error, in order to destroy it."[275]

In the process of the essay, Franklin also discusses the idea of the British government collecting "tythes and taxes" from the Dissenters. In the article, he argued in favor of the dissenters, pointing out that they find themselves in the midst of what amounts to the conflict of two moral duties or obligations.

On the one hand, the dissenters should be afforded the same opportunity to express their chosen religious beliefs that are afforded to all other subjects of the Crown. On the other hand, the Crown puts on the dissenters the added obligation to support the government's coffers, even if that is decidedly against the religious beliefs of the dissenters.[276]

At the end of his essay on toleration, Franklin raised the additional question about whether there should be "Any kind of religious test in order for the Crown to certify one's religious faith." He goes on to point out that in America—particularly in New England, where the legislators almost to the man are dissenters from the Church of England—there are:

1. No test to prevent churchmen from holding office.
2. The sons of churchmen have the full benefits of the universities.
3. The taxes for the support of public worship, when paid by churchmen, are given to the Episcopal minister.[277]

Then, in Old England:

1. Dissenters are excluded from all offices of profit and honour.
2. The benefits of education in the universities are appropriated to the sons of churchmen.
3. The clergy of the dissenters receive none of the tythes and taxes paid by its people who must be at an additional charge of maintaining their own separate worship.[278]

Even as early as Franklin's time in Boston, he was cognizant of the intolerance of Puritans in the colony. He saw the Puritans as being intolerant of everyone except for other Puritans. Franklin's free thinking in Philadelphia, when he worked as an apprentice to his brother James, unnerved his parents back in Boston. His father wrote to his youngest son stating his concern about what Josiah called "erroneous opinions."[279] In turn, Franklin responded to his father, sketching out his philosophy based on the idea of tolerance that would last for the remainder of his life.

In the letter to his father Josiah that responded to the "erroneous opinions" letter from his parents, Benjamin wrote:

> It would be vain for any person to insist that all the doctrines that he holds are all true and all that he does not hold are false.[280]

The same held true for Franklin to the opinions of various religious sects like his mother's Congregationalist theology and his father's Calvinists Presbyterian beliefs.

Another way to see his commitment to his lifelong idea of tolerance is the fact that he built a non-denominational new hall in Philadelphia expressly for the use of "any preacher of any religious persuasion who might desire to say something there."[281] Franklin added:

> Even if the Mufti of Constantinople were to send a missionary to preach Mohammedanism to us, he would find a pulpit at his service.[282]

We also argued earlier in this study that one of the best ways to see the American statesman's views on religious toleration is to look carefully at his defense of the Rev. Samuel Hemphill against the Philadelphia Presbyterian Synod, who removed the minister from the pulpit.

In his "A Defence of the Reverend Hemphill's Observations," Franklin related words like,

> Though I believe nobody will deny their undoubted Right to declare their Opinions, yet 'tis certain that to go farther and to deprive him as far as they can of Liberty...to deprive him of the exercise of his Ministerial Function and of his livelihood, will provide him with a Persecuting Spirit.

For Franklin, the Presbyterian Synod of Philadelphia had acted toward Rev. Hemphill as an example of religious intolerance. He believed that the synod was depriving the reverend of his religious freedom by acting in a way that kept him from making a living. And in Franklin's understanding, that was an arch-case of nothing less than religious intolerance.

Finally, Franklin's opinion against the idea of a "Religious Test" in both England and America is an attestation to his view that all people should be left to worship his God whatever way he sees fit and that all citizens have a moral obligation not to infringe on the practice of any other person's religious views.

In short, Franklin was in favor of citizens expressing their God-given right to worship in whatever ways they wish to do so while also being committed to the idea that one has a moral obligation in America to not impinge upon how other citizens wish to exercise their right to free worship.

This brings us to the major conclusions we have made in Chapter Five. The principal subject matter of Chapter Six in the study of Benjamin Franklin's religion is what America's first great statesman wrote, believed, and said about the idea of ethics and the nature of the moral good.

Conclusions to Chapter Five

In the Introduction to Chapter Five, we suggested that the chapter would be divided into four major sections. These were: Franklin on religious freedom; the founding documents on religious freedom and toleration; other Founding Fathers on religious toleration; and Franklin on religious toleration.

We began the first of these sections by supplying some background information on the demographics of the make-up of early American religion. We pointed out that, at the time of the American Revolution, 98 percent of all Americans were Protestant Christians and that three-quarters of those would have considered themselves to have been "Reform Christians."[283]

In the beginning of section one, we also spoke of the wide range of Christian views in America, from the most Orthodox believers to those who would have identified themselves as freethinkers, skeptics, or deists.

In that initial section of Chapter Five, we indicated that, as early as the age of fifteen in his Silence Dogood letter number 8, Franklin first expressed his deep commitment to the ideas that would become the First Amendment of the US Constitution, including religious freedom and religious toleration.

We have shown that same commitment at the very end of Franklin's life when he committed funds to every religious sect in Philadelphia, including support for a synagogue, as well as selecting his pallbearers from the leaders of the various religious congregations in the city.

Along the way, in the first section of this chapter, we maintained that the first American statesman's views on religious freedom can be seen in his parody "A Witch Trial at Mount Holly," as well as his writing on the religion of Native Americans in Pennsylvania and Delaware. Franklin's comments in "A Narrative of the Late Massacres" was another example of his commitment to the idea of religious freedom.

Another way we have suggested that Franklin's dedication to religious freedom may be seen is how many religious congregations at the middle to end of the eighteenth century claimed the first American statesman as "one of their own." This included the Congregationalists, the Presbyterians, the Church of England, the Society of Friends, and, if we take John Adam's views into account, the Roman Catholics as well.

We also pointed out that for many Americans, the idea of religious freedom and its original meaning is in the process of experiencing an onslaught of attacks on the idea, beginning in a case in 1993 and continuing all the way to 2017 and two cases about a cake for a gay couple and contraceptives for Roman Catholic nuns.

In the second section of Chapter Five, we sketched out what the Founding Fathers in our Founding documents had to say about the ideas of religious freedom, the separation of church and state, and the notion of religious toleration. Relying mostly on the US Constitution, we spoke of the central place of faith in America, the centrality of religion in America, the protection of religious rights, religious liberty as the "First Liberty," the guarantee of religious liberty, and religion in public life and politics.

In this second section of Chapter Five, we spent considerable space writing about the "Establishment Clause" and what the US Supreme Court meant by the expression "free exercise" in regard to religious belief and practice, or what is sometimes called the "Liberty Clause."

In the third section of this chapter, we explored what many of the other Founding Fathers had to say about the idea of religious toleration in the early American context.

Among the other Founding Fathers besides Franklin, we discussed the idea of religious toleration were George Washington; Thomas Jefferson, the author of the "Virginia Bill Establishing Religious Freedom;" James Madison, who helped Jefferson on the Virginia Bill; George Mason; and Patrick Henry.

The perspective of Franklin on the idea of religious toleration was the major focus of the fourth and final section of Chapter Five. We began that section with a description of his childhood views of the religious intolerance he had seen at the hands of the Puritans in his native Boston.

In section four of Chapter Five, we shifted our attention to Franklin's article "Religious Tolerance in Old and New England" for the *London Packet* from June 3, 1772. The context of this essay, as we have shown, was whether religious dissenters in England should be required to pay "tythes" and taxes to the Crown, even if their religious convictions expressly forbid it. Franklin took the side of the dissenters and gave an excellent analysis of the conflicting moral rights and duties of the religious dissenters in the episode in question.

In the fourth section, we have also shown that Franklin's lifelong commitment to the idea of religious toleration may be seen in his building of a non-denominational new building in Philadelphia for the use of "any preacher of any religious persuasion who might desire to say something there."[284] And that included even the Mufti of Constantinople, "who would find a pulpit at his service."[285]

We also indicated at the close of Chapter Five, that Franklin's defense of the Reverend Samuel Hemphill against the Presbyterian Synod of Philadelphia was one of the American statesman's most eloquent expressions of his views on religious toleration in the American context.

Additionally, we have shown that, for the most part, Franklin was diametrically opposed to the idea of any "Religious Test" that might have been imposed by a state or the federal government. Ultimately, we maintained that he was in favor of the right of a citizen to express his God-given right to worship the Divine in whatever ways he wishes to do so while at the same time being committed to the idea, which he appears to have held his entire life, that one has a moral obligation not to impinge or limit in any way, the exercise of other citizens to express those religious rights.

This brings us to Chapter Six, where we shall explore what Franklin had to say, believe, and to have written about the philosophical phenomena of morality, ethics and moral virtue.

Franklin's return to Philadelphia in 1785. Benjamin Franklin, Richard Bache, his wife Sarah, Franklin's daughter, and her son Benjamin Franklin Bache at dockside in Philadelphia. Franklin is greeted by Judge Thomas McKean, who stands on the right. A sedan chair with two African American porters awaits Franklin on the left. Courtesy of the Library of Congress, Prints & Photographs Division, artist Jean Leon Gerome Ferris.

Chapter Six
Franklin on Morality, Ethics and Virtue

> The greatest virtues are those which are
> most useful to other persons.
> —Aristotle, *Nicomachean Ethics*

> Whatever is, is right. Though purblind man sees but a
> part of the chain, the nearest link; his eyes nor
> carrying to the equal beam that poises all above.
> —John Dryden

> Father of light and life, Thou Good Supreme!
> O teach me what is Good; teach me Thyself!
> Save me from folly, vanity, and vice,
> From every lowly pursuit, and fill my soul.
> With knowledge, conscious peace, and virtue pure;
> Sacred, substantial, and never-fading Bliss!
> —Benjamin Franklin

Introduction

The major purpose of Chapter Six is to describe and discuss what American statesman Benjamin Franklin believed, wrote and had to say publicly about the nature and extent of the moral good. In the opening section of this chapter, we will provide some background information that is important for understanding Franklin's sense of moral, goodness and virtue.

This will be followed by a second section on what he had to say, more specifically about the notion of moral virtue as opposed to non-moral virtue. In the third section, we shall turn our attention to what might be called Franklin's "Moral Method." We will see that he conducted a kind of experiment involving his thirteen virtues and how he measured up to them.

And in the fourth and final section of Chapter Six, we will identify and discuss what Franklin wrote and had to say about particular issues, including, among other things, his position on slavery. We move first, then, to some background information on Franklin's ethics. We will also provide a catalog and discussion of his general comments and observations on both virtue and ethics.

Background Information on Franklin's Ethics

By the late eighteenth century, there were in Europe and America four different philosophical theories about the nature of the moral good. These were known as Deontological Theory, Teleological Theory, Divine Command Theory, and a fourth theory known as Virtue Ethics.

German philosopher Immanuel Kant championed the first of these theories. He held a view called the Categorical Imperative, which suggested that all human beings have a set of universal moral duties that have no exceptions. Kant had in mind duties such as "Tell the truth," "Keep one's promises" and "Don't harm innocent people."[286]

Our second moral theory, Teleological Theory, was based on producing the best consequences for most people rather than on universal moral rules and duties like Kant's theory. Thinkers like Englishmen Jeremy Bentham and John Stuart Mill held the Teleological Theory. This theory is also sometimes known as Utilitarianism. The Utilitarian says that the moral good is nothing more than producing the best consequences for the most number of people. However, Bentham and Mill disagreed about how to define the most good. Bentham thought it was measured by the most pleasure for the most number, while Mill's standard was the most happiness for the most number. Another difference between the two forms of Teleological Theory is that Bentham's view is called Act Utilitarianism, while Mill's theory is called Rule Utilitarianism.

The third moral theory popular in Franklin's day was called Divine Command Theory. This view essentially says that the moral good is whatever God commands it to be. Since God is said to be Omnibenevolent, or "All Good," then ethics is nothing more than following the pronouncements of that Deity, such as the Ten Commandments and the Golden Rule.[287]

The fourth and final moral theory of Franklin's day was what is known as Virtue Ethics. This theory was developed in ancient Greece by the philosopher Aristotle. His Virtue Theory suggests that the nature of ethics is more about one's moral character and habits than it is about duties or consequences.[288]

In the case of Franklin, as we shall see in this chapter, Franklin put more reliance on the third and fourth theories outlined in this analysis of the nature of the Moral Good. At times, he seems to assent to Divine Command Theory, such as with his atheist friend, T. H., for example, but he more often appears to have relied on Virtue Ethics, as we shall see with his notions of virtue. There can be no doubt that the earliest and most long-lasting source for understanding Franklin's ethics was the Puritan-Congregationalist-Calvinist background of his childhood. From the Puritans, he learned the high standard for virtue and the moral life. He also understood his moral belief that one ought to imitate the moral life of Jesus to be a position he had adopted from his childhood upbringing. He was also influenced by the moral values of his parents, his Uncle Benjamin, as we have shown in Chapter One, as well as those of his parents' Congregationalist Church in Boston, known as the "Third Church," or South Church Congregationalist in Boston.

As a child, Franklin also relied on the set of moral rules that all Puritan and Calvinist children learned very early on in their lives, such as the Ten Commandments in the Old Testament and Jesus' pronouncement in the New Testament to "Do unto others as you would have them do unto yourselves."

In several places in his autobiography, Franklin provides some hints about his basic views on ethics. In most of these instances, when it comes to God and ethics, he observed that the most important aspect of moral behavior was to do good when it came to the individual as well as the good of the state.

> The important thing is to believe in something, and
> the idea of service is the highest form of worship.[289]

More specifically, what Franklin meant by the highest form of worship is that the best way to serve God is also "to serve your fellow Man."[290] In regard to his own life, even early on, he expressed an interest in achieving what he called "Moral Perfection," which can only be achieved, he thought, by embodying certain moral virtues.[291] We will say more about these thirteen moral virtues that Franklin had in mind in the second section of this chapter.

Franklin also sincerely believed that the idea of strict, moral self-awareness and moral control are both crucial in becoming an honest and virtuous citizen.[292] He also claimed on several occasions that a person should act morally for himself, not just for God. And for the American statesman, two ways one may act morally are by imitating the lives of Jesus Christ and Socrates, as he tells us in his autobiography.[293] Franklin also agreed with Aristotle that the process of doing the Good is good "in itself." In other words, good is good in and of itself.

In a letter to his friend, Scottish philosopher and jurist Lord Kames, dated February 25, 1767, Franklin reveals that "For nearly thirty years, I have had in preparation a book on Ethics." He goes on to tell us, "I planned it first in 1732, and since then, I have made Experiments of the Method with success." Later in the letter, he states that the book was "intended for the Benefit of the Youth." And it was to be called *The Art of Virtue*. At the end of the letter to Lord Kames, he says that the object of the work was practical to show "those who wanted to be good how to achieve that goal." "Many people," Franklin explained to Kames, "lead bad lives that would gladly lead good ones but know not how to make the change."

In his book *Benjamin Franklin: The Religious Life of a Founding Father*, Thomas Kidd points to another piece of background information on the statesman's views on ethics. Kidd tells us, "In the early 1730s, he had begun tinkering with what he wryly called 'the bold and arduous project of arriving at moral perfection.'"[294] Kidd then proceeds to speak of the formation of Franklin's "Book of Virtues," suggesting Joseph Addison's drama *Cato: A Tragedy*, the ethics of Cicero, and the Biblical book of Proverbs, Chapter Three, as sources for Franklin's understanding of virtue.

In the third chapter of the Book of Proverbs, in its 34 verses, the writer of the book mentions faithfulness, trust, love, wisdom, honor, discipline, peace, goodness and understanding. It is easy to see why this Biblical chapter was one of the principal sources of Franklin's views on virtue and ethics.[295]

The Roman poet Cicero wrote about four "Cardinal Virtues." They are wisdom, justice, courage, and temperance. As we shall see, Franklin employed Cicero's comments on justice and temperance, but he did not include courage and wisdom in his list of thirteen virtues.[296]

Through the character called Juba in his drama *Cato*, Joseph Addison demonstrates that neither culture nor ethnicity constrains the human capacity for virtue. Juba came from Numidia, a Black culture. Juba is embarrassed with his fellow Numidians who acted with traitorous intentions, particularly in front of Cato.[297]

For Cato, a man's actions determine his character and moral value, not his race nor even where he is from. With his dying breath, Cato proclaims, "Whoever is brave and virtuous is a Roman." This, of course, is a cosmopolitan call to the universal brotherhood of those who are virtuous, and Franklin deeply respected the values and the moral principles of Addison's drama.

In 1728, in his "Articles of Belief and Acts of Religion," at the age of twenty-two, Franklin observed this about achieving moral perfection when he wrote:

> It was about this time that I conceived the bold and arduous project of arriving at moral perfection. I wished to live without committing any fault at any time. I would conquer all that either natural inclination, custom, or company might lead me into. As I knew or thought I knew what was right and wrong. I did not see why I might not always do the one and avoid the other.[298]

In the same section of the *Articles*, Franklin continues his analysis of his quest to achieve moral perfection. He wrote:

> But I soon found I had undertaken a task of more difficulty than I had imagined. While my care was employed in guarding

> against one fault, I was often surprised by another. Habit took the advantage of inattention. Inclination was sometimes too strong for reason.[299]

Franklin continued his analysis of his inability to achieve moral perfection:

> I conclude, at length, that the mere speculative conviction that it was our interests to be completely virtuous was not sufficient to prevent our slipping, and that the contrary habits must be broken and good ones acquired and established, before we can have any dependence on a steady, uniform rectitude of conduct.

Here he again seems to agree with Aristotle's idea that moral traits are acquired principally through habit or habitual behavior. Ethics, for both men, is about character and the developing of that moral character through habit.

In the "Articles of Belief and Acts of Religion," Franklin ended his discussion of moral perfection by simply pointing out that the quest appears to be a tree that does not bear the hoped-for outcome. In his autobiography, as well, he again admits that he fell "far short of achieving my goal, but I am much better off for having tried to sanctify myself."[300] His early life, as Thomas Kidd indicates, "was heavy on self-improvement and light on God's intervention." Kidd indicates that one scholar believes that Franklin's exploration was a version of "secular pietism."[301]

From this discussion of background materials on the ethical views of Franklin, we may make the following conclusions:

1. In Franklin's day, there were four different theories on the nature of moral goodness, which were the Deontological Theory, Teleological Theory, Divine Command Theory, and Virtue Ethics.
2. Franklin employed Divine Command Theory and Aristotle's Virtue Theory more than the other two perspectives.
3. He attributed his emphasis on virtue and the desire to imitate the life of Jesus to be bequeathed to him from his parents' Puritanism.

4. We have learned in a Franklin letter to Lord Kames that since the 1730s, the statesman was developing a work to be entitled *The Art of Virtue*.
5. Franklin intended this work to be written for the moral development of American youth. Even early on, Franklin understood that one ought to do the Good for its own sake, not simply for the sake of God.
6. Franklin spoke regularly about the possibility of achieving what he called "Moral Perfection."
7. He admits in his autobiography that he had "fallen far short of his goal of moral perfection."

This brings us to the second and central section of Chapter Six, in which we will specifically explore the understanding of moral virtue in the life and times of the earliest American statesman Benjamin Franklin. It is to virtue, then, to which we turn next.

Franklin on Moral Virtue

Much of what Franklin had to say and write about the idea of virtue comes directly from the ancient Greek moral theory of Aristotle, whose theory itself is sometimes called "Virtue Theory." Aristotle made an important distinction between a "Moral Virtue" and a "Non-Moral Virtue." For him, the former is a "disposition to act in a certain manner so that the emphasis is on the moral character of the individual."[302]

For Aristotle, moral virtues are acquired over time until they become habitual character traits of the person. This is a careful, conscious, rationally inculcated habit that is done for its own sake. An honest person is one who has inculcated the habit of speaking the truth because he prizes the value of the truth, or honesty, for their own sake.[303]

For Aristotle, then, the ideas of morality and virtue are fundamentally about character and the habits or tendencies to behave in particular moral ways. Aristotle also tells us that, in general, a moral virtue is a mean between two extremes. Usually, those two extremes are the excess and the deficiency of the virtue. Thus, courage is a moral virtue between rashness, or courage in excess, and cowardice or courage in deficiency.[304]

Patience, to cite another example, is a moral virtue that is the mean between impatience, which is deficient and irascibility that is patience in excess. The virtue shyness is between shame and modesty, at least according to Aristotle.[305] And one of the greatest of the moral virtues, justice, which Aristotle defines as "getting what one is due," is the mean between the deficient injustice, and giving one more than he is due, the excess.

For Aristotle, the sum total of the moral virtues is what the philosopher called *Eudaimonia*, or in English, "happiness." The aim of a moral life for Aristotle is the achievement of human happiness.[306]

On the other hand, non-moral virtues are not habitual, nor are they acquired through acting in consistent ways. Moral virtues, like wisdom, for example, are sometimes innate, while moral virtues are always learned. Moral virtues require a deliberate choice, while non-moral virtues do not.

We know that Franklin had a copy of Aristotle's *Nicomachean Ethics* in his personal library. He also possessed several of the works of Cicero that dealt with ethics and virtue, and he quoted Cicero on these matters.

Again, in his "Articles of Belief and Acts of Religion," Franklin also provided an introduction to his thoughts about the moral virtues. He related:

> In the various enumerations of the moral virtues I had met with my reading, I found a catalogue more or less numerous, as different writers included more or fewer ideas the same name. Temperance, for example, was by some confined to drinking and eating, while by others it was extended to mean the moderating every other pleasure, appetite, inclination, or passion, bodily or mental, even to our avarice and ambition. I proposed to myself for the sake of clearness to use rather more names with fewer ideas annexed to each, than a few names with more ideas; and I included under thirteen names of virtues all that occurred to me as necessary or desirable and annexed to each a short precept, which fully expressed the extent I gave to its meaning.[307]

Next, Franklin sets out a catalog of his thirteen virtues, some of which appear to be moral virtues, while others are non-moral virtues. Nevertheless, the statesman's list is the following and includes descriptions for each. These virtues can be found in the *Articles*, as well as in the first section of Franklin's autobiography:

1. Temperance. Eat not to dullness; drink not to elevation.
2. Silence. Speak not but what may benefit others or yourself; avoid trifling conversations.
3. Order. Let all your things be in their places; let each part of your business have its time. [So pick up after yourselves.]
4. Resolution. Resolve to perform what you ought; perform without fail what you resolve.
5. Frugality. Make no expense but to do good to others or yourself, i.e, waste nothing.
6. Industry. Lose no time; be always employed in something useful; cut off all unnecessary actions, so you will be doing things that benefit you.
7. Sincerity. Use no hurtful deceit; think innocently and justly, and if you speak, speak accordingly.
8. Justice. Wrong none by doing injuries, or omitting the benefits that are your duty.
9. Moderation. Avoid extremes; forbear resenting injuries so much as you think they deserve.
10. Cleanliness. Tolerate no uncleanliness in body, clothes, or habitation.
11. Tranquility. Be not disturbed at trifles, or at accidents common or unavoidable.
12. Chastity. Rarely use venery but for health or offspring, never to dullness, weakness, or the injury of your own or another's peace or reputation. [There is nothing there about being faithful to your wife.]
13. Humility. Imitate Jesus and Socrates. [Rather than giving Jesus this special elevated divinity, he is compared to Socrates. So yes, Jesus has his place, but it is a bit diminished.][308]

Among the sections of Addison's play that Franklin was most fond were statements like,

Modesty is only an ornament but also a guide to virtue.[309]

Or consider this Addison quote:

> A true critic ought to dwell rather upon excellencies than imperfections, to discover the concealed beauties of a writer and to communicate to the world such things as are worth their observation.[310]

Addison was speaking of virtue when he wrote:

> Justice discards party, kindred, and is therefore always represented as blind.[311]

In another place of his drama, Addison wrote:

> If there is a power above us, He surely must delight in virtue.[312]

And along the same lines, Joseph Addison relates in *Cato*:

> Justice is that which is practiced by God himself and to be practiced in its perfection by none but him. Omniscience and Omnipotence are requisite for the full exertion of it.[313]

And in all of these lines, Franklin was in full consent about virtue, ethics and his belief in God.

In Franklin's account of virtue, he both agrees and disagrees with Aristotle's account of moral and non-moral virtue. He agrees with the Greek philosopher's judgment that moral virtues are formed habitually. Franklin disagreed, however, about the definition of a virtue. Whereas Aristotle told us a moral virtue is a "Mean between two extremes," Franklin defined a virtue as "A fundamental positive characteristic." But he does realize the importance of Aristotle's notion of moderation in his own theory.[314] In this regard, Aristotle and Franklin seemed to be in agreement that virtues are primarily moral traits of a human being.

The first great American statesman also agrees with Aristotle on the importance of the virtues of justice and temperance, as well as the centrality of the idea of moderation and frugality in the making of a moral life as well as the idea that virtues involve habitual behavior and traits of character.

Originally, Franklin had planned his virtue list to only include twelve virtues. But after discussing his list with a Quaker friend, the friend asked the statesman why "Humility" was absent from the list. Soon after, humility was added to the collection of virtues. Franklin tells us that his friend said, "Ben, if you are serious, you need to add a thirteenth virtue, Humility, because you don't have any."[315]

After adding "humility" to his list of virtues, Franklin went on to define what he meant by the term, "It is to emulate Christ and Socrates in all things."[316] After developing his collection of virtues, he set out again to reorder his moral life. Each day he would look at his list, and for a week, he would focus on a different virtue. He was to repeat this process over and over again until "I knew what mattered most about that particular virtue."[317]

In his memoir, shortly before his death, Franklin reflected on the story of his view on the virtues. He noted that he has "come to feel a oneness with each of the twelve." But when he thought about the thirteenth, he realized that he was simply not humble. He had failed at the thirteenth virtue. He wondered why the final item on his list of virtues also was the most difficult to embody.

The first twelve virtues were all the products of his own imagination, while the thirteenth was provided by the Quaker friend who told him that he did not have much humility. Franklin had failed at a virtue that he did not originally value. Now maybe that was because he did not have it, or maybe it was for another reason.

At any rate, Franklin's account of virtue was not without its critics. Many Christian critics complained that the statesman's list was "doctrineless, moralized Christianity." They said the account of virtues appears to be "without God."[318] One of the best critics of Franklin on virtue was British writer D. H. Lawrence, who, in 1924, reviled the collection as the "barbed wire of moral enclosure that Poor Richard had rigged up."[319] Later in the same review, Lawrence observed that "Franklin preferred to be the servant of his own Holy Ghost."[320]

This third section of Chapter Six will be followed by a fourth section on specific moral issues on which Franklin made some comment or about which he had written something. This brings us to an analysis of Franklin's method in regard to achieving his goal of moral perfection in regard to his thirteen virtues, the topic of the next section of this chapter.

Franklin's Moral Method

In order to keep track of his thirteen virtues, Franklin carried around with him a small notebook related to the virtues. He made a chart that consisted of a column for each of the virtues on the vertical axis and the seven days of the week on the horizontal axis. He evaluated himself at the end of each day according to how well he exemplified each virtue.[321] The great American statesman placed a dot next to the virtues he believed he had been deficient in on any given day. His goal was to minimize the number of dots and thus to make a clean life free of vice.

Each week, Franklin would concentrate on a single virtue and then, after the week, move to the next virtue. After thirteen weeks, he had moved through his entire list, only to begin the process all over again. Thus, in the first week, he did his best to follow the virtue of temperance without thinking too much about the other virtues. This one would be tough for him because he loved his beer.

After temperance, Franklin then proceeded to "silence," followed by "order," and so on. After thirteen weeks, he had gone through all thirteen virtues and his analysis of how well he had lived up to them in his quest for what the American statesman called "Moral Perfection."

Every evening, he would do a self-examination of sorts and mark his progress in his special notebook. He speaks about the notebook this way:

> I made a little book, in which I allotted a page for each of the virtues. I ruled each page with red ink, so as to have some columns, one for each day of the week, marking each volume with a letter for the day. I crossed these columns with thirteen red lines, marking the beginning of each line with the first letter of one of the virtues, on which line, and in its proper column. I might mark by a little black spot, every fault I found upon examination to have been committed respecting that virtue upon that day.[322]

When Franklin first began this method of evaluating himself on the thirteen virtues, he found himself putting more marks in the little book than he had originally wished to make. As time went by, however, the number of dots in his notebook was greatly diminished, and he became gradually closer to his goal of moral perfection.

Even though he never achieved his goal of moral perfection, he still had some notable moral flaws in relationship to the thirteen. His incessant womanizing and love of a good glass of beer most likely gave him problems with keeping number twelve, chastity, and virtue number one—temperance. Franklin's Quaker friend who suggested including the thirteenth virtue, humility, said he primarily did so because the statesman "so rarely exhibited that virtue."[323]

This brings us to some general comments that Franklin made or wrote about ethics in general, or about virtue in particular, in his other principal works in addition to his autobiography. These include "Articles of Belief and Acts of Religion," the fourteen Silence Dogood letters, "On the Providence of God," and "Dialogue Between Two Presbyterians."[324]

Franklin's General Comments on Ethics and Virtue and His Responses to Particular Moral Problems in His Life

Among the many general observations about virtue found in the other written works of Franklin, we will point to several. First, in a summary of his religious beliefs to which we have referred in Chapters One and Two, the statesman related in regard to belief number six, "And that God will certainly reward virtue and punish vice either here or hereafter."[325]

In the Silence Dogood letters, Franklin observed that "Virtue alone is sufficient to make a man great, glorious and happy."[326] From the same source, he also related this about virtue:

> Only a virtuous people are capable of freedom. As nations become corrupt and vicious, they have more need of masters.

Franklin spoke of virtuous character when he related, "Words may show a man's wit, but actions his meaning."[327] He again was referring to virtuous character when he related in the autobiography:

> The best thing to give your enemy is forgiveness.
> To an opponent, tolerance; to a friend, your heart; to
> your child, a good example; to a father, deference; to
> your mother, conduct that will make her proud of you;
> to yourself, respect; to all others, charity.[328]

Franklin spoke of two non-moral virtues when he observed in the "Dialogue Between Two Presbyterians" that "Without freedom of thought there can be no such thing as Wisdom and no such thing as public liberty, without freedom of speech."[329] Franklin was speaking of the ideas of joy and happiness when he told us in one of his letters, "Joy is not to be found in things. It is in us." This is another example of him believing that virtue is an internal character trait, much like Aristotle.

General comments about ethics and the nature of the moral good can also be seen sprinkled throughout his written works and letters. Among some of the most memorable of these general observations about the good are the following:

1. Never ruin an apology with an excuse.
2. Make yourselves sheep, and the wolves will eat you.
3. He that is good at making excuses is usually not good for anything else.
4. God heals, and the doctor takes the fees.
5. Keep your eyes open before marriage and half shut afterward.
6. My father convinced me that nothing was useful, which was not honest.
7. You may delay, but time will not.
8. To succeed, jump as quickly at opportunities as you do at conclusions. Strive to be the greatest Man in your Country and you may be disappointed. Strive to be the best and you may succeed.[330]

During his life, he also made comments about particular moral issues of his day. In the fourth and final section of Chapter Six, we will speak of some of those issues. Most of these we have mentioned and discussed earlier in this study.

One of these issues is the final moral matter in his public life to which he gave some attention, the issue of slavery. In 1787, Franklin was elected the first president of the Pennsylvania Society for the Abolition of Slavery. This was a cause that the statesman had committed himself to as early as the 1730s. His final public act on February 15, 1790, was the signing of a memorial to Congress recommending the dissolution of the system of slavery in America. Two months later, on April 17, 1790, at the age of eighty-four, Franklin passed away.[331]

Earlier in this study, we mentioned another moral issue in Franklin's life. It involved the treatment of Native Americans and the wish by some Christian missionaries to disregard the beliefs of the Natives in favor of Christianity. We have shown the statesman's concerns for Native Americans in both the Pennsylvania and Delaware colonies.

A third moral issue and the great statesman's response was the move among Puritans to expel the Jews from certain colonies. Franklin was so staunchly against this idea that he contributed five pounds to a Jewish group in Philadelphia to build a synagogue.

Another moral issue that he was involved in was the defending of, or simply the supporting of, what were seen as religious dissenters, both here and abroad, as we have shown in Chapter Five. Franklin's "A Defence of the Reverend Hemphill's Observations" also should be seen as another example of this moral issue.[332]

A fifth moral issue that concerned Franklin was the treatment of the poor. In fact, earlier in this study, we have shown that the statesman believed that society and its members who are well-off have a moral obligation to those who are poor and less fortunate.

This concern of his went all the way back to his childhood when, at the age of thirteen, he witnessed the effects of a great fire in his hometown of Boston. In his autobiography, he speaks of this event and the desolation of many families who had become poor because of the blaze. This incident may well be one of the impetus for Franklin establishing the fire department in Philadelphia later in life in 1736.

During his life, Franklin made several observations and pronouncements about ethics that were specifically related to Christianity. Some of these put Jesus and his followers in a good light, while others did not. Among these moral pronouncements were the following:

1. To follow by Faith alone is to follow blindly.
2. When a Religion is good, I conceive it will support itself; and when it does not support itself... the professors are obliged to call for help from the civil power. This is a sign of being a bad Religion.
3. Whoever shall introduce into public affairs the principles of primitive Christianity will change the face of the world.
4. The way to see by Faith is to shut the eye of Reason.
5. How many observe Christ's birthday. How few, His precepts.
6. I wish Christianity were more productive of good works... I mean real good works... not holy-day keeping, sermon-hearing... or making long prayers, filled with flatteries and compliments despised by wise men, and much less capable of pleasing the Deity.
7. Many have quarreled about a Religion that never practiced it.[333]

In addition to these seven observations about the relationship of religious practice to ethics, he also offered an eighth pronouncement about that relation, one that was extremely self-reflective. He said this:

> It is much to be lamented that a man of Franklin's general good character and great influence should have been an unbeliever in Christianity, and also have done much as he did to make others unbelievers.[334]

What is significant about this eighth moral pronouncement about the relation of religious belief to ethics is how self-reflective it is. Franklin knows he is not terribly religious, at least according to traditional Christian beliefs. Yet, at the same time, he is also cognizant of the fact that he is capable of bringing people to the true foundations of the Christian Church and the imitation of the life of Jesus Christ.

Several other conclusions may be made about his overall perspective on the relation of religion to ethics. Among these are the following:

1. That faith alone is to disregard reason.
2. The person of Jesus and his original teachings were the best ethical system ever created, a view shared with Thomas Jefferson.
3. Many claim to be Christians, but few really live by its principles.
4. Good works are more productive morally than attending church services, listening to sermons, and the use of prayer.

Finally, we will end Chapter Six on Franklin's views on ethics and virtue by pointing to a catalog of personal moral and non-moral characteristics for which he was familiar. Some of these are moral traits, and some of them are not.

First, he cultivated productive habits in both moral and non-moral ways. Secondly, he took many risks.

Third, Franklin was better at controlling and helping to create his public image than any other figure of his time or since. Fourthly, more than any other of the American Founding Fathers, Franklin was a champion of the common man. Fifth, for his entire adult life, he was an early riser. He was the man who famously observed:

> Early to bed and early to rise makes a
> man healthy, wealthy, and wise.[335]

Sixth, Franklin was what might be called the "First great networker." He made friends and business connections everywhere he went, including England and France. He was always very good with people and had a happy talent of being at ease in almost any company, from the scrappy tradesman to wealthy merchants and members of the European nobility.[336]

Many biographers of Franklin have pointed out that his most valuable trait was his personal magnetism, not to be confused with his scientific work on magnetism. This trait was a huge asset in his business life and in his political and personal endeavors.

Seventh, he was an extremely creative thinker. What one might even say, "He always thought outside the box." Franklin is quoted as saying:

> In order to create, we must first identify the
> problem and then offer the best possible solution.³³⁷

Among his most creative projects were the following:

> The Franklin stove.
> The first public library.
> His experiments on electricity, lightning rods and magnetism.
> His development of the glass armonica.³³⁸

Eighth, Franklin was better at using and prioritizing his time than any Colonial American. He found ways to increase his daily productivity, from his daily hourly schedule to his rising at 5:00 a.m. every morning. As he is frequently quoted as having observed:

> Waste no time, always be employed in some
> activity that is useful and cut off all unnecessary actions.³³⁹

Ninth, he was extremely frugal, so much so that he included frugality as one of the thirteen virtues. Franklin realized the importance of living debt-free and only spending minimally. Again, he is quoted as saying:

> A penny saved is a penny earned.³⁴⁰

And,

> When you occur a debt, you give to
> another the power over your liberty.³⁴¹

He understood that to live a productive and moral life, it is helpful not to be plagued by the stress of debt.

Tenth, he was very good at identifying unmet demands or needs and often stepped forward in an effort to fill those needs. One fine example of this phenomenon is the amount of German Americans in the colonies. He responded by identifying the fact that there was no German newspaper. In response, he launched the *Philadelphische Zeitung*, the first German newspaper printed in America.³⁴²

Eleventh, Franklin was good at "seeing the whole picture." His *Pennsylvania Gazette* and *Poor Richard's Almanack* were the most successful publications in America, in large part because of the statesman's congenial and witty prose style. His serving as Postmaster is a fine example of this phenomenon. He saw a need with the state of the postal system in the new America and set out to fix the problem by serving as the bringer of a solution to that need that was much greater than for himself, his family, and his friends.[343]

Benjamin Franklin (1706–1790), first Postmaster-General, handing mail to postrider, Philadelphia, 1775.
Credit: New York Public Library / Art Resource, NY

Twelfth, and finally, Franklin was ambitious, hard-working and trustworthy. In fact, this last characteristic was clearly one of his most important personal moral characteristics. He kept his promises and expected others to do the same.[344]

Franklin's lifelong search for a better world and a better America did not always result in personal profit for the statesman. Nonetheless, he said many times very clearly that his personal motto was:

Doing well by doing Good.[345]

And this was, undoubtedly, the real secret of his success, both as an entrepreneur and as a moral human being.

This brings us to the major conclusions we have made in this chapter. The content of Chapter Seven of this study of Benjamin Franklin's religion, as we shall see, will be what the American statesmen believed, wrote, and had to say about religions other than his own, more specifically about Judaism, Catholicism and Islam.

Conclusions to Chapter Six

In the Introduction to Chapter Six, we suggested that the chapter had four separate goals, as well as four separate sections. The first of these was "Background Information on Franklin's Ethics." In that opening section, we spoke again of the Puritan-Calvinist background in which he was raised. We also pointed out that for more than thirty years, Franklin prepared a work he was to call "The Book of Virtue."

We began the section on Franklin's ethics by describing four major moral theories that were current in the second half of the eighteenth century and the first half of the nineteenth century. These were Deontological Theory; Teleological Theory, or Utilitarianism; Divine Command Theory; and Virtue Ethics. We also indicated that he occasionally referred to Divine Command Theory but more often relied on the idea of virtue ethics. In the first section of Chapter Six, we maintained that three of the sources on virtue that Franklin consulted in terms of cobbling together his understanding of the idea of virtue were Cicero's sense of cardinal virtues, Joseph Addison's characters Jubo and Cato in his drama *Cato: A Tragedy,* and the third chapter of the Biblical Book of Proverbs that mentions and discusses several moral virtues.

In the second section of the chapter, we began with a summary of the views of ancient philosopher Aristotle on the idea of virtue and his distinction between moral virtues and non-moral virtues. We followed this description with a summary of how Franklin's work on virtue both agreed and disagreed with the account given by the Greek philosopher.

Additionally, our next task in the second section was to provide a catalog of sorts of Franklin's thirteen virtues and a short description of what each of these virtues consisted of for him. We also pointed out that he had originally planned to include twelve virtues but added a thirteenth when an anonymous Quaker friend of his pointed out that the list lacked any mention of humility, a virtue that, in the view of the friend, was something that Franklin was missing.

At the close of section two, we pointed out that Franklin's account of ethics and virtue was not without its critics. Among those were Puritans, who said the list lacked God and doctrine, and British writer D. H. Lawrence, another critic of both Franklin's desire to achieve moral perfection and his account of moral virtue.

The chief task of section three of Chapter Six on Franklin's views on ethics and virtue was to give a summary of his moral method. In that section, as we have indicated, he devised a plan or method for cultivating his thirteen virtues, spending a week at a time on each virtue and recording when he did and did not embody that particular virtue.

In the fourth and final section of Chapter Six, we set out two separate goals. The first was to supply some general observations of Franklin on the ideas of ethics and virtue. As we have seen, we supplied a summary of several of these general observations, as well as another list of many of the ways that he understood the relationship of religious belief to the ideas of ethics and virtue.

We also included in section four a summary of twelve personal moral characteristics for which Franklin is mostly known. Among these personal characteristics were his champion of the common man, his being the "First Great Networker," his being very good with people, his trustworthiness, and many other moral characteristics of the statesman.

The other task of the fourth section was to identify and discuss various moral issues that Franklin was concerned about over the years. They included his dedication to the poor, his treatment of the religious views of Native Americans, his abolitionist stance on slavery, and his being against the colonial idea of expelling the Jews and Catholics from America.

We also pointed out that he believed that when the Presbyterian Synod revoked the license of the Rev. Samuel Hemphill to preach, that action for Franklin was entirely a moral one.

Indeed, we have also shown that his "A Defence of the Reverend Hemphill's Observations" was an example of a larger moral issue about how dissenters, in general, were treated by the traditional religious figures in both Europe and America. In fact, we showed how he defended dissenters in England when the Crown required them to pay "tythes" and additional taxes. For Franklin, this too was a moral issue, one like the issue of the Rev. Hemphill when the religious authorities meddled in the ability of certain people to make a living.

This brings us to the end of the sixth chapter. In Chapter Seven to follow, we will analyze and discuss what Franklin had to say about religious traditions other than his own—Judaism, Catholicism and Islam.

Franklin and his son William flying a kite
during an electrical storm.
Courtesy of the Library of Congress.

Chapter Seven
Franklin on Other Religions

> The United States of America... has itself no character of enmity against the laws, religion, or tranquility of Muslims.
> —President John Adams

> Freemasonry more than fulfilled Benjamin Franklin's Enlightenment dreams of establishing a party of virtue and he became a hard-working a nd enthusiastic member of the fraternity.
> —Shai Afsai, "Benjamin Franklin and Virtue"

> Were I a Roman Catholic, perhaps I should on this occasion, vow to build a chapel to some saint; but as I am not, if I were to vow at all, it should be to build a lighthouse.
> —Benjamin Franklin, Letter to his wife, July 17, 1757

Introduction

The major purpose of Chapter Seven is to explore and discuss what Benjamin Franklin believed and said about religious traditions other than his own family's Protestant Congregationalism and Presbyterianism. We will accomplish this goal by first looking at Franklin on Judaism, then the statesman on Roman Catholicism, and finally, what he said and wrote about Islam. In this sense, Chapter Seven will have three principal parts, one each for the three religious traditions.

Franklin on Judaism

In Chapter Six of this study on Franklin's religion, we have suggested that, as a young man in his twenties, he resolved to perfect his moral character, so he devised a unique method to aid in the challenging task of becoming what he called "Moral Perfection."[346]

Franklin's moral method, as described in his posthumously-published autobiography, became incorporated into the practical Jewish ethical tradition called *Mussar* in 1808 when Rabbi Mendel Leflin (1749–1826) of Satanov—a proponent of the Jewish Enlightenment—published a book entitled *The Book of Spiritual Accounting*.[347] What is significant about the rabbi's work for our purposes is that his book advocates a nearly identical method to that proposed by Franklin as expressed in his autobiography. Leflin's book continues to be studied in Jewish religious academies, and in many ways, his work underpins Jewish ideals of character development and Jewish self-improvement programs. Judaic scholars have been reluctant, however, to acknowledge Franklin's method or that there might have been any actual borrowing from Rabbi Leflin. For the most part, Franklin scholars have been unaware of the similarities between the two moral methods found in both works.

Recently, one exception to these general rules has been the work of Shai Afsai, whose research has focused on the works of Thomas Paine, Jews in the Enlightenment, and Freemasonry. His article, "Benjamin Franklin's Influence on Mussar Thought and Practice: A Chronicle of Misapprehension," was published in the *Review of Rabbinic Judaism*.[348] Afsai's work *Franklin and the Art of Virtue* is another by-product that came out of this research.[349] What Afsai has shown in these two works is that both Franklin's autobiography and Rabbi Leflin's *Spiritual Accounting* put forth a year-long, quarterly repeated self-examination program that focused on thirteen character traits. In both methods, each trait is given a week of close examination and daily journaling in similar grid charts, with the seven days of the week running horizontally and the thirteen desired traits that Franklin calls "Virtues" running vertically on the chart.

Afsai also suggests that the organization of Freemasonry played a key role in Franklin's account of virtue. He quotes Franklin biographer Gordon S. Wood that "In the Masons, Franklin discovered just the organization he was looking for."[350] Wood adds:

> Freemasonry more than fulfilled Franklin's Enlightenment dreams of establishing a party for virtue, and he became an enthusiastic and hard-working member of the fraternity... Eventually, he became the Grand Master of all the lodges in the Colony of Pennsylvania. No organization could have been more congenial to Franklin, and although he seldom mentioned the organization in his correspondence, he remained a Mason throughout his life. Not only was Masonry dedicated to the promotion of virtue throughout the world, but this Enlightenment fraternity gave Franklin contacts that helped him in his business.

Some Franklin scholars, such as Norman Fiering, for example, have suggested that Freemasonry was the impetus for Franklin's work on virtue.[351] Others like Gordon Wood believe that the Freemasons may have hindered and or complicated Franklin's thoughts about virtue and ethics.[352]

What is clear, however, is that twenty years after Franklin died in 1790, halfway across the world from Philadelphia, Rabbi Leflin of Satanow published his own book on a moral self-improvement method. Franklin had planned on his book being used by "Virtuous and good men of all nations," who he envisioned as members of his "Party of Virtue." Leflin's *Spiritual Accounting* was written solely for the religious and moral edification of his fellow Jews.[353]

One of the students of Rabbi Leflin, a prominent scholar named Jacob Samuel Bick, wrote about the self-improvement method of the *Spiritual Accounting*. Bick even made the connection to Franklin when the rabbi told us this:

> A wonderful technique invented by the sage Benjamin Franklin from the city of Philadelphia in North America. This scholar is renowned in all corners of the Earth...

Thus Rabbi Leflin has prepared a delicacy for his nation—and taught a clear and simple solution for the broken but still precious soul to speedily return from the bad to the good. In their approbation, the rabbis of the generation said that this thing is beneficial and new. And the nation replied in turn "Sanctified! Sanctified!"[354]

Another early example that recognized the influence of Franklin on Rabbi Leflin is the work of Rabbi Meir Halevi's Hebrew biography of Rabbi Nahman Krochmal, another disciple of Rabbi Leflin. Halevi says in a letter that:

> The Spiritual Accounting teaches ...good conduct according to the way of the English sage, Mister Franklin, whose approach Leflin often embraced in his manner of inquiry and acquisition of wisdom.[355]

Rabbi Leflin's book was first published in 1808 in Lemberg, Austria, although the rabbi was from Poland. In her essay, "Benjamin Franklin in Jewish Eastern Europe," Nancy Sinkoff describes the core of *Moral Accounting*, a method that sounds very familiar. She tells us:

> The core of Moral Accounting was a boxed grid, seven lines by thirteen, which correlate, respectively, to the days of the week and to thirteen virtues in need of improvement. The grid was to be used daily throughout a thirteen-week cycle which repeated four times in the course of a year.[356]

Rabbi Leflin himself tells us that he had not invented this method. He related,

> Several years ago a new method was revealed, and it is [such] a wonderful invention for this [kind] of [moral] education that it seems that its renown will spread as quickly, if God desires it, as that of the invention of printing which brought light to the world.[357]

Professor Sinkoff also suggests that the conduit between Franklin and Rabbi Leflin was Adam Kazimierz Czartoryski (1734–1823), a Polish friend of Leflin who was also a Mason. At one point, Sinkoff flatly comes out and says that Czartoryski was "the connective tissue between the American and the Eastern European."[358] Czartoryski knew Franklin personally; they were both members of the Mason Lodge in Paris called "*Les Neuf Soeurs*" established in 1776. Franklin was elected a member of the "Venerable" of that Paris lodge in 1781.

Another similarity to Franklin's account of virtue is that Rabbi Leflin's book also included thirteen virtues, six of which are the same in both accounts. These were order, cleanliness, righteousness or justice, frugality, silence and calmness; but the Rabbi's account includes equanimity, patience, truth, diligence and what he calls "separation," which cannot be found in Franklin's summary of the thirteen virtues.

In short, the conclusion of this material should now be clear—Franklin was a precedent and source for the work on virtue and moral character of Rabbi Mendel Leflin's book *Sefer Heshbon ha Nefesh*, or *The Book of Spiritual Accounting*, written and published in 1808.

Already in this study, we have pointed to two other examples of Franklin's treatment of Judaism. The first of these was the financial support that the statesman gave to the construction of the Mikveh Israel Synagogue in Philadelphia in 1740 when Franklin was thirty-four years old.[359]

The other example of Franklin's commitment to the Jews and Judaism in Philadelphia is to point out that one of the clergymen that the statesman had designated as a pallbearer at his funeral was Manuel Josephson, the Rabbi of Mikveh Israel in 1790. He was the president of the congregation at the time of Franklin's death.[360]

Over and against this analysis of Franklin and the faith of Israel and the Jews in Philadelphia was his general demeanor regarding all religions. As we have shown in the chapter on religious toleration, the statesman fully believed in, and was committed to, the First Amendment guarantee of Religious Liberty and Religious Tolerance for everyone in Pennsylvania, as well as in the new republic—the United States of America—and Franklin's support of Article VI, Clause 3 of the US Constitution's prohibition against any religious test in America, as we shall see in Chapter Nine of this study.

This brings us to the second section of Chapter Seven of this study of Franklin's religion in which we will describe and discuss the many relationships that the first great American statesman had with Roman Catholics, the Vatican, and with the Catholic Church in the eighteenth century.

Franklin and Catholicism

The attitudes and treatment of Roman Catholics and the Catholic Church in the life and times of Franklin might be called ambivalent at best. On the one hand, while he was a British subject in colonial times, he shared with many of the other Founding Fathers the Anglican Church's rejection of Rome and beliefs like transubstantiation promulgated by the Catholic Church. On the other hand, he was asked by the Papal Nuncio to recommend a possible bishop to be the head of the American Catholic Church.

In fact, John Adams believed that Franklin became "more Catholic in his approach to religion," as suggested earlier in this study. At that point, we suggested that John Adams said to Franklin:

> The Catholics thought him a Catholic. The Church of England claimed him as one of them. The Presbyterians thought him half a Presbyterian and the Friends believed he was a Quaker.[361]

John Adams thought that Franklin was more chummy to the Roman Catholics than he ought to have been, perhaps because the Roman Church claimed him, much like the Anglicans and the Presbyterians, as well. Clearly, the Congregationalists, his mother's denomination, also had some claim to the statesman's being included on the rolls of their believers.

Many historians generally cast the founding of the University of Pennsylvania or the College of Philadelphia in 1755 as a step toward secular education. The Academy, as it was called, first met in the building constructed for the arrival of Rev. George Whitefield in 1739 in Philadelphia.[362]

Although Whitefield contributed to the development of the Academy, the real brains behind the idea were those of Franklin. He wanted the Academy to be based on the liberal arts, while Whitefield said, "Christianity seems to be an afterthought in the formation of the Academy."

The foundation of what was to become the University of Pennsylvania also shared a pro-Protestant and anti-Catholic sentiment to which both Whitefield and Franklin adhered. In 1755, Franklin and other members of the original board of the new academy swore an oath of fidelity to King George II. They also repudiated Catholic power and beliefs.[363] Indeed, for the new college to show support and loyalty to the British Crown, especially in light of the Seven Years War that had started the year before and which matched Europe's great Catholic and Protestant powers in the struggle for the control of religion in North America.[364]

The most distinctive theological commitment Franklin and the other board members made was the repudiation of the Roman Catholic doctrine of transubstantiation, or the idea that during the Lord's Supper the bread and wine become the body and blood of Jesus Christ. Franklin and the first provost of the university, William Smith, and the remainder of the board agreed to vow to follow the "True Faith of a Christian," meaning the Protestant variety.[365]

Many of the religious wars in Europe in the eighteenth century cut across main religious lines. The Protestant Lutheran Sweden, for example, sided with Catholic France in the Seven Years' War. Catholic Portugal, on the other hand, allied with the British Protestants. Anti-Catholicism, however, was very much a part of British life both in Britain and the American colonies. In fact, some historians argue that the American colonists, and Franklin among them, were much more anti-Catholic than the British Parliament that had passed the Quebec Action 1774. This British act protected the Roman Catholic faith in Quebec and provided religious freedom in the province, much like that in the First Amendment of the US Constitution.[366]

These anti-Catholic sentiments in Colonial America were not limited to Franklin, Adams, Whitefield and William Smith. The establishments of other colleges at Harvard, Yale, the College of New Jersey, and William & Mary College were all founded by Protestant denominations and shared anti-Catholic sentiments.[367]

In his book *Recovering Benjamin Franklin*, scholar James Campbell speaks of the statesman's relation to the Roman Church when he writes, "Franklin displayed elements of anti-Catholicism throughout his life."[368] Dr. Campbell adds:

> He writes, for example, on April 13, 1785, about the conversion of a Boston Protestant clergyman to Catholicism.

"Our ancestors from Catholic became first Church of England men and then refined into Presbyterians. To change now from Presbyterianism to Popery seems to me refining backwards, from white sugar to brown."[369]

The Protestant minister Dr. Campbell refers to is the Reverend John Thayer, a New England Presbyterian pastor who converted to Catholicism in 1761. Franklin returned from England a year later in 1762, where he immediately attended to family and business matters as well as the advocacy of more royal authority in the Pennsylvania Colony.

On the one hand, then, there seems to be a strain of anti-Catholicism in Franklin's life. On the other hand, while he was the ambassador in Paris, the Papal Nuncio consulted with him about the head and the organization of the American Catholic Church in America.[370]

In fact, Franklin recommended that a young priest named John Carroll become the head of the Catholic Church in the new United States. In 1776, Franklin journeyed to Canada with John Carroll, so he was in a position to recommend Father Carroll, who became a member of the Jesuit community in 1753 and was ordained a priest in 1769, seven years before Franklin and Father Carroll would meet and travel together.[371]

Four years later, however, Pope Clement XIV issued a Papal Bull that dissolved the Society of Jesus, or the Jesuits. Nevertheless, the following spring, Father Carroll returned to Maryland, where, at the time, local laws discriminated against Catholics. There was no Catholic Church in Maryland, so the priest began the life of a missionary in Maryland and in Virginia. John Carroll built a small chapel on his mother's estate and offered mass there on Sundays for any who wanted to attend.[372]

Meanwhile, the American Revolutionary War had begun in 1775, and it was in the interests of the colonies to enlist the aid of their neighbor to the north, but Canada remained neutral in the conflict. Franklin led a delegation from the Continental Congress to Canada to again seek an alliance in February of 1776. The delegation included Charles Carroll of Carrollton, the only Catholic signer of the Declaration of

Independence. Charles Carroll asked his cousin, Father John Carroll, to join him in the delegation.[373]

In the meantime, in the wake of the Revolutionary War, John Carroll and other priests in America began to meet regularly in the new United States to ensure that their apostolic mission would continue.

On November 6, 1783, in response to a petition sent to Rome by the Maryland Catholic clergy asking if they could nominate a superior who would lead the Catholic Church in America. It was at this point that John Carroll became the Bishop of Baltimore, appointed by Pope Pius VI. John Carroll then went on to serve as bishop and as archbishop for the next thirty-five years until his death in 1815.[374]

Among his many accomplishments, Archbishop Carroll was instrumental in founding Georgetown University in Washington, DC. For the training of his Baltimore priests, Carroll invited the Sulpicians who established Saint Mary's Seminary in Baltimore.[375] He also encouraged Elizabeth Seton to establish the Sisters of Charity in the United States for the education of girls.[376] Another of his many accomplishments included his nomination by Franklin to be the head of the Catholic Church in America. And a year later, became the Bishop of Baltimore.

Benjamin Franklin also had some experiences with other Catholic women he met in London near the "Romish Chapel" on Duke Street while living there. This was in the parish of Saints Anselm and Cecilia, which the Portuguese and Sardinians started in the early eighteen century. It is one of the rare Catholic churches still in operation in Britain.[377]

Near the church, Franklin found lodgings in the house of a Catholic widow. She was an elderly shut-in whose conversation he very much enjoyed. In her youth, she had planned to become a Catholic nun. Unable to find a suitable place on the Continent to join, she returned to Britain, where convents were now outlawed. Instead, she vowed to live the life of a nun on her own. Franklin admired the simplicity and discipline of the woman.[378] He noted that one of the priests from the church could be seen entering the woman's house on a regular basis. When he asked her about it, she informed him that the priest was hearing her confession and bringing her the sacrament. Given her lifestyle and keeping his own behavior with the ladies in mind, he asks the would-be nun how she could find enough behavior to confess. The woman answered directly, "It is always impossible to contain one's vain thoughts."[379]

One time Franklin visited the ascetic nun's flat, which he "detailed with his curious Protestant eye." She was "cheerful and polite, and full of pleasant conversation."[380] There was nothing but a mattress on the floor, a table, a crucifix, a book, and a stool on which Franklin was invited to sit. There was a picture over the chimney of Veronica's Veil. Embossed with an image of the bleeding face of Christ, which the would-be nun explained to him to be "a very good likeness."[381] He, not surprisingly, was not convinced of the miraculous nature of the piece of art but was convinced of the Catholic woman being a fine example of the personification of two of his virtues—frugality and temperance.

When Franklin visited the European Continent for the first time in 1761, he had his son William along on the trip. In Holland, even though it was a Protestant city, the main attractions were the Catholic churches, "which surpassed anything I had ever seen before or conceived."[382] In Holland, the two also visited some Catholic convents where some English women were in residence. He wrote a letter home to his friend Polly Hewson and told her that contrary to the awful view of Catholics with which he was raised, these Catholics on Holland were "admirably zealous." He told Polly Hewson that "The English protestants were lukewarm in comparison."[383]

In his autobiography, Franklin mentioned several other Roman Catholic friends and acquaintances he had encountered over the years. In general, however, he extended the same first amendment rights of religious freedom and religious toleration that he extended to the Jews we saw in the previous section of this chapter. And this surely was the overarching theory that lay at the heart of Franklin's understanding of what today might be called "Comparative Religion."[384]

This brings us to the third and final section of Chapter Seven of this study on Franklin's religion, in which we will identify, explore, and discuss what the first great American statesman had to say and write about the religion of Islam and its followers, the Muslims.

Franklin on Islam and Muslims

We will begin this third section of Chapter Seven by pointing out that the British North American colonial period was a time when there were many Muslim slaves in America, a number of prominent members of those Islamic slaves, as well as many references to Islam and particular Muslims among the Founding Fathers of America. We know, for example, that George Washington had several Muslim slaves on the farms at his Mount Vernon estate.

Among these was a carpenter known as Sambo Anderson, who was afforded many privileges not usually given to Washington's slaves, such as owning his own rifle or owning his own house on a Washington property.[385] Phillis Wheatley, to cite another example, was a Muslim slave that came across the Middle passage and eventually became the first well-known female African-American poet in America.[386]

We also know of several Muslim slaves who served in the Continental Army. Among these were Peter Salim, Yusuf ben Ali, and brothers Francis and Joseph Saba. Peter Salim is said to have fired the shot that killed John Pitcairn at the Battle of Bunker Hill.[387] Yusuf ben Ali was an aide to General Thomas Sumter during the war against the British.[388] The Saba brothers, who were born in North Africa, were sold into slavery in Annapolis and later served in the Continental Army.[389] Another early Virginia Muslim slave who also served in the Continental army was Bampett Muhamed. He served as a corporal in a Virginia regiment from 1775 until 1783.[390]

In an article entitled "Islam at Mount Vernon," Mary V. Thompson suggests that it is likely that besides Sambo Anderson, at least three other George Washington slaves were Muslims. One of those was a young woman named "Nila," whose African name was most likely Nailah.[391]

Among the prominent Muslim slaves in Maryland in the colonial period up to the American Civil War were the ancestors of Harriet Tubman, Frederick Douglass and Kunta Kinte, the forefather of Alex Haley of "Roots" fame.[392] Another prominent Muslim slave in Maryland was a man named Job Diallo, who was born in Senegal, came to America on a slave ship, and eventually in 1734 was repatriated back to Africa.[393]

In 1785, George Washington welcomed good Muslim workers at his Mount Vernon estate. He said, "As long as he is a good worker, I will accept any man who would do an honest day's work in my home."[394]

Another prominent Maryland Muslim slave was Yarrow Manout (1736–1824). He was born in Guinea, kidnapped and enslaved in Africa, and then in America sold to the Samuel Beall Jr. family in Montgomery County, Maryland.[395]

During the Civil War period, a group of Muslims resided in the Dismal Swamp of southern Virginia and northern North Carolina. Their leader was a man named Black Mingo Pocosin, who was also most likely from northwest Africa in the early nineteenth century.[396]

The upshot of all of this should be clear. In the period from the Continental Army until the America Civil War, there were a significant number of Muslim slaves in what became the United States. There are also other ways, as well, as we can see what relations Franklin may have had to Islam and/or to Muslims. Earlier in this study, we mentioned another example where Isla, or a Muslim, was a subject of discussion.

In 1739, when Franklin supervised the building of the new lecture hall in which the Rev. George Whitefield would speak, in the dedication of that building, which would become the first structure of the University of Pennsylvania, the first great American statesman told his crowd gathered that day:

> Even if the Mufti of Constantinople were to send a missionary to preach Islam to the US, he would find a pulpit at his service in which he could preach.[397]

Another way the presence of Islam in early America can be seen is by the fact that both Thomas Jefferson and John Adams both owned copies of the Muslim Holy Book, Al-Qur'an. There are even reports that Jefferson attempted to teach himself Classical Arabic, the language of the Holy Book.[398]

When Keith Ellison, the first Muslim member of the US Congress from Minnesota, took the oath of office, he was not sworn in with his hand on the Bible. Instead, Ellison was sworn in using Jefferson's Qur'an.[399]

John Adams also spoke of owning a Qur'an in a letter to Jefferson on Christmas day 1813, in which he spoke of both the Muslim and the "Hindoo" Sacred Scripture. Adams even offered the hope that there soon "would be available in English of the Sacred books of the Persians, the Chinese, and the Hindoos."

In another letter from Adams to Jefferson from September 24, 1821, the former tells the latter that, "Some hundreds of millions of Musselmen [Muslim], expect another Prophet more powerful than Mahomet who will spread Islam over the whole world before it is burned up."

A letter was presented to George Washington from the Touro Synagogue in Newport, Rhode Island, when he visited there on August 18, 1790. In a speech at the ceremony, Washington mentioned all three Abrahamic faiths, the exercise of religion and religious toleration that should be "afforded to all citizens in America." Several other early American documents also show that Islam served many roles in early America.

We have established the fact that the Islamic faith in the seventeenth and eighteenth centuries was well-known and even prominent in the form of some Muslims in early America. There was also, however, in the same period, some great concern about the growth of Islam in both Europe and America.

Cotton Mather (1663–1738), for example, fulminated against what he called "Mohometan Turks and Moors and Devils" when he received word that Americans were being taken hostage in North Africa. Mather said to his congregation, "We are afar off, in a Land, which never had (that I ever heard of) one Mahometan breathing in it."[400]

Little did Mather know that the first Muslims arrived in the New World around 1527 with the Conquistadors. The first documented Muslim settlers arrived in the Dutch province of New Netherland around 1630. In the book *A History of Islam in America*, historian Kambiz Ghanea Bassiri establishes that many of the slaves dragged ashore in irons in America were Muslims captured by rival tribes and enslaved.[401] Similar conclusions have been made by Professor Michael Gomez of New York University.[402]

By 1698, noted Arabic scholar and Catholic Evangelical, Ludovico Marracci, published the first historically-accurate Latin translation of the Qur'an, as well as a refutation of the Muslim Holy Book.⁴⁰³ In 1798, James Lyon published *The True Nature of the Imposture Fully Displayed in the Life of Mahomet*, an exposé on the salacious life of the Prophet Muhammad. Lyon was the son of a congressman who was jailed for sedition. In fact, John Adams labeled the father of James Lyon, the "New Muhammad," for his supposed religious zeal in stifling dissent.⁴⁰⁴

Not to be outdone, John Quincy Adams compared Thomas Jefferson to the "Arabian Prophet" because Jefferson had referred to Adams' father, John Adams, as a "heretic," as Robert Allison reported in his work *The Crescent Observed*.⁴⁰⁵ This may have been because earlier, Adams, America's second president, named the Prophet Muhammad as one of the world's "greatest seekers of truth alongside Socrates and Confucius."

Thomas Jefferson, the country's third president and the author of the Declaration of Independence, tried to learn Arabic from his copy of Al-Qur'an and hosted the first presidential *Iftar*, a ceremony that marks the end of the month-long fast of *Ramadan*.⁴⁰⁶

Although Franklin mentioned the "Mufti of Constantinople" in a speech from 1739 in Philadelphia, he still would have had a difficult time convincing the citizens of Philadelphia to believe that the asserters to the religion of the Prophet Muhammad should be afforded the same rights to religious freedom and to religious toleration as the rest of the citizens of the new republic.

Thus, the views of Franklin and the other Founding Fathers of America appear to have been, in general, quite ambivalent. On the one hand, Franklin, Jefferson and John Adams at times praised the Prophet Muhammad and the followers of his faith. On the other hand, people like Cotton Mather, James Lyon and Ludovico Marracci worried gravely about the influence that the Muslim faith may have on the United States. The criticisms of Islam in America, in some ways, were an extension of Enlightenment attitudes developed in France and Britain in the seventeenth and eighteenth centuries by people like Montesquieu, Voltaire and Gibbon, who all studied and critiqued Islam along with Christianity, giving the contributions of Islam a new importance on the European continent. In fact, in 1736, Voltaire wrote a five-act drama entitled *Mahomet*, whose only expressed goal appears to have been the ridicule of the Prophet Muhammad and the faith of Islam.[407]

Edward Gibbon devoted three chapters of his *Rise and Fall of the Roman Empire* to Islam. These were called "Mahomet and the Origins of Islam," "Mahomet as Preacher and Warrior," and "The Crusades: Christianity and Islam in Conflict." Like Voltaire, in these three chapters, there is little that is positive about the Prophet Muhammad, his religion and his Holy Book, Al-Qur'an.[408]

In his *l'Esprit des lois*, Montesquieu also offers a fundamentally negative view of Islam. He says that any religion that does not promote the well-being of its believers is morally flawed and the numbers Islam among the faiths he had in mind.[409] In short, then, the views of Cotton Mather on Islam in America had European precedents in France and Britain in addition to Ludovico Marracci mentioned earlier.

In Franklin's essay, "A Narrative of the Late Massacres," he described the treatment of prisoners of war and pointed out that when word of the benign treatment of his men came back to the Prophet Muhammad, he applauded his men for their humanity. Franklin greatly admired Muhammad, but the American statesman also quotes the prophet as saying to the leader of his enemy:

> Oh Khaled, you butcher, cease to molest me with
> your Wickedness. If you had a heap of gold as large as
> Mount Obod, and should expend it all in the cause of Allah,
> your merit would not efface the guilt incurred by the Murder
> of the meanest of these poor Captives.[410]

In the same essay, Franklin goes on to give three more examples of how the earliest armies of Islam treated their captives. The final of these examples was the story of a Moor who lived in Spain. The Moor was sitting in his garden when a Spanish cavalier jumped over his garden gate. He explained to the Moor that he was running from his enemies, so he asked for protection. The Moor gave the cavalier protection, and the Spaniard went on his way. Later, some fellow Moors came to the garden looking for the cavalier, and the Moor realized that the other Moors were in pursuit of his son's killer. When the cavalier was finally captured and was on his way to prison, the Moor said to the captive:

> You are indeed guilty of my Son's Blood, but God is just and good, and I thank Him that I am innocent of your blood and my faith shall be preserved.[411]

Franklin used this narrative for several reasons. One of these was the role that forgiveness should play in religious discourse. Another important reason why the narrative about the Moor in the garden is important is the overall understanding that the first great American statesman had in regard to religious freedom and religious toleration to the followers of Islam, as well as other Christian sects that were not his own.

This brings us to the major conclusions we have made in this seventh chapter on Franklin's views of other religions—Judaism, Catholicism and Islam. This will be followed by Chapter Eight, an analysis of what he and other people in his time believed about American immigration.

Conclusions to Chapter Seven

In this chapter, we have had three principal goals regarding the overall task of discussing the views of the American statesman on religions other than his own. More specifically, we introduced and discussed, in turn, what he believed and wrote about Jews and Judaism, Roman Catholicism, and the Prophet Muhammad and the advocates of his Islamic faith.

To those ends, in the first section, we have shown two most important things. The first was that Franklin contributed funds to the construction of the Mikveh Israel Synagogue in Philadelphia, just as he had supported other religions and denominations, such as the construction of a bell tower and a new bell in a Christian church. The other important idea about Franklin and Judaism has to do with his development of the thirteen virtues and what appears to be an appropriation of his scheme by Eastern European Rabbi Mendel Leflin.

As we have shown, the rabbi outlined thirteen different virtues that are mostly similar to those of Franklin. Rabbi Leflin also proposed using a grid so one could keep track of how well a believer could live up to the high standard of his virtues.

The views of Franklin and Leflin were different in some important respects. The main difference is that Franklin believed his scheme of virtues was universal and could be used by all religions, while Rabbi Leflin's formulation of moral virtue was primarily aimed at Jewish believers.

In the second section of Chapter Seven, we turned our attention to the phenomenon of Franklin on Roman Catholicism. We began by suggesting that he grew up in a very anti-Catholic environment that had been imported from Britain and Enlightenment thinkers on the Continent.

We also indicated that there were some incidents in his life where these anti-Catholic sentiments could clearly be seen, such as his boarding with a would-be Catholic nun widow in London and the repudiation of transubstantiation by the original board of the University of Pennsylvania.

On the other hand, we have also shown that at times Franklin embraced Roman Catholics and their faith, such as the 1783 incident when he recommended to the Papal Nuncio in Paris that Father John Carroll of Maryland should be considered as the first head of the Catholic Church in America. And in 1783, that is precisely what happened.

We also indicated that when Franklin and his son William traveled to Europe for the first time, among the most important sites seen by the two were the "magnificent Catholic Churches of Holland," even telling Polly Hewson in a letter that the Protestant churches in Britain and America were, "lukewarm" compared to the Roman structures in Holland.[412]

The third section of Chapter Seven was devoted to what Franklin and the other Founding Fathers believed and wrote about what today might be called "comparative religion" with respect to the Prophet Muhammad and the Muslim faith. We began this section by pointing out that Islam appears to have served many roles from the time of the Spanish in early America until the Founding Fathers. Indeed, we began by cataloging many prominent Muslim slaves in America in the eighteenth century, including some at George Washington's Mount Vernon estate and several North African Muslims who served in the Continental Army.

In section three of Chapter Seven, we indicated that many of the Founding Fathers of America, including George Washington, John

Adams, Thomas Jefferson and Benjamin Franklin, had many positive things to say about Muhammad, Islam and the Qur'an. In fact, we pointed out that both John Adams and Thomas Jefferson owned copies of the Muslim Holy Book.

As we indicated, however, there was another strain in Colonial America regarding the religion of Islam in the seventeenth and eighteenth centuries. That strain, as we have shown, was a negative one about the Muslim faith, and its banner was taken up by figures like Cotton Mather and Ludovico Marracci.

We have shown that the views of Cotton Mather and Marracci on Islam had corresponding negative judgments about Islam and the Prophet Muhammad to be found in the works of Voltaire, Edward Gibbon and Charles-Louis Montesquieu. This second attitude toward Islam was exemplified by a belief that the Muslim faith, in some ways, could be detrimental to the American way of life, and the Reverend Mather and Marracci made that very clear in the late seventeenth century, as did James Lyon at the close of the eighteenth century.

Also, the bottom-line conclusion regarding the Founding Father's attitudes toward Muhammad, Islam and the Muslim Holy Book, Al-Qur'an, were ambiguous at best, at times critical, and at others very positive in their assessments.

This brings us to Chapter Eight, where we will introduce, analyze and discuss the phenomenon of religious tests in Britain, America and in the thought of Benjamin Franklin.

Benjamin Franklin helped raise funds for the first Pennsylvania Hospital building, the east wing, designed by Samuel Rhoads and constructed in 1755. The hospital is located on Pine Street between 8th and 9th Streets in Philadelphia. It is now part of the University of Pennsylvania Health System. Courtesy of the Library of Congress.

Chapter Eight
Franklin on Immigration

> He that is willing to tolerate any religion that is not
> his own, unless it be matters merely indifferent,
> either doubts his own or is not sincere in it.
> —Nathaniel Ward, *The Simple Cobbler of Aggawam in America*

> God is only father in the sense of being father to all. When
> I hate someone or deny that God is his father—it is not
> he who loses, but me, for then I have no father.
> —Soren Kierkegaard, *Repetition*

> The Spaniards, Italians, French, Russians and Swedes
> are generally of what we call swarthy Complexion; as
> are the Germans also, the Saxons only being excepted.
> —Benjamin Franklin, *The Autobiography of Benjamin Franklin*

Introduction

A prominent American once said this about immigrants,

> Few of their children learn English... The signs in our streets have inscriptions in both languages... Unless the stream of their importation could be turned, they will soon outnumber us all so that we will not be able to preserve our language and even our government will be precarious.[413]

The author of this quotation is not President Donald Trump, nor is it a contemporary Republican pundit. Rather, the source of this quote is none other than the subject of this study, the first great American statesman, Benjamin Franklin.

Voicing this grievance was Franklin, who spoke these words in the 1750s, during a wave of immigration of a people whom he referred to as the "most stupid of the nations."[414] He was speaking of Germany and the German immigrants to the British colonies of North America.

Franklin was not alone. At about the same time, a Lutheran minister named the Reverend Henry Muhlenberg, himself a recent arrival to the American colonies from Germany, also worried that:

> The whole country is being flooded with ordinary, extraordinary, and unprecedented wickedness and crimes... Oh what a fearful thing it is to have so many thousands of unruly and brazen sinners come into this free air and unfenced country.[415]

The purpose of Chapter Eight should be obvious. The goal is to catalog and discuss what the first great statesman of the United States had to say and to write about the phenomenon of immigration.

To that end, this chapter will have three main sections. In the first of these, we will comment on the history of attitudes toward immigration in America. In the second section, we will introduce and discuss beliefs and attitudes toward immigration during Franklin's lifetime, from 1706 until his death on April 17, 1790. In the third section, we will examine more specifically what the first great American statesman said and wrote about the phenomenon of immigration.

A History of Attitudes Toward Immigration in the United States

By the mid-eighteenth century in the United States, many prominent Americans, Franklin included, worried about the British practice of dumping its felons on American colonies. In fact, with typical wit, he suggested that America send rattlesnakes to Britain in return.[416] Franklin, a patriot committed to the ideals of human liberty, decried these policies of the British government that sent ships loaded with convicts and criminals to America. In 1749, as a reaction to this practice, the Assembly of Pennsylvania passed a bill forbidding the importation of convicts, but the British Parliament rejected the measure on the grounds that "Such Laws are against the Publick Utility, as they tend to present the Improvement and the Well Peopling of the Colonies."[417] Franklin responded in his *Pennsylvania Gazette* by asking, "In what other way can Britain show a more Sovereign Contempt for us, than by emptying its Jails into our Settlements."[418]

In the Pennsylvania Colony, the Scotch-Irish had bred discontent at their penchant for squatting on land that was not their own. This ran counter to the Penn family and its genteel views about who owned what in the colony. By 1790, the year of Franklin's death, the United States Constitution firmly established the idea of naturalization only to "free white persons" who had been in the country for two years. That requirement was later pushed back to five years and, in 1798, to fourteen years."

Once America was independent, the new nation began to carve its collective beliefs about who was and who was not an American. In 1790, for example, John Jay, the author of the New York Constitution and later a US Supreme Court Justice, suggested erecting a "wall of brass around Catholics" to keep them isolated from the real Americans.[419]

At the end of the eighteenth century, the Federalists feared that too many immigrants were joining the opposition, meaning, of course, the British and French. In 1798, the Alien Act was passed with the threat of war in the air over French attacks on American shipping. Our second president, John Adams, claimed to have a license to deport "anyone he considered dangerous." Although his own secretary of state favored mass deportation, Adams never actually put anyone on a boat.[420]

By the beginning of the nineteenth century, the French warranted the most suspicion, but there were other "worrisome aliens" as well. "Wild Irish" refugees were thought to harbor "dangerous radicals." Harsh "anti-coolie" laws were passed against the Chinese. And, of course, there were the more than ten million "involuntary" immigrants from Africa, who, along with their offspring, were regarded as "people held in service," that is, slaves.[421]

In the early nineteenth century, there were frequent signs in American cities that simply said, "No Irish Need Apply." And with each new wave of immigration, new arrivals had to face a rich glossary of epithets. Disdain for what was foreign is and was, sad to say, as American as apple pie, slavery and lynching.

The wall along the Mexican border in contemporary America is simply the latest vestige of the venerable tradition that is at least as old as John Jay's "wall of brass." "Don't fence me in" has been a frequent anthem over the history of the United States, but it is perfectly acceptable to fence in everybody else.

In the 1860s, Chinese immigrants were very desirable to American employers. With the 1868 Burlingame-Seward Treaty, however, immigration from China began to be limited because many of the Chinese took jobs with the American railroads, and this caused a stir that these Asian immigrants were taking too many jobs of "real Americans."[422]

In the 1870s, the state of California pushed the federal government to pass the Chinese Exclusion Act, which was not passed until 1882. The act banned all immigrants from China and marked the first federal government involvement in the process of immigration. Another restriction on immigration in 1917 was known as the Asiatic Barred Zone Act, which required a literacy test and excluded certain categories of "undesirables, including anarchists, paupers and prostitutes, from seeking immigration."[423]

Equally undesirable, at least according to the act, were people from most Asian and Pacific nations, with the exceptions of those from Japan and the Philippines. By 1924, immigration from Asia was still barred, and quotas were now introduced, but a new immigration threat began to appear from Italians, Greeks and from Eastern Europe.

Beginning in the 1890s, these new immigrants from southern and eastern Europe were thought to be swarthy. The dark complexions of the Italians and Greeks were again seen as a threat. Anti-immigrant sentiments, this abiding fear of the "huddled masses" emerged again in the late nineteenth and early twentieth centuries. The new anti-Catholic and anti-swarthy immigrant posture picked up steam in American nativism political parties and the Klu Klux Klan.[424]

This brings us to the second section of Chapter Eight, where we will speak more specifically about what Americans in Franklin's time believed about immigration.

American Attitudes Toward Immigration in the Eighteenth Century

In the eighteenth century, Benjamin Franklin was not alone in his views about Germany and the Germans as immigrants to America. Alexander Hamilton, for example, an immigrant himself, had his doubts. He supported John Adams' 1798 Alien and Sedition Act that increased the US residency requirement for US citizenship from five years to fourteen years, and it allowed the president forcefully to deport immigrants.[425]

In his *Papers*, Hamilton wrote of the dangers of letting aliens into the country, arguing that:

> The influx of foreigners must, therefore, tend to produce a heterogeneous compound to change and corrupt the national spirit and to complicate and confound public opinion; to introduce foreign propensities.[426]

On another occasion, Hamilton again turned his attention to what he called "Foreigners" when he related:

> Foreigners will generally be apt to bring with them attachments to the persons that they have left behind; to the contrary of their nativity, and to its particular customs and manners. They will also entertain opinions on government congenial with those under which they have lived; or, if they should have been led hither from a preference to ours, how extremely unlikely is it that they will bring with them that temperate love of liberty, so essential to real Republicanism.[427]

And Franklin and Hamilton were not alone. Thomas Jefferson, even though he saw emigration as a fundamental right, was not, nevertheless, too keen on German immigration, whom apparently he saw as setting a "bad example for other immigrants."[428] Jefferson observed about the matter, "As to other foreigners it is thought better to discourage their settling together in large masses." Jefferson added, "Wherein, as in our German settlements, they preserve for a long time their own language, habits, and principles of government."[429]

Jefferson also commented on the hospitality of the natives in America in regard to newcomers when he observed:

> Had it all been true, prudence requires us to trace the history further and asks what has become of the nations of savages who exercised this policy, and who now occupy the territory which they then inhabited? Perhaps a lesson is here taught which ought not to be despised.[430]

Here Jefferson speaks of immigrants who came from savage nations, how they have become assimilated into America, and that a lesson may be learned by the practice of what today would be called xenophobia. Often the disdain for foreigners in America was inflamed by religion. Boston's Puritans in the eighteenth century hanged several Quakers in the Massachusetts Bay Colony.[431] In the colony of Virginia, the Anglicans arrested many Baptists in the same period.[432] By the turn of the eighteenth century, anti-Catholic sentiments were so strong that only in the Rhode Island Colony were the religious rights of Catholics respected.[433] The new colony of Georgia was kept free of Papists. Inspectors were appointed in the colony to make sure no followers of the "Roman errors would enter the region."[434]

In 1716, the Maryland Assembly passed a law forbidding officeholders from "attending Popish assemblies or attending mass." In 1718, residents who did not take the required Protestant oaths were disenfranchised. By 1740 in the Maryland Colony, Catholics were banned from serving in the state militia for fear that they would start an "armed insurrection."[435] Any Roman priests who attempted to make converts in the Maryland Colony was tried for treason and subject to the death penalty.[436]

In Massachusetts in 1750, the Rev. Paul Dudley gave a series of lectures at the Harvard Divinity School. The Rev. Dudley said the purpose of these lectures was:

> The detecting and convicting and exposing of idolatry of the Roman Church. Their tyranny, usurpation, damnable heresies, fatal errors, abominable superstitions, and other crying wickedness in her high places.[437]

We see how much Boston changed, however, when Bishop John Carroll traveled there just a few decades later. When the cleric spoke of his acceptance in the city, he related:

> It is wonderful to tell what great civilities have been done to me in this town, where a few years ago a Popish priest was thought to be the greatest monster in creation. Many here, even of their principal people, have acknowledged to me that they would have crossed the street rather than meet a Roman Catholic some time ago.[438]

In 1776, the New Jersey Constitution forbade Catholics from serving in public offices. Connecticut passed similar laws. Vermont required all voters to profess allegiance to the "Protestant faith."[439] New Hampshire developed a series of state constitutions, each successive one containing anti-Catholic provisions.[440] The New York State Constitution of 1777, under the leadership of John Jay, had a provision barring from citizenship all who failed to repudiate allegiance in spiritual matters to any "foreign prince or potentate."[441] Presumably, this meant Roman bishops and the pope. This provision of the New York State Constitution lasted until 1790 when the federal government took charge of naturalization issues.

By the third decade of the nineteenth century, many English anti-Catholic tracts were imported to America. Anthony Gavin's *Master Key to Popery*,[442] Scippione de'Ricci's *Female Convents: Secret of Nunneries Disclosed*,[443] and the 1835 work *Six Months' Residence in a Convent* by Rebecca Theresa Reed, published in Boston, was perhaps the most popular of this genre.[444] The social antipathies, class conflicts, and unbridled religious jealousies of the period all can be seen in Reed's volume.

The American Catholic hierarchy's response to these anti-Catholic sentiments came in the form of a pastoral letter issued on April 22, 1837. It calls to task members of the legislatures of Massachusetts and South Carolina for not censuring Protestant members of the clergy in their states who were critical of Roman Catholics. The letter also raised the issue of whether Catholics and Jews in America are to be granted the same religious freedom and religious toleration that are extended to the Protestant denominations.[445]

As suggested earlier in this chapter, the immigration patterns in the first decades of the twentieth century began to change dramatically from those of the post-Civil War years. The predominant ethnic groups were now from southern and eastern Europe, particularly Italians and Jews.

Given the history of America, the results of these new immigrations were predictable. There was a new wave of American nativism against the "Swarthy Italians and Eastern European Jews." And in what may be one of the greatest ironies was that the Irish, whose fathers and grandfathers had been victims of the same kind of oppression now reserved for Italian Catholics.[446]

The amount of anti-Catholicism in early America was great. One of the causes of the American Revolution was opposition to King George III's granting of religious rights to the Catholics of Quebec after the British defeated the French in the Seven Years' War. The New England worthies, as well as people like Benjamin Franklin and George Whitefield in the Pennsylvania Colony, were worried that the king intended to reinstitute Catholicism throughout the colonies.

Most rational people would appear to have laughed at such a proposal, but there were plenty of religious bigots in New England and elsewhere, including in Franklin's home in Pennsylvania. The Puritans who came to New England did not come to practice religious freedom. They came to practice their religion and to persecute anyone who would not conform to their brand of Calvinism.

Many of the Founding Fathers, including Franklin, condemned King George III for his restrictions on immigration to the New World. Well-designed states, the new patriots believed, should promote immigration, and this was why they denounced the king for endeavoring to "prevent the population of these states."[447] Thus, another aspect of Franklin's views on American immigration had to do with the lack of support from the English Crown in supporting the English-speaking population of the Pennsylvania Colony and state and its growth in population.

This brings us to the third section of Chapter Eight, in which we will examine the issue of immigration in the modern period of American history, particularly from the early twentieth century until the present time.

American Immigration in the Modern Period: 1920s to the Present

We have shown in this chapter that by the early decades of the twentieth century, some immigrants were denied US citizenship because of what was called their "Swarthy Complexion." In the 1920s, the US Supreme Court held two cases directly related to the issue of what it meant to be "White."

In 1922, the limits of what it meant to be White were tested by two Japanese Americans named Takao Ozawa and Takuji Yamashita, whose naturalization cases were brought before the Supreme Court. The two Japanese Americans filed a petition to the court on the basis that, in general, Japanese people were white-skinned. The Supreme Court ruled against both petitioners on the same day, ruling that "A White person is a categorization that could only apply to people who were Caucasian."[448]

The following year, a Punjabi man named Bhagat Singh Thind, a member of the Sikh faith, applied for naturalization on the basis that, like many Europeans, northern Indians were Aryans and hence of the Caucasian race. The Supreme Court denied his petition, which argued that "The petitioner did not fit the common understanding of what it means to be Caucasian."[449]

It is of some interest that for a long time, restrictions on US citizenship did not apply to Mexicans. With the Great Depression, however, and the scarcity of resources that followed, there was the idea that Mexicans were already competing for rare jobs in the United States. So between 1929 and 1944, two million Mexicans became the targets of so-called "Repatriations." Effectively, these people became the scapegoats of the day, as many other groups had been long before them.[450]

Scholar Francisco Balderrama, a California State University historian who has written about mass deportation, told National Public Radio that,

> Whether they were American citizens or whether they were Mexican nationals, in the minds of the American industry leaders, they were all Mexicans, so ship them back home.[451]

After the attack on Pearl Harbor prompted the American entry into World War II, President Franklin D. Roosevelt ordered the internment of many Japanese Americans, who may have been sympathetic to Japan. The government sent these people to live in areas designated by the US military. People of Japanese descent were kept in internment camps or relocation camps under the suspicion that they may be sympathizing with the enemy.[452] In all, more than 130,000 Japanese American detainees were sent to these camps. Later, many returned to Japan rather than returning to their homes in America, which were mostly in the state of California.[453]

For most of its history, as we have shown so far in this chapter, American immigration was based on a quota system that privileged Caucasians and Western Europeans. That is, until 1965. Then came President John F. Kennedy's vision that "America is a Nation of Immigrants," which he laid out before his election in 1960, going all the way back to 1958.

Kennedy's approach established a new rhetoric for reframing the identity of Americans. Since Kennedy, for decades, no one group was specifically targeted or marginalized until September 11, 2001. After 9/11, states like Arizona and Georgia started pushing for anti-immigration policies. Certain Republican politicians took part in the new anti-immigration movement, this time in relation to Muslims.

Finally, the only consistent statistical recording of attitudes toward immigration in the United States in the modern era is the answers to a survey question that has been asked of Americans by the researchers of the Gallop Company since 1965. At that time, Americans began to be asked, "In your view, should immigration be kept at its present level, increased, or decreased?"[454]

Most respondents have always said to either keep the present level or decrease it. That was true from 1965 until 1999. Only since 1999 have more than ten percent or more of the respondents in a given sample have started speaking of increasing immigration.[455]

Enter the illegal immigration problem in contemporary America from Mexico and Latin America. Some say illegal immigration is out of control when, in fact, it is historically at some of its lowest levels. In the latest Gallup polls on immigration from 2016, we see the highest percentage of respondents suggesting that immigration should be decreased to 35 percent.[456]

This brings us to the fourth section of this chapter, where we will speak more specifically about what the first great American statesman said and wrote about the phenomenon of immigration.

Franklin on Immigration

The two major sources for understanding Benjamin Franklin's views on the issue of immigration are his essay, "Observations Concerning the Increase of Mankind," written in 1751, and in a May 9, 1753, letter to British statesman Peter Collinson. In the former, he made several observations about population statistics, including the issue of immigration.

Franklin's "Observations" was a short essay circulated by the statesman in manuscript form to his circle of friends, but in 1755, it was published as an addendum in a Boston pamphlet on another subject. From 1755 until 1780, the pamphlet was issued ten times during that period. The pamphlet in question was entitled "Americanization: What is it and What to Do?" It was originally published on May 19, 1755, by the American Philosophical Society in Philadelphia. He was one of its founding members.

The pamphlet warns businessmen to stop "Anti-American propaganda and agitation the instant it raises its head." It implores immigrants to "learn English, the mother tongue of over seventy million of our native and foreign-born." The pamphlet advises parents to "discourage any tendency to accept gratuitous benefits" and to "teach that it is un-American to ask for charity or accept tips." The pamphlet even closes with appeals to "Colonial Ancestors, like Benjamin Franklin." It should be clear that the fingerprints of Franklin were all over the pamphlet called "Americanization: What is it and What to Do?"

His "Observations" examines population growth and what he believed were its limits. Writing at the time as a British subject, the statesman argued that the British population and power should expand in North America, while he also argued that Britain and the rest of Europe were too crowded.

Franklin projected that America's exponential growth would see the population doubling every twenty-five years "so that in a century, the greatest number of Englishmen will be on this side of the water." He thought the land in America was underutilized and thus available for farming and cultivation. Historian Walter Isaacson points out that Franklin's theory was empirically based on population data at the time and that Franklin was essentially correct that the United States population did continue to double every twenty years until the 1850s when it surpassed Britain's population by a great margin.

While Franklin's "Observations" was an important contribution to economic theory and population growth, more recent treatment of the essay has focused on its final two paragraphs. He was alarmed by the influx of German immigrants into Pennsylvania. The Germans, he believed, did not have a liberal, political tradition, nor the English language nor English culture.

He goes on to make it clear that he believed the growth of unassimilated Germans was a threat to the English language and culture. In fact, at one point in the essay, Franklin turned his attention to race and argued that Germans, Italians and other groups are not really "White People" because, among other things, their "Swarthy Complexion."

In paragraph number twenty-three of "Observations," Franklin asked,

> Why should the Palatine Moors be suffered to swarm into our settlements, and by herding together establish their language and manners to the exclusion of ours?"

The first great American statesman added,

> Why should Pennsylvania, founded by the English, become a Colony of Aliens, who will shortly be so numerous as to Germanize us instead of Anglifying them...

Realizing the potential offense that his comments might cause, at the end of his life, Franklin deleted the final two paragraphs from the "Observations." His derogatory comments about both the Germans and the Dutch, however, were picked up and used by his opponents in Philadelphia. This led to a decline in support among the Pennsylvania

Dutch. As a result, he was defeated in the October 1764 election to the Pennsylvania Assembly. In great irony, he was responsible for publishing the first German newspaper in the Pennsylvania Colony. In the letter to Collinson dated May 9, 1753, he again speaks about the issue of American immigration and refers to concerns he had in the early 1750s about immigrants from Germany, finding them undesirable to his Pennsylvania Colony.

Among the things that Franklin particularly said or wrote about German immigrants were the following:

1. They are not as smart as the people already living in the colonies.
2. They are unable to adapt to local values.
3. Not being used to liberty, they know not how to make a modest use of it.
4. They are endangering New England's Whiteness.
5. The Spaniards, Italians, French, Russians and Swedes, are generally of what we call a swarthy complexion, as are the Germans also, the Saxons only excepted.

In the letter to Collinson, the first great American statesman turned his attention to a familiar theme. He observed:

> Those who come hither are generally of the most ignorant Stupid Sort of their own nation, and as Ignorance is often tended with Credulity when knavery would mislead it, and with Suspicion when Honesty would set it right.

Franklin also told Collinson about the Germans and Dutch in Philadelphia,

> The signs in our Streets have inscriptions in both languages and in some places only German. They begin of late to make all their Bonds and other legal Writings in their own language which, although I think it not to be are allowed as good in our Courts.

He goes on in the same letter to tell the Englishman Collinson:

> Where the German Business so increases that there is a continual need of interpreters. And I suppose in a few years,

> they will also be necessary in the Assembly, to tell one half of
> our Legislators what the other half had said.

Franklin continued his assault on the Dutch and German immigrants of Pennsylvania:

> In short, unless the stream of their importation could be turned
> from this to the Colonies, as you very judiciously propose, they
> will soon so outnumber us that all the advantages that we have
> will not, in my opinion, be able to preserve our language and
> even our Government which will become precarious.

To be fair to Franklin, he acknowledged the importance of immigration as a source of growth for the colony and the country, but he did not declare himself to be against German immigration. Rather, he was in favor of the controls on it. As Franklin wrote in his letter to Collinson, "I am not against the admission of Germans in general, for they have their virtues, their industry, and frugality is exemplary."

In the same letter from May 9, 1753, he added, "They are excellent husbandmen and contribute greatly to the improvement of a country." Thus, not all that he said about German immigrants was negative. He found some positive things to say about them, as well. Nevertheless, in addition to the great irony of Franklin publishing the first German newspaper in Philadelphia, in another irony, the wave of German immigrants about whom he was so worried, rather than destroying American culture and the use of the English language, hundreds of thousands of these German immigrants became the backbone of the nation's agriculture, particularly in the Midwest. The Germans also played an integral role in the pushing westward, many settling in Texas, the Dakotas, and eventually, California.[457]

German immigrants were also the source of another very American tradition—the decoration of fir trees during Christmas time, as well as the painting of eggs during the Easter season. In fact, more Americans trace their ancestry back to Germany than any other foreign nation, and this would surely come as a big surprise to Franklin.

In some ways, he was correct about German immigration to Pennsylvania. The first group of German settlers to the colony arrived in 1683, whereupon they immediately founded the city of Germantown.

In 1702 the town of Skippack was established, and in 1709, Oley and Conestoga in Pennsylvania.[458]

Between 1727 and 1777, when Franklin was concerned about the effects of German immigration, approximately 65,000 Germans landed in Philadelphia alone. The largest wave of these Germans was between 1749 and 1754. By the time of the Revolutionary War, Philadelphia had about 75,000 ethnically German residents. Some historians have estimated the number to have been as many as 100,000.

In the same period, Franklin observed that a third of all White citizens of Philadelphia were of German stock.[459] Another aspect of his view on immigration can be seen in another section of the "Observations," in which he bemoans the number of genuine "White People" in the world. He said, "The number of purely white people in the world is proportionally very small." He goes on to speak of the other colors of human beings: Africans are black or tawny; Spaniards, Italians, and Greeks are of a "Swarthy Complexion." French, Russians and Swedes make "the principal Body of White People on the face of the Earth."

Franklin goes on to lament about White people,

> I could wish their Numbers to be increased. But perhaps
> I am partial to the Complexion of my country, for
> such kind partiality is natural to Mankind.

Many critics in contemporary America look at these comments as being little more than racist, but clearly, he is lamenting the fact that the "New America" will no longer be as "White" as it was in his day.

Franklin first came into contact with German immigrants when he heard evangelist Michael Welfare, a German Seventh Day Baptist, preaching in Philadelphia in 1734. Even earlier, beginning in 1731, the statesman printed two German books for the German Baptists.[460] In 1740, he published a German edition of Gilbert Tennent's sermon "The Danger of an Unconverted Ministry." Tennent (1703–1764) was a prominent Scots-Irish Presbyterian evangelist during the First Great Awakening.[461] And he published a German Moravian catechism at a Moravian conference in 1742.[462]

While Franklin was showing interest in these Germans, making friends with them and doing business with them, he also began to lament the number of German immigrants who were, he believed, overrunning the colony. At best, he had an ambivalent attitude toward the German immigrants that is not often pointed out by his critics.

This brings us to the major conclusions we have made in Chapter Eight on Benjamin Franklin's views on immigration.

Southern Border Addendum to Chapter Eight

It goes without saying that the period of the early twenty-first century in the United States has been the most significant in changes and numbers regarding American immigration. The federal government estimated in 2018, during the Trump Administration, that there were 11.4 million illegal immigrants in the country. The number of people turned away or apprehended at the southern border reached 2.8 million in 2022, the highest number since 1980.

In 2018, the government also announced that the total foreign-born population of the United States was 44.7 million. The Department of Homeland Security, however, has yet to publish new data on this foreign-born population. The number of illegal immigrants to the US fluctuated greatly during the Trump Administration from a low in April 2017 at 11,127 to a high in May 2019 with 132,859.

After countless comments about the border leading up to the 2020 presidential election—in which Biden spoke many times of America "being an asylum for immigrants" and what he called "dreamers," several media outlets reported in September of 2022 that "Border Crossings are Three Times Higher under Biden Than Trump."

Data from the US Border Patrol in that same year suggested that 189,000 immigrants per month have been recorded in the Biden Administration, compared to an average of just under 51,000 per month during the Trump tenure. By 2022, the new rate was so significant under Biden that, in fewer than two years, had admitted more illegal crossings than Trump did throughout his whole administration. That included more than 2 million crossings in 2022 alone. The figures for Biden's first year—that is 2021—was 1.7 million. Early signs from figures for 2023 suggest the final number will be somewhere between 2.5 and 3 million.

These immigration figures are not only alarming, but they also show up in many polls of US citizens in America. On May 9, 2023, a Reuters poll announced that Biden's approval rating was at 40 percent, slightly higher than the 39 percent the month before. The Reuter's poll, which was conducted for three days in May 2023, found that 54 percent of respondents—including 77 percent of Republicans and 34 percent of Democrats—were against the idea of raising the number of immigrants allowed into the country every year. Only 26 percent said that they "approved of Biden's handling of immigration."

While various periods of American history have worried about the number of Chinese, Japanese and "swarthy" people from Italy and Greece, and Franklin's concern about Germanic immigrants, the contemporary phenomenon unfurling at the US southern border dwarfs any of these earlier efforts.

Conclusions to Chapter Eight

In the introduction to Chapter Eight, we indicated that the chapter on Franklin on immigration would have four sections. In the first of those, we commented upon the history of attitudes toward immigration in the history of the United States. In the second section, we turned our attention to a more specific treatment of immigration during Franklin's lifetime, from 1706 until April 17, 1790, the date of the statesman's death.

The subject matter of the third section, as the introduction to the chapter has indicated, was the history of attitudes toward immigration in more modern times from the beginning of the twentieth century until the present time.

And in the fourth and most important section, we devoted our time to an examination of what the first great American statesman wrote and had to say about issues related to immigration in the Pennsylvania Colony and state, as well as the nation as a whole.

In the first section, we began by speaking of the British practice in the 1740s of emptying their prisons and transferring these convicts and criminals to America. We also indicated that Franklin wished to send rattlesnakes in return for the prisoners.

We continued by speaking of the Scotch-Irish immigrants, the "wild Irish," and the anti-coolie legislation in America.

In our continuance of this section, we spoke of the successive waves of American immigrants from China and the passing of the Asiatic Barred Zone Act in 1917 that required a literacy test for admission into the United States.

We also spoke of the new immigrants from southern and eastern Europe beginning in the 1890s, principally the Italians, Greeks and Jews from Eastern Europe.

In the second section of Chapter Eight, the subject matter was American attitudes toward American immigration during the life of Benjamin Franklin. In that section, we cataloged the perspectives of John Adams, John Jay, Alexander Hamilton, Thomas Jefferson, the Rev. Paul Dudley and many other eighteenth-century Americans.

American immigration in the modern period from 1920 to the present was the principal focus of the third section. We analyzed three petitioners to the US Supreme Court—two Japanese and one Indian—who unsuccessfully argued that they should be considered "White."

We also examined the immigration of Mexicans to America during the Great Depression and the internment of Japanese people after the bombing of Pearl Harbor. We suggested that President John F. Kennedy was the first to change the rhetoric regarding immigration by calling America "a Nation of Immigrants."

At the close of section three, we introduced the Gallup Poll company's tracking of attitudes toward immigration in America from 1965 until 2016 and how American attitudes have changed over time to the point in 2016 where 35 percent of all Americans have suggested that we should have more restrictions on immigrants coming to the United States.

In the fourth and most important section of Chapter Eight, we introduced and discussed a number of perspectives held by Franklin's views on immigration. The two main texts in support of those beliefs were his "Observations Concerning the Increase of Mankind" written in 1751 and a letter written to British statesman Peter Collinson on May 9, 1753.

What we have seen in these two sources was that Franklin had an antipathy toward the immigration of German nationals into the colony/state of Pennsylvania and that he believed that they were unable to adjust to American values and mores. We have also shown that he was entirely correct about the number of Germans who became residents in Philadelphia and Pennsylvania. Between 1749 and 1754, there were some estimates that up to 100,000 residents in Philadelphia alone were of German descent.

We also indicated that there were two great ironies in regard to Franklin's views about German immigrants into Pennsylvania. First, his printing company was the publisher of the first German newspaper in the colony of Pennsylvania. And secondly, the Germans in America were the backbone of the farming industry, first in the Midwest and later in the far west of the US.

We will turn our attention to Chapter Nine and to a subject of what has sometimes been called "religious tests" in both Great Britain and the United States, as well as what Franklin had to say and write about the phenomenon of religious tests in Pennsylvania and America.

Deborah Read Franklin (ca. 1708–1774), common-law wife of Benjamin Franklin. Courtesy of the Library of Congress.

Chapter Nine
Franklin on Religious Tests

> This clause is not introduced merely for the purpose of satisfying of scruples of many respectable persons who feel an invincible repugnance to any religious test or affirmation. It had a higher object, to cut off every pretense of any alliance between church and state in the national government.
> —Justice Joseph Story, *Commentaries on the Constitution of the United States*

> ...but no religious Test shall ever be required as a Qualification to any Office or public Trust under the United States.
> —The Constitution of the United States, Article VI, Clause 3

> That no further or more extended profession of faith should be exacted. I observe to you too that the evil of it was less, as no inhabitant, nor any officer of government, except the members of the assembly, was obliged to make the declaration.
> —Benjamin Franklin to a "Friend in England," October 3, 1775

Introduction

The purpose of this chapter is to explore the phenomenon of what in the seventeenth and eighteenth centuries in the English-speaking world were referred to as "religious tests." A religious test at that time referred to the requirement that governments sometimes made requiring its citizens who wished to hold public office to make a religious oath to the government, clarifying that the oath-taker was of the government-sanctioned religious point of view of the Church of England.

The idea of religious tests or religious oaths for public office began developing in Great Britain as a response to Roman Catholics and "non-conformists" who did not hold the sanctioned religious point of view.

Chapter Nine will unfold in the following parts. First, we will provide an analysis of the history of religious tests as they developed in Britain in the seventeenth and eighteenth centuries. In the second section, we will introduce and discuss the US Constitution, Article VI, sections 2 and 3, where the idea of religious tests is mentioned.

In the third section, we will examine what many of the other American Founding Fathers, besides Franklin, had written or spoken about the idea of religious tests in the eighteenth century. And in section four—the final section—we will identify and discuss what he believed, wrote and spoke about the phenomenon of religious tests.

The History of Religious Tests in Great Britain

Laws that made the holding of public office in Britain that were conditional upon subscribing to the established religion began in Scotland shortly after the Scottish Reformation imposed such a law in 1567. In this Scottish law no one was to be appointed to a public office, or to become a notary who did not profess Calvinism, that is, the Presbyterianism of John Knox's revolution.[463]

The following century, in 1681, the Scottish Test Act was passed and was rescinded nine years later in 1690. Later attempts to exclude Scotland from the English Test Acts were rejected by the Scottish Parliament.[464] By 1707, anyone bearing an office in a university, college, or school in Scotland was required to profess and subscribe to the Confession of Faith of the Protestant Religion, that is, Calvinism or Reform Presbyterianism [465]

The reception of the Eucharist in its Presbyterian form and thus against transubstantiation, became a Scottish requirement in the early eighteenth century in Scotland and this requirement was not removed until an act in 1853.[466] Before that time in Scotland, anyone opposed to the Divine authority of Scripture or the Scottish Confession of Faith, and to do nothing to prejudice the Church of Scotland or its "doctrine and privileges" were finally abolished by an act in 1889.[467] Thus, the idea of a religious test in Scotland was finally rejected in 1889.

Meanwhile, in England, a series of test acts were passed, beginning in the "Corporation Act of 1661" passed during the reign of King James I. It required that all naturalized or restored in blood citizens should receive the sacrament of the Lord's Supper, meaning the Anglican, or Church of England rite that rejected transubstantiation.[468]

It was not until the time of King Charles II, however, that the receiving of Communion in the Church of England was made a precondition for holding public office in the country. The earliest English imposition of this religious test was the "Corporation Act," passed by Parliament in 1661. This act required that, in addition to taking the "Oath of Supremacy," all members of the corporations were required to receive the Sacrament of the Lord's Supper within a year of taking public office, according to the rites of the Church of England.[469]

The Corporation Act was followed twelve years later by what was known as the "Test Act of 1673," the long title of which was "An Act for preventing dangers which may happen from Popish recusants."[470] This English act required all persons filling any office, civil or military, to take the "Oath of Supremacy" and to declare allegiance to the Crown and to declare opposition against transubstantiation.[471] The 1661 act also required the Anglican rite of Communion be received within three months after receiving an office.[472]

The wording of the Test Act of 1673 included specific instructions regarding "proper beliefs about the elements of bread and wine at the consecration thereof." This wording aimed, of course, at the idea of transubstantiation. The act was passed in the English Parliament session that began on February 4, 1673, according to the Gregorian calendar. The act was dated in 1672; however, according to the Julian calendar, then in force in England.[473]

Initially, the Test Act of 1673 did not extend to peers, so in 1678, the act was extended by an additional act in 1678 that required all peers and members of the House of Commons to make a declaration about transubstantiation, the invocation of saints, and the sacrament of the mass. The effect of this 1678 act was to exclude Catholics from both houses of Parliament. It was also aimed at what came to be known as the "Five Popish Lords," who were excluded from serving in either house.[474]

This was a change largely motivated by what was known as the "Popish Plot," a fictitious conspiracy invented by Titus Oates that, between 1678 and 1681, gripped the kingdoms of England and Scotland in anti-Catholic hysteria. Oates and others alleged that there was an extensive Catholic conspiracy to assassinate King Charles II and accusations that led to the executions of twenty-two "conspirators."[475]

This Catholic hysteria in England and Scotland also led to the precipitation of what was called the "Exclusion Crisis."[476] Eventually, Oates's intricate web of accusations fell apart, leading to his arrest and his conviction for perjury.

The Exclusion Crisis ran from 1679 until 1681, during the reign of King Charles II of England. It sought to exclude the king's brother and the presumptive James, the Duke of York, from the English, Scottish and Irish thrones because he was a Roman Catholic. In 1673, the Duke of York refused to take the oath prescribed by the new Test Act.[477] King Charles had no legitimate children, so the English feared that James would become king.

Sir Henry Capel summarized the general feeling of the country when in a Parliamentary debate in the House of Commons on April 27, 1679. Sir Henry said this:

> From Popery came the notion of a standing army and arbitrary power... Formerly the crown of Spain, and now France, support this root of Popery amongst us; but lay properly flat, and there's an end to arbitrary government and power. It is a mere chimera, or notion, without Popery.

These developments in England and Scotland were the backdrop of the idea of discussion in the British North American colonies about the phenomenon of religious tests in the United States and Canada, including the mention of "no religious test" found in Article VI, Clause 3 of the US Constitution, which is the subject matter of the second section of Chapter Nine to follow.

No Religious Test in US Constitution

As an outgrowth of the Corporation Act of 1661, the Tests Act of 1673 and 1678, as well as the Popish Plot in late seventeenth-century

England in the first two centuries of the British American colonies, the issue of whether the US should have a religious test in its constitution was debated.

The US Constitution, Article VI, Clause 3, contains the following language:

> ...but no religious Test shall ever be required as a Qualification to any Office or public Trust under the United States.

This ban on religious tests was proposed at the Continental Congress in 1787 by Charles Pinckney, a young South Carolina delegate. But the notion of a "no religious test" clause was a departure from the prevailing state government restrictions, and Pinckney's proposal was adopted with relatively little debate on August 30, 1787, in Philadelphia at the Continental Congress. Only a Connecticut delegate, Roger Sherman, and a few other delegates complained about Pinckney's proposal, but only Sherman voted against it.

Some of the delegates present thought the clause was unnecessary since the Constitution gave the new federal government no authority over religion. Both the North Carolina delegation and part of the Maryland delegation voted to exclude Article VI, but it is not clear what provisions of the article had troubled them.[478] It was clear, however, that initially the "no religious test" clause only applied to the federal government and not to states.

The clause on "no religious test" was met with more stringent opposition in the ratifying debates that took place in the states. Anti-Federalists in North Carolina, Massachusetts and Connecticut voiced concerns that government would suffer without an assurance that all public servants were religious. Others wanted to limit public service to Christians for fear that "Pagans, deists and Mahometans" might seek public offices among them.[479]

But there were also those who came to the aid of religious freedom's aid. This was particularly true in religious tests and oaths in state constitutions from 1776 to 1784. The Delaware State Constitution of 1776, for example, required the following oath:

> I do profess faith in God the Father and in Jesus Christ, His only Son, and in the Holy Ghost, one God, blessed for evermore;

> and I do acknowledge the Holy Scriptures of the Old and New Testaments to be given by Divine inspiration.

The Maryland State Constitution of 1776 required all state officeholders to declare "a belief in the Christian religion." In the same year, the New Jersey State Constitution excluded Catholics and Jews when it declared:

> No Protestant inhabitant of this Colony shall be denied the enjoyment of any civil right merely on account of his religious principles.

The 1776 constitution of Pennsylvania required assent for public office in the following oath:

> I do believe in one God, the creator and governor of the universe, the rewarder of the good and the punisher of the wicked. And I do acknowledge the Scriptures of the Old and New Testament to be given by Divine inspiration.

As we shall see later in this chapter, Franklin was decidedly against this provision of the Pennsylvania Constitution of 1776, while at the same time, he was very much in favor of Pinckney's proposal regarding Article VI, Clause 3 for the US Constitution.

What was true in Delaware, Maryland and Pennsylvania was also true in the state constitutions of North Carolina, Georgia, Vermont, Massachusetts and New Hampshire.

Indeed, the New Hampshire constitution of 1784 related that "Every member of the house of representatives shall be of the Protestant religion." The 1784 document in New Hampshire added:

> That no person shall be capable of being elected a senator who is not of the Protestant religion... The President shall be chosen annually, and no person shall be eligible to this office unless, at the time of his election, he... shall be of the Protestant Religion.

Similarly, the 1777 state constitution of Georgia mandated that "All representatives shall be of the Protestant Religion." In the 1777 Vermont state constitution, each member of state office shall make the following declaration:

> I, _____, do believe in one God, the Creator and Governor of the universe, the Rewarder of the good and punisher of the wicked. And I do acknowledge the Scriptures of the Old and New Testaments to be given by Divine inspiration, And own and profess the Protestant Religion.

Finally, the state of Massachusetts, in its 1780 constitution, included the following oath for all its state office seekers:

> I do declare that I do believe in the Christian Religion, and have a firm persuasion of its truth; and that I am seized and possessed, in my own right, of the property required by the constitution as one qualification for the office or place to which I am elected.

The conclusion of this analysis of the state constitutions from 1776 to 1784 should be obvious. Although Article VI, Clause 3 of the US Constitution specifically forbade any religious test for serving federal public office, at least nine of the thirteen state constitutions required a religious test.

This brings us to the third section of Chapter Nine, in which we will identify and discuss the views of other Founding Fathers of the United States—other than Benjamin Franklin—on the phenomenon of religious tests in America.

Religious Tests of Other Founding Fathers

The purpose of this third section of Chapter Nine is to identify and discuss the perspectives of other American Founding Fathers on the issue of religious tests in the United States of America in the late eighteenth century. Among those figures who have commented on the phenomenon of religious rests and the clause found in Article VI of the US Constitution were the following:

1. Charles Pinckney (1757–1824)
2. James Iredell (1751–1799)
3. James Madison (1751–1836)
4. Oliver Ellsworth (1745–1807)
5. John Adams (1735–1826)
6. Thomas Jefferson (1743–1826)

7. Alexander Hamilton (1755–1804)
8. John Jay (1745–1829)
9. Edmund Randolph (1753–1813)
10. George Mason (1725–1792)

Each of these ten American Founding Fathers has made explicit his views on the idea of a religious test, as contained in Article VI, as well as references to the phenomenon in many state constitutions. In this section, we will identify and discuss the points of view of these ten Founding Fathers, other than the first great American statesman, Franklin.

We have already commented on the views of Charles Pinckney on the question of religious tests. He was the delegate at the Constitutional Convention who proposed Clause 3 of Article VI of the US Constitution to include the wording that "no religious Test shall ever be required as a Qualification to any Office or public Trust under the United States."

James Iredell, a member of the North Carolina ratifying convention and who later became one of the original nine justices of the US Supreme Court, also favored the "no religious test" view. In July 1776, he wrote:

> Men of no religion at all have no scruple to qualify themselves for office through a Religious test... No test can bind such a one. I am therefore clearly of the opinion that such a discrimination would neither be effectual for its own purposes, nor, if it could, ought it by any means to be made... A religious test would not answer the purpose, for the worst part of the excluded Sects would comply with the test, and best men would only be kept out of our counsels.

Iredell appears to make four points in regard to the idea of a national religious test. First, it would be ineffectual; second, it will not serve its purpose; third, evil people would not comply with it; and finally, good people would comply with no real effect.

James Madison also saw religious tests as unnecessary, at least in so far as the tests would only require belief in God. Madison asked,

> Is not a religious test as far as it is necessary, or would operate, involved in the oath itself? If the person swearing believes in the supreme being who is invoked, and in the penal consequences of offending him, either in this or the future world, or both, he will be under the same restraint from perjury as if he had previously subscribes to the test requiring the belief.[480]

Thus, he believed that requiring individuals seeking public office to swear a belief in God as part of a separate test would be unnecessary for both believers and for non-believers alike.[481]

Oliver Ellsworth, another delegate to the Continental Congress in 1797, US Senator and third Chief Justice of the US Supreme Court, at one point both defined what a religious test is, as well as supporting the provision outlined in Article VI, Clause 3. Judge Ellsworth related:

> A religious test is an act to be done , or profession to be made, relating to religion, such as partaking of the sacrament according to certain rites and forms, or declaring one's belief of certain doctrines, for the purpose of determining whether his religious opinions are such that he is admissible to a publick office.[482]

After sketching out this definition of what a religious test is, Ellsworth added:

> If any test-act were to be made, perhaps the last exceptionable would be one requiring all persons appointed to office to declare their belief in the being of God. But I answer that his dedication of making such a belief is no security at all. Test laws are totally ineffectual. They are no security at all because men of loose principles will rather suffer an injury than to act contrary to the dictates of the conscience.

Ellsworth seems here to make two conclusions about religious tests—that they would be totally ineffective and that bad people would not follow them. This brings us to the views of John Adams on religious tests.

The same view on the issue of religious tests can also be found in the writings of John Adams and Thomas Jefferson. We have linked these two men together because much of what we know of their attitudes toward religion comes from letters to each other from 1811 until 1826.

Like Franklin, John Adams believed in the utility of religion, even when he often had doubts about specific Christian theological teachings. This point of view about utility is how he also approached the issue of religious tests. In that regard, in a letter to Jefferson, Adams believed that the use of any religious test in a nation's founding documents "will have no social utility in its entirety."[483] In short, Adams was against the idea of religious test—even though the Constitution says there should be none in America—because, at least according to John Adams, the second President of the United States, those tests have no beneficial consequences to the society as a whole.

Thomas Jefferson fervently opposed the idea of a religious test in adopting the state of Virginia's Constitution. This is made clear in the first draft of Jefferson's "A Bill for Establishing Religious Freedom." In the final draft of that document, Thomas Jefferson wrote this:

> We the General Assembly of Virginia do enact that no man shall be compelled to frequent or support any religious worship, place, or ministry whatsoever, nor shall be enforced, restrained, molested, or burthened in his body or goods, nor shall otherwise suffer, on account of his religious opinions or belief; but that all men shall be free to profess, and by argument to maintain, their opinions in matters of religion, and that the same shall in no wise diminish, enlarge, or affect their civil capacities.

In this comment, Jefferson says more about the first amendment and the separation of church and state than he does about the idea of a religious test in Virginia or in the US Constitution for that matter.

In a letter dated July 31, 1788, to Jefferson, James Madison, however, told us that he feared the New Englanders were worried that the prohibition of a religious test, would "open the doors to Jews, Turks, and Infidels." And Jefferson responds to this missive by expressing his long-held belief that religious tests are unnecessary.

Edmund Randolph, Governor of Virginia and later the first Attorney General of the United States, also commented on the phenomenon of religious tests in America, such as in these comments from "The Exclusion of Religious Tests," June 10, 1788, during the ratification of the convention:

> The exclusion of religious tests is an exception from this general provision, with respect to oaths or affirmations. Although officers, etc., are to swear that they will support this constitution, yet they are not bound to support one mode of worship, or to adhere to one particular sect. It puts all sects on the same footing.

Randolph, along with Madison and George Mason, two other members of the Virginia delegation to the Continental Congress in 1787, developed something they called the "Virginia Plan," an outline for the new federal government that included three branches of government (legislative, executive and judicial), as well as a bicameral congress consisting of the Senate and the House of Representatives. When the vote in Charles Pinckney's wording on the question of a religious test came to a vote, Randolph, Madison and George Mason were in favor of the South Carolinian's suggestion.[484]

Finally, of the ten Founding Father's views on the phenomenon of a religious test, the most contradictory point of view about the matter was the perspective of John Jay. He was the first Chief Justice of the Supreme Court and co-author of some of the *Federalist Papers*, and wrote as a judge, "It is the duty as well as the privilege and the interests of our Christian nation, to prefer Christians for their rulers."[485]

This comment suggests two things. First, that John Jay believed the United States is a Christian nation. And second, it appears that he was in favor of a Christian religious test when it comes to the Constitution. What Judge Jay meant by Christian, however, is another matter entirely.

In 1777, in the New York state discussions of their state constitution, he was in favor of excluding Catholics from the protections afforded to citizens by its constitution. Jay said at the time about Roman Catholics:

> They renounce and believe to be false and wicked, the dangerous and damnable doctrine, that the Pope, or any other earthly authority, have power to absolve men of sins.

Ultimately, Jay's proposal to ban Catholics from New York was defeated, but he was able to insert a provision barring Catholics from immigrating to the state of New York, but only if they first "renounce all allegiance and subjection to all and every foreign king, prince, potentate and state in all matters, ecclesiastical as well as civil." It is likely that Judge Jay had Roman bishops and the pope in mind here. John Jay saw himself as being a "New Light" advocate of the First Great Awakening, much like George Whitefield. He called himself a "Christian enthusiast" and "fell among the most Orthodox Christians." Thus, it would appear that John Jay would have been entirely in favor of instituting a religious test in his state of New York. But it is not clear how he would have reconciled that position with Charles Pinckney's wording in Article VI, Clause 3 of the US Constitution.

This brings us to the fourth and final section of Chapter Nine on the phenomenon of religious tests in America. That is, what Benjamin Franklin had to say and wrote about the issue of a religious test in his colony/state of Pennsylvania, as well as in the national Constitution.

Franklin on Religious Tests

There are three most important sources for understanding Benjamin Franklin's views on the phenomenon of religious tests. The first of these is his vote at the Continental Congress on George Pinckney's proposal regarding his wording of Article VI, Clause 3 of the US Constitution. The second source is a letter dated October 3, 1775, to "A Friend in England" that most interpreters now believe was to the English scientist Joseph Priestly.

The third and most definitive text for determining his views on religious tests is an October 9, 1780, letter to his friend Richard Price now owned by the US Library of Congress. In this final section, we will examine these three sources one at a time in the hope of ascertaining where the first great American statesman stood on the issue of religious tests.

Franklin returned to Philadelphia in 1775. There he served as a delegate to the Continental Congress, where he became instrumental in drafting the Declaration of Independence and the Articles of Confederation to form the new union—the United States of America.[486] Because of his international experience in England, France and Holland, he was chosen by the Continental Congress as one of the first ministers, or ambassadors, to France. While in Paris, as we have suggested earlier in this study, he reached his peak of international fame. He became the focal point for a European Franklin-mania among the French intellectual elite, including many French ladies of the upper class.[487]

He ultimately helped to negotiate a cessation of hostilities and a peace treaty called the Treaty of Paris. It was signed by representatives of King George III of Great Britain, by Benjamin Franklin as representative of the United States of America and a representative from Canada, and was signed on September 3, 1783, in Paris. It officially brought an end to the American Revolutionary War.

The first great American statesman was present at the Continental Congress in late May and early June when the delegates to the convention voted on many proposals regarding the content of what was to become the US Constitution. Among those proposals was that of the young South Carolina delegate, Charles Pinckney, who suggested the wording of the passage in Article VI, Clause 3 regarding the idea of a religious test and the federal government of the new nation with a new constitution on May 31, 1787.

Article VI, Clause 3 of the original constitution was drafted at the convention in Philadelphia in 1787 and ratified by the states in 1788, including the clause that provided that,

> ...but no religious Test shall ever be required as a Qualification to any Office or public Trust under the United States.

Franklin was present for the vote when Charles Pinckney's language was proposed for Article VI, Clause 3. The only dissent from the proposal was Roger Sherman of Connecticut, who was against the idea of banning religious tests in the new constitution.[488] He objected to the proposal not because he favored a religious test but because he thought it "unnecessary, the prevailing liberality being a sufficient security against such tests." Other delegates, however, had some misgivings about Pinckney's proposal, but they did not vote against it in the end.

All the other delegates at the Continental Congress were in favor of Pinckney's proposal, and that included a delegate from the Pennsylvania Delegation, Benjamin Franklin. Thus, our first clue for discerning Franklin's views on a religious test is how he voted for

Pinckney's proposal and, thus, the idea of no religious test in the US Constitution.

The second source for understanding his views on a religious test is an October 3, 1775, letter to an anonymous "Friend in England." As suggested earlier, many historians believe that the English friend is none other than Joseph Priestly (1733–1804), an English chemist, natural philosopher, separatist theologian and liberal political theorist.

In the Franklin letter, his attention turns to some passages in the Old Testament. He related,

> I agree with your sentiments concerning the Old Testament, and though the clause in our Pennsylvania Constitution, which required the members of the Assembly to declare their belief that the whole of it was given by Divine inspiration, would have had better been omitted.

He goes on to say he had been opposed to the clause,

> ...but being over-powered by numbers, and fearing that more in the future might be grafted onto it, I prevailed to have an additional clause: That no further or more extended profession of faith should be exacted. I observe to you too that the evil of it was the less, as no inhabitant, nor any officer of government, except the members of the Assembly, was obliged to make the declaration.

In these two comments of Franklin's about religious tests, several conclusions can be made. First, the Pennsylvania Constitution initially required an assenting to the belief of the Divine inspiration of the Old Testament. Secondly, he was decidedly against that provision. Thirdly, he believed the provision of assenting to Divine inspiration was some kind of evil. And finally, his perspectives in the letter to the English friend on the issue of the phenomenon of religious tests were more or less consistent with his voting on the proposal of Charles Pinckney about the wording of Article VI, Clause 3. That is, Franklin was against the idea of having a religious test in regard to the US Constitution on May 31, 1787.

The third source for constructing his views on the idea of a religious test is a letter he wrote to his friend Richard Price on October 9, 1780. In that letter, he said to Price:

> I am fully aware of your opinion respecting religious tests, but though the people of Massachusetts have not in their new constitution kept quite clear of them, if we consider what the People were 100 years ago, we must allow that they have gone great lengths in Liberality of Sentiment on religious Subjects; and we may hope for greater Degrees of Perfection when the Constitution some years hence shall be revised.

In the letter, he closes the missive by pointing to a few examples from the Old Testament that he thought could not have been divinely inspired. Franklin spoke, for example, of "The approbation ascribed to the Angel of the Lord of that abominably wicked and detestable action of Jael, the wife of Heber, the Kenite." He concluded, "In the rest of the book were like that I should rather it be given by inspiration from another quarter, and to renounce the whole of it." It is not clear what Franklin meant by "another quarter," it may well have been the devil. Or Satan that he had in mind. Given the nature of the message from the angel of the Lord.

Here he is referring to an incident in the Book of Judges, chapters four and five, where Jael, the wife of Heber, slays Sisera in the war of Deborah and Barak against the Canaanite when the Israelites were wrestling the land of Israel from the Canaanites. Canaanite general Sisera's army is routed by Israel and Sisera fled on foot to Jael's tent, where he was offered hospitality and security, only to be slain by Jael while he slept. Jael killed Sisera by striking him with a sharp object in the skull, killing him instantly.

Franklin found it unlikely that such an episode was divinely inspired, and he points to other narratives in the Old Testament where the American statesman had some reservations about their Divine origins as well. Rather than simply renouncing the Divine inspiration of these episodes, he chose instead, as he said, to "renounce the whole of it."

Thus, from these three sources, it appears that the first great American statesman was consistent in his views on the phenomenon of religious tests from a 1775 letter on the question, to a second letter to Richard Price from 1780, and finally to his vote on the proposal from

Charles Pinckney on the suggestion by him that the US Constitution should be devoid of any religious test in regard to the holding of government offices on May 31, 1787.

This brings us to the major conclusions of Chapter Nine on the phenomenon of religious tests in Britain and America. Chapter Ten to follow should be seen and understood as a catalog and summary of the major conclusions of this study on Benjamin Franklin's religion.

Following Chapter Ten, we have also included an extensive bibliography on many aspects of this study, as well as an appendix on the many foreign words and expressions that have been featured in this study. But first, we turn to the major conclusions to Chapter Nine.

Conclusions to Chapter Nine

The overall purpose of this ninth chapter of this study of Franklin's religion has been to discuss the phenomenon of religious tests in Great Britain and the United States in the sixteenth, seventeenth and eighteenth centuries and, more specifically, to present what several of the American Founding Fathers—including Franklin—said and wrote about the regulation of religious tests in America.

We have attempted to meet these two fundamental goals of this chapter by dividing it into four main sections. In the first of these, we introduced and discussed the idea of religious tests in Great Britain from the 1567 Scottish law to the 1681 Scottish Test Act that required assent to the Presbyterian Confession of Faith in Scotland.

Next, we introduced and discussed the series of religious test acts in England, beginning with the Corporation Act passed in 1661 during the reign of King James I. This act, as we have shown, required that all subjects take an Oath of Supremacy, an allegiance to the Crown, and an opposition to the idea of transubstantiation. The 1661 act also required that anyone holding an English office must receive Anglican communion within three months of receiving the office.

In the same section of Chapter Nine, we then turned our attention to the 1673 Test Act, which also aimed to prohibit anyone who held an English office to believe in transubstantiation at the time. As we have indicated, the English Parliament passed the 1673 Test Act on February 4, 1673. We also indicated that since the 1673 act did not extend to peers, it was extended in 1678 to exclude Roman Catholics from both houses of the English Parliament.

At the close of the first section, we discussed the "Popish Plot," or "Catholic Hysteria," between 1678 and 1681, led by Titus Oates, who was later convicted of perjury and led to the executions of twenty-two "conspirators" of Oates' plot.

In the second section of Chapter Nine, we continued our discussion of religious tests by introducing a proposal put forth by delegate Charles Pinckney of the South Carolina Delegation at the Continental Congress in which Pinckney suggested the following wording for Article VI, Clause 3 of the US Constitution:

> ...but no religious Test shall ever be required as a Qualification to any Office or public Trust under the United States.

As we indicated, Pinckney's proposal passed with dissent only coming from delegate Roger Sherman of the Connecticut Delegation. Next, we introduced the state constitutions of nine American colonies or states that all required certain religious tests for the holding of public offices in those places.

In the third section of Chapter Nine, we introduced ten separate American Founding Fathers who all commented in the eighteenth century about the phenomenon of religious tests in America. These views we have identified and discussed were those of Charles Pinckney, James Iredell, James Madison, Oliver Ellsworth, John Adams, Thomas Jefferson, Alexander Hamilton, Edmund Randolph, George Mason, and Judge John Jay of New York.

As we have seen, the predominant view of these ten American Founding Fathers is that they all were decidedly against the idea of any religious test in the US Constitution and thus in favor of Pinckney's proposal.

In the fourth and final section, we devoted our attention to the views of Franklin on what he said and wrote regarding the notion of religious tests in the Pennsylvania and US Constitutions.

In that section, we indicated that he was against the idea of a religious test as it was written in the original Pennsylvania state constitution, particularly the stipulation that certain Old Testament narratives were not, in his view, divinely inspired. More particularly, he was skeptical that the narrative of Jael killing the Canaanite general, Sisera, could have been an action fully sanctioned by the Divine.

Regarding his perspectives on religious tests at the federal level, we identified three principal sources for determining his views. One was his vote on Pinckney's May 31, 1787, proposal pertaining to the language of Article VI, Clause 3 of the US Constitution, which Franklin fully endorsed.

The second source we pointed to regarding his views on an American religious test was a letter the statesman had written to an anonymous "Friend in England," whom many historians now identified as English scientist Joseph Priestly. Franklin pointed out in that letter that he was against the religious test first proposed in the Pennsylvania Constitution and favored Pinckney's proposal regarding the wording of Article VI, Clause 3 of the US Constitution.

As indicated in the final section of Chapter Nine, we introduced and discussed the third source of Franklin's views on the phenomenon of religious tests. That is, a letter he wrote to his friend Richard Price on October 9, 1780, where he discussed at some length the phenomenon of religious tests in America.

The major conclusion we made regarding the 1780 correspondence to Price is that Franklin was completely consistent with what the statement said regarding religious tests about the State of Pennsylvania and his vote on Pinckney's proposal at the Constitutional Convention in 1787.

The bottom-line conclusion, then, of Franklin on the issue of a religious test in his home of Pennsylvania and the Constitution of the United States is that he was decidedly against the idea of having any religious test as a precondition for holding office in either Pennsylvania or the United States of America.

This brings us to the final chapter of this study on Benjamin Franklin's religion. In Chapter Ten, we will describe and discuss the major conclusions we made on the issues of God, religion and ethics.

Ezra Stiles (1727–1795) was an American educator, academic, Congregationalist minister, theologian and author. He was the seventh president of Yale College and one of the founders of Brown University. Courtesy of the Yale University Art Gallery, artist Reuben Moulthrop.

Chapter Ten
Major Conclusions of this Study on Franklin's Religion

Benjamin Franklin made enough money to retire from active business by the age of 42. How did he do it? Well, it was not by patenting his most famous invention, the lightning rod. In fact, he did not patent any of his inventions or scientific discoveries.
—Philip Slater, "Benjamin Franklin"

At this critical moment, the octogenarian Benjamin Franklin took the floor. Calling for unity, he asked the delegates to open sessions with prayer. As they were "groping in the dark to find political truths.
—Thomas Kidd, *Benjamin Franklin*

Motivation is when your dreams decide to put on work clothes.
—Benjamin Franklin, *The Autobiography of Benjamin Franklin*

Introduction

The general purpose of this study of America's first great statesman Benjamin Franklin's religion has been to describe and discuss what the Boston-born man has written or has had to say about God, religion and immortality. To achieve those major aims in this study, we have provided descriptions and discussions of his earliest religious life with his parents and the Third Church of the Congregationalist in Boston, also called the "Old South Church" at the time.

We also provided a description and discussion of what he had written and said about the phenomena of God and Jesus Christ, the Bible, his intellectual sources, his views on religious freedom and religious toleration, as well as his perspectives on the nature of moral goodness and the idea of virtue and his views on comparative religion, his perspectives on immigration and his views on religious tests and the US.

The purpose of this tenth and final chapter is to provide a summary, or a catalog, if you will, of the major conclusions we have made about Franklin's religion. To that end, this chapter will consist of nine sections, one each dedicated to the previous nine chapters, beginning with Franklin's early religious life.

Franklin's Early Religious Life

In this study, we divided our discussion of Franklin's earliest religious life into three parts. In the first of these, we provided and discussed a short biography of his life in nine parts from his birth in 1706 until his death on April 17, 1790.

These nine sections of his life were the following:

1. Franklin's birth, early life and schooling
2. His apprenticeship with his brother James' printing firm
3. Franklin's escape to Philadelphia
4. Franklin and the *Pennsylvania Gazette*
5. Franklin's early civic work
6. Franklin's inventions and discoveries
7. Franklin and politics
8. Franklin and the New Nation
9. Franklin's death and influences[489]

In each of these sections, we have described and discussed his relation to religion, such as the fact that he only had two years of formal education. At the age of about fifteen, he began to have some doubts about many of the Christian doctrines he had learned from his Calvinist parents and from his theological mentor, his uncle Benjamin Franklin the Elder.

In section two, we showed that Franklin, although he was a lowly apprentice to his brother at the age of sixteen, began to write clandestine letters under the guise of Mrs. Silence Dogood, a minister's widow, and placed them under the door of his brother's printing shop. In the pseudonym of Mrs. Dogood, Franklin made several theological observations in the fourteen Dogood letters.[490]

In the first section of Chapter One, we have shown in our short biography of Franklin that in the fifth part of that biography, the statesman contributed to the building projects of nearly every religion and denomination in Philadelphia. We have also shown that in the other sections of his life, he wrote books about religion, published articles and some books of others about religion, and mentioned God, religion and ethics in many of his letters.

In the second section of Chapter One, we began cataloging eight different published works of Franklin's about God, religion and immortality. These works with religious themes were the following:

1. "Articles of Belief and Acts of Religion" (1726)[491]
2. The Silence Dogood letters (1727)
3. "Doctrine to be Preached" (1731)
4. "On the Providence of God in the Government of the World" (1732)
5. "Self-Denial is Not the Essence of Virtue" (1735)
6. "Dialogue Between Two Presbyterians" (1735)
7. A letter to Madame Brillon (1781)
8. Benjamin Franklin's autobiography (1778 to 1790)

In our analysis of each of these works on religion, we have attempted to show the various perspectives on God, religion and immortality that can be found in them. For example, in the "Articles of Belief," he flirted for a while with the idea of polytheism, in which he believed there are many gods, each in charge of his own solar system and the god of Judaism and Christianity being the creator of those other multiple gods.

To mention another example of what we have shown in our exploration and explication of Franklin's eight written works on religion, we have shown that in his "On the Providence of God in the Government of the World," he was fully dedicated to the theological idea of the Argument from Design, also called the Teleological Argument for God's existence.

In his 1735 essay entitled "Self-Denial is Not the Essence of Virtue," he vociferously argued against the idea that enlightened self-interest is at the heart of ethics and virtue while at the same time replacing it with an idea akin to the ancient Greek philosopher, Aristotle's account of virtue ethics.[492]

In the "Dialogue Between Two Presbyterians," also written and published in 1735, Franklin, in dialog form, sketches out what he apparently saw as a traditional Presbyterian theology and the views that he held, which contained many skeptical and radical beliefs characterized by the deists of his day.[493]

In a 1781 letter Franklin wrote to Madame Brillon, he wrote about his theological beliefs when the French noble lady inquired about them. In that letter to her, he expressed six separate theological beliefs that can be summarized this way:

1. Belief in one God.
2. That God created the Universe.
3. That God is owed adoration and service.
4. The best service to God is doing good service to man.
5. The human soul exists and is immortal.
6. Vice will be punished and virtue rewarded in the afterlife.[494]

These pronouncements in the letter to Madam Brillon are significant because gone from this collection of Franklin's beliefs about God is the polytheism from the "Articles of Belief" and the deism found in "On the Providence of God in the Government of the World." In the letter to Madame Brillon, as well as in a letter to President Ezra Stiles of Yale College nine years later, Franklin appears to have returned to the set of monotheistic beliefs he had learned from his parents and his uncle Benjamin in childhood.[495]

In the third section of Chapter One, we supplied an account of the religious views in the earliest period of Franklin's life. In that section, we indicated that his parents came from two distinct Christian traditions, his mother's Congregationalism and his father's Presbyterianism, though we also indicated that the Franklin family worshipped at the Third Church in Boston, a Congregational Church. It is also important to remember that in the mind of the young Benjamin Franklin, there were little to no distinctions between the two sects. In his eyes, they were both Calvinist and Presbyterian.

We also indicated that at around the age of fifteen, he began to doubt his parents' religion and began to be persuaded by the philosophical arguments of the seventeenth- and eighteenth-century European deists. We also have shown that in the early period of Franklin's life, he became enamored with the Argument from Design, also called the Teleological Argument for God's existence.

Additionally, in 1735, Franklin defended the Rev. Samuel Hemphill after the Presbyterian minister had been dismissed from his pulpit by the Philadelphia Synod of the Presbyterian Church. Indeed, He wrote two separate tracts about Hemphill's dismissal—the "Dialogue Between Two Presbyterians" and his "A Defence of the Reverend Hemphill's Observations."[496]

Along the way in the first chapter, we outlined an evolution of Franklin's beliefs about God from his early childhood to his polytheism in the "Articles," to his deism in the "Providence of God," and finally to his return to Christian monotheism at the end of his life.

We also indicated some of the earliest theological and philosophical influences on the great American statesman in Chapter One. These included deists like Voltaire and the Great Awakening theologian George Whitefield, not to mention the theological influences of Franklin's sister, Jane Mecom, an Evangelical Christian in Boston and a great influence on her brother's religious beliefs.[497]

This brings us to the second section of Chapter Ten, in which we will discuss the major conclusions about Franklin on what he said and wrote about God and Jesus Christ.

Franklin on God and Jesus

In the second chapter of this study of Franklin's religion, we set out to fulfill two separate goals. The first was to introduce and then discuss what he believed about God at any given time in his life.

Then, introduce and discuss what he believed about the figure of Jesus Christ.

Regarding the former goal of Chapter Two, we suggested that he went through a series of six stages throughout his life regarding what he said and believed about the God of the Judeo-Christian tradition. These six phases about God included the following:

1. His early childhood monotheism.
2. His period of deistic beliefs.
3. His polytheism in his "Articles of Faith."
4. His understanding of God in "On the Providence of God."
5. His beliefs stated in the letter to Madame Brillon.
6. His return to his childhood monotheism in the letter to Ezra Stiles.

In the first section of Chapter Two, we indicated the various churches attended by Franklin, including the Congregationalist Old South Church in Boston and the Anglican Christ Church in Philadelphia, where he was active in the community life of that congregation. And where he and his wife are interred.

Franklin's earliest religious beliefs about God were most likely little more than a mirroring of his parents and his uncle Ben's beliefs, a man who often tutored his nephew in theological matters. We have shown that early in his life, the American statesman borrowed books from his father's personal library, as well as books borrowed from his friends, in developing those early perspectives on God.

We indicated that among the volumes Franklin borrowed were John Bunyan's 1673 classic *The Pilgrim's Progress* and Philip Doddrige's 1745 book *The Rise and Progress of Religion in the Soul*.[498]

In the opening section of Chapter Two, we introduced Sir Isaac Newton's metaphor about God and the Universe at the close of his *Principia Mathematica*, in which he argued that the Universe is like a watch and God is like a watchmaker. We also pointed out that a Swiss watch at the time was one of the most complicated devices made by human beings, a device where all of the pieces fit together in a complicated way in much the same way that all the pieces of the Universe fit together in some grand design.[499]

The nature and extent of deism was another topic discussed in the first section of Chapter Two, as well. Franklin brushed with that theological view when he was in his late teens. In his 1732 work "On the Providence of God in the Government of the World," he became enamored with the design argument for God's existence, much like English philosopher William Paley or Frenchman Voltaire.[500]

At the very end of the first section of Chapter Two, we spent considerable time and space discussing two letters about God, religion and immortality, written by him to his French friend Madame Brillon and to the President of Yale College, Ezra Stiles, who, just a month before Franklin's death, had inquired of the statesman what his religious beliefs were, particularly about Jesus.[501]

In these two letters, we summarized the six beliefs that the statesman sent to Madame Brillon, and in the letter nine years later to Ezra Stiles where Franklin expressed his final views about God, religion and immortality.

Indeed, at the very end of section one of Chapter Two, we made some observations of what he had to say about atheism. We introduced a letter sent by an anonymous friend of Franklin's, only identified as "J. H.," an atheist who had sent Franklin a tract on his atheistic metaphysical views while asking Franklin for comment.[502]

Franklin's response to J. H. was critical of his friend's views on God, and the statesman raised several theological objections to them that were mostly pragmatic and ethical in nature, including the idea that if there is not God, then there is no standard for ethics and morality, a nod in the direction of what is called Divine Command Theory, a view of ethics we saw in Chapter Six in this study of Benjamin Franklin's religion.[503]

At the close of the first section of Chapter Two, we have also shown what Franklin said to his friend J. H. were perfectly consistent with the statesman's other observations about the Divine and His existence and his belief in the Argument from Design or Teleological Argument for God's existence.

In section two of Chapter Two, we moved our attention to what Franklin believed about the person and nature of Jesus Christ. We began by reiterating the statesman's skepticism concerning the Divinity of Jesus. We then provided a catalog of beliefs that, from his mid-teens, he began to hold about Jesus of Nazareth. These beliefs included the following:

1. That Jesus was not fully human and fully Divine.
2. That Jesus was not God.
3. That Jesus died for all people, not just Christians.
4. That Jesus came to restore his natural religion.
5. That Jesus was committed to the idea of charity for the poor.
6. That Jesus made no comment on the subjects of dancing and dance halls.
7. That Franklin was skeptical about Jesus' temptation in the desert by Satan.
8. That Franklin frequently discussed the figure of Jesus with his friend, the Rev. George Whitefield.[504]

Most of the second section of Chapter Two was taken up with a discussion of these eight beliefs of Franklin about Jesus. We also indicated that in his letters and personal conversations with one of his dearest friends, Polly Stevenson Hewson (1739–1795), the two friends often spoke about God, religion, ethics, the Bible, and the immortality of the soul.

Included in these conversations with Hewson can be seen Franklin's doubts about Jesus being tempted in the desert by the devil. He asked her about the matter:

> Could the Devil really show Jesus all the kingdoms of the Earth at the same time? How and why would Satan attempt to perform miracles before the Son of God? And why would an Omnipotent Jesus allow the devil to carry him to the top of a mountain to observe all of those earthly kingdoms?[505]

It is clear that in these letters and conversations with Hewson, and in his defense of the Rev. Samuel Hemphill, he had many reservations about the person of Jesus Christ regarding certain narratives found in the four Gospels. And the biggest reservation he had was that he believed that Jesus Christ was not God.

Finally, after George Whitefield visited Franklin at his home in Philadelphia, the Evangelist sent him a thank you note "for his kind offer for Christ's sake." Franklin immediately responded by saying, "It was not for Christ's sake but for your sake."

True to the principles sketched out in the first two chapters of this study, his response to the Rev. Whitefield spoke of the priority and the humanity of the statesman's views on the person of Jesus Christ—that his moral and ethical views were the most important elements in the man from Nazareth's philosophical, religious, and, above all, ethical views.

This brings us to the third section, where we will review what the first great American statesman believed and wrote about the Judeo-Christian Holy Scriptures. It is to the Bible, then, to which we turn next.

Franklin and the Bible

In the Introduction to Chapter Three of this study, we indicated that the chapter would have four parts about what Franklin had to say and write about the Bible. The first of those four parts was an analysis of what he related in general comments about the Holy Scriptures. In these general comments, we have indicated that at the age of fifteen, he began to doubt the idea of Biblical Revelation, that he was in favor of a diligent daily reading of the Holy Scriptures, and that he thought that there should be a Bible in every home.[506]

We also have shown in another general comment of Franklin regarding the Bible that at times he often quoted from the Bible if he believed that he could advance an argument he was making. For example, when Franklin was against the British government's plan to add taxes to the poor, the American statesman quoted Second Thessalonians 3:10 in support of his rebuke of the government.

In the remaining two sections of Chapter Three, we have shown several passages of the Old Testament that Franklin was particularly fond of in one section and a passage from the New Testament that he liked in the other section.

In section two of Chapter Three, we enumerated and discussed seven peculiar sets of circumstances in which his views on the Bible can more easily be seen. These seven circumstances can be summarized this way:

1. Mrs. Silence Dogood on the Bible.
2. Franklin and the Great Seal the United States.
3. Franklin's New Version of the Bible.
4. The Bible in the Pennsylvania Constitution.
5. Benjamin Franklin as a Bible Merchant.
6. Franklin's Bible Hoaxes.
7. The Franklin Family Bible.[507]

In each of these seven circumstances, we have shown how the Bible came to the fore in Franklin's life, the first great statesman in America and one of the United States' first great authors, as well. Among these seven sets of peculiar facts, we also pointed out many relevant facts in each of these circumstances.

Mrs. Dogood was fully cognizant of both the Old and New Testament and in letters eight and nine made several traditional comments about the Scriptures, not surprising given the fact that her husband was a Preacher. Franklin chose a passage from the Book of Exodus to express the yearnings of the new nation and the desire to be a new Chosen People in the World.[508]

In his new version of the Bible, he seemed primarily interested in making the Bible more relevant to eighteenth-century standards and mores. We also have seen in the second section of Chapter Three of this study that he was in favor of the reading of the Bible and the mentioning of it in the Pennsylvania Constitution, that he sold Bibles at his shop on Market Street in Philadelphia, that the Franklin family Bible was a King James Version from Britain passed down through the family, and that he perpetrated many Bible hoaxes, including the construction of a fifty-first chapter of the Book of Genesis, the text he called "Hezekiah 6:1" and an apocryphal tale about the sons of the patriarch Jacob of the Old Testament.

In the third section of Chapter Three, we provided a summary of the passages from the Old Testament that he appears to have been familiar with. In that section, we indicated that in his written works and letters, Franklin quoted directly from the following Old Testament books:

> Genesis
> Exodus
> Leviticus

Judges
Psalms
Proverbs
Samuel
The Book of Job
Ecclesiastes
The Book of Daniel[509]

We also indicated that he was much more comfortable with the books of the Torah and the writings than with the major and minor prophets. This was mostly because, we would think, of his overall interests in justice, virtue and ethics.

In the fourth and final section of Chapter Three, we identified and discussed the passages in the New Testament where Franklin quoted directly from the New Testament or commented upon it. In this final section, we have suggested and then shown that he made four separate kinds of comments about the New Testament. They were the following:

1. General remarks on the New Testament.
2. Franklin's comments about the poor in the New Testament.
3. Places in the New Testament that mirror the values of Benjamin Franklin.
4. Passages he employed while defending the Rev. Samuel Hemphill.

Among the general comments that he made concerning the New Testament is a belief in what the Letter to the Hebrews calls "evidence for things unseen" in the first verse of chapter eleven of the work. In another general comment, he suggests that human beings have a moral status closer to God's than any of the other animals because of the human capacity to reason that the animals do not possess.

We have also shown that Franklin believed in the possibility of salvation even for those who did not know about Jesus Christ and his possibility of healing grace.

In the material about the poor in section three of Chapter Three, we introduced and discussed ten adages when he appeared to reflect the moral values of the New Testament. Among these sayings were:

Do not fear, for as soon as we die, we will be immortal.
That the end of passion is the beginning of repentance.
That one should love his neighbor but not pull down his hedge.[510]

We have shown that he employed his knowledge of the Bible, most likely learned as a child, to respond to the Presbyterian Synod of Philadelphia when it branded the Rev. Samuel Hemphill as a heretic of his church. We have also shown that Franklin very adeptly employed many passages from the New Testament in his effort to vindicate the character and beliefs of his friend, the Rev. Samuel Hemphill. Indeed, in his "A Defence of the Reverend Hemphill's Observations," written on October 30, 1735, we have shown that Franklin responded to the synod in defense of his friend by implying that his accusers were "makers of myths and old wives tales," and that the accusers "may not have been sound in their faiths."

Indeed, we have shown that the first great American statesman very slyly suggested that Hemphill's accusers, at least for Franklin, were very much akin to the old Greek adage, "'All Cretans are liars,' said the Cretan," and in Franklin's mind, the accusers of Hemphill were Cretans, as well. The implications of Franklin should have been clear enough to the members of the Philadelphia Presbyterian Synod.

In defense of Hemphill, Franklin quotes eight Biblical passages, one from the Old Testament, Psalm 41:4, and four from the New Testament. These were Romans 8:18; Acts 24:25; the Gospel of Mark 16:16; Acts 10:34; two passages from the Gospel of Matthew, 18:3 and 19:14; and Paul's letter to the Ephesians, 3:8. The implication of all of these uses of Scripture is that he believed that the Rev. Hemphill's accusers were guilty of falling short in their own supposed orthodoxy.[511]

This brings us to the fourth section of this final chapter, in which we have explored the phenomenon of the intellectual sources that went into the making of the philosophical and theological views of Franklin.

Franklin on Deism and Other Intellectual Sources

We began Chapter Four of this study by suggesting that there were four major kinds of intellectual sources in the life of Franklin. These can be summarized this way:

1. Deism
2. The Enlightenment
3. The Great Awakening
4. Other relevant sources

In the first of these sources, we have said more about the philosophical origins of the movement of deism in England, as well as in the French-speaking world. That is, Lord Herbert of Cherbury in England and Pierre Viret in sixteenth-century France. We also indicated other seventeenth- and eighteenth-century deists such as Matthew Tindal in Britain and Voltaire in France.[512]

We also have shown that the most prominent American deist in the eighteenth century was Thomas Paine and his book, *Of the Religion of Deism Compared with the Christian Religion*.[513] In fact, we have shown that in this work, he set out six characteristics of his version of deism. These may be summarized this way:

1. God exists.
2. God created the universe.
3. God endowed humans with reason.
4. Written religious texts are rejected.
5. Demagogy is rejected.
6. Miracle and Mystery are Rejected.

In the second section of Chapter Four, we turned our attention to the eighteenth-century philosophical movement known as the Enlightenment. We began this section by sketching out several major beliefs in the movement, including the rejection of Roman Catholicism in both Britain and among the French proponents of the Enlightenment.

We introduced and then discussed four other ideas that all who claimed to be Enlightenment thinkers in the eighteenth century appear to have believed. These characteristics of the Enlightenment were the following:

1. Rationalism
2. Empiricism
3. Progressivism
4. Cosmopolitanism

We also indicated how Franklin was an advocate of all four of these Enlightenment ideas, sometimes as a philosopher, sometimes as a scientist, and sometimes as a citizen or a great American statesman.

Next, in the third section of Chapter Four, we turned our attention to the phenomenon of the First Great Awakening, to its nature and extent, as well as some of its major proponents, including Jonathan Edwards and English preacher George Whitefield. Indeed, we have written extensively about the relationship and friendship between the Rev. Whitefield and Franklin, pointing out that at times their relationship appeared to be ambivalent and at other times as if Whitefield gave theological guidance to the American statesman.[514]

In the fourth and final section of Chapter Four, we identified and discussed two other intellectual sources for the life of Franklin. These were his father Josiah's child-rearing practices set forth by Franklin in his autobiography and the reading material throughout his life. Regarding the former intellectual source, he identified what he called the following:

       1. Instant learning possibilities
       2. Introduction of new possibilities
       3. Observant interests
       4. Practiced kind correction[515]

What Josiah Franklin meant by number one above is that he always invited learned friends and family members to dinner so his children could learn from these guests. What Franklin's father referred to as "New Possibilities" was the introduction of new ideas that his children had not previously thought to explore. "Observant Interests" referred to Josiah Franklin keeping tabs on what his children were into at any given time. And the son, Benjamin, tells us that his father sometimes chose to "correct" or to "change" the wishes of his children but always with what the son called "Kind and gentle correction."[516]

At the close of Chapter Four, we also introduced a final intellectual influence on the life of Franklin, that is, his reading habits over the years. More particularly, we identified and discussed five books from the statesman's library that he saw as intellectual influences. In that portion of that chapter, we enumerated these books of his this way:

1. Cotton Mather's *Essays to do Good*
2. Plutarch's *Life of Pericles*
3. John Locke's *A Letter Concerning Toleration*
4. Samuel Seward's *The Selling of Joseph*
5. Joseph Addison's drama *Cato: A Tragedy*[517]

We have indicated in Chapter Four that he admired these five books for different reasons. Mather because of its views on virtue and the good. Plutarch because of Pericles' dedication to Republicanism. John Locke's essay because it is the foundation of modern theories about religious freedom and religious toleration. Franklin admired Samuel Sewall's 1700 work, *The Selling of Joseph*, because it sketches out several perspectives on personal property and other civil issues among the sons of Jacob in Sewall's account, like Sewall's views on slavery, for example.

And the principal reason that Franklin admired Joseph Addison's play *Cato: A Tragedy* was how Cato stood up to the tyranny of Julius Caesar, which reminded him of how America stood up against the tyranny of King George II in his time.

He mentions these five books as playing a role in forming the statesman's intellectual life, going back to the age of eleven when he first read Mather's *Essays to do Good*, also known by its Latin title *Bonifacius*.

Franklin admired these books for other reasons as well. He liked very much Samuel Sewall's views on slavery, as well as witch hunting. In his last public act, he supported an anti-slavery bill and quoted Samuel Sewall in describing his views about the matter. He admired Cotton Mather as a man, as a preacher, as well as in terms of being a great colonial writer.

This brings us to the fifth section of this final chapter, where we will summarize the views of Franklin on the two political issues of religious freedom and religious toleration.

Franklin on Religious Freedom, Toleration, and Church and State

Chapter Five of this study on Benjamin Franklin's religion was divided into four sections. These sections can be summarized this way:

1. Franklin on religious freedom.
2. The Founding documents on religious freedom and toleration.
3. Other Founding Fathers on religious toleration.
4. Franklin on religious toleration.

We began the first section of Chapter Five by supplying some background information on the demographic makeup of the early American colonies before the American Revolution. In that background information, we pointed out that 98 percent of all Americans at the time of the Revolution were Protestant Christians and that three-quarters of those people would have considered themselves to have been Reform Christians, including Franklin's mother and father and his theological mentor, Uncle Benjamin.[518]

At the beginning of section one, we spoke of the wide range of Christian views in America, from the most orthodox believers to those who would have identified themselves as freethinkers, skeptics or even as deists.

In that same initial section of Chapter Five, we indicated that as early as the age of fifteen in his Mrs. Silence Dogood letters, he first expressed his deep commitment to deism and to the ideas that would eventually become the First Amendment to the US Constitution, including its references to religious freedom as well as religious toleration.

We also saw a commitment to these same ideas at the end of his life when he dedicated funds to every religious sect in Philadelphia, including support for a synagogue.[519] Franklin also left instructions that his pall-bearers should be chosen among the leaders of the various religious congregations and religions in the city; and that is exactly what occurred as the statesman was laid to rest next to his wife in the Christ Church, Anglican cemetery in the city.[520]

Another way in the first section of Chapter Five where Franklin's views on religious freedom can be seen is in his parody of the

Massachusetts witch trials, "A Witch Trial at Mount Holly," as well as in his writings and discussions about the religions of Native Americans in Pennsylvania and Delaware. Another writing of his entitled, "A Narrative of the Late Massacres," as we have indicated, was another example of the statesman's commitment to the idea of religious freedom, even for Native Americans. In still another way that his commitment to religious freedom can be seen is how many different religious congregations in the middle of the eighteenth century claimed the statesman as "one of their own." These included, as we have shown, the Congregationalists, the Presbyterians, the Church of England or Anglicans, the Society of Friends, or the Quakers, and if we take John Adams' view into account, the Roman Catholics, as well.

All of these denominations claimed Franklin because, presumably, of the ways they each had been treated by him. In his life, he was numbered among the faith of his parents' denominations—the Congregationalist and the Presbyterians, but he is buried next to his wife and near his parents in an Anglican cemetery in Philadelphia.

We also indicated in Chapter Five that for many conservative religious Americans, the idea of religious freedom and its original meaning in the Constitution is in the process of the erosion of these God-given rights, beginning in a 1993 court case and continuing to 2017 when two cases about a cake for a gay couple and contraceptives for nuns and religious postulants.

In the second section of Chapter Five, we sketched out what the Founding Fathers of the nation in our Founding documents had to say about the ideas of religious freedom and religious toleration. Relying primarily on the US Constitution in that discussion, we mainly spoke of the central place of faith in America, the protection of religious rights, religious liberty as the "first liberty," and religion in public life and politics.

Along the way, in the second section, we spent a considerable time writing about the "Establishment Clause," as well as what the US Supreme Court meant by the term "free exercise" regarding religious beliefs and practices, or what is sometimes called the "Liberty Clause."[521]

In the third section, we turned our attention to what many of the other Founding Fathers, besides Benjamin Franklin, had to say or write about the idea of religious toleration in America in the eighteenth century. In that portion of Chapter Five, we identified and discussed some of the perspectives of George Washington; Thomas Jefferson, the author of the "Virginia Bill Establishing Religious Freedom;" and James Madison, who helped Jefferson in the writing of the Virginia bill, as well as George Mason and Patrick Henry.[522]

Franklin's perspectives on religious toleration were the major focus of the fourth and final section of Chapter Five. We began that section by describing his childhood and what he saw as the religious intolerance of many of the Puritans of his day.

In section four, we then shifted our attention to his article for *The London Packet*, a London daily newspaper, on June 3, 1772, entitled "Religious Tolerance in Old and New England." The contents of this essay, as we have shown, was whether religious dissenters in England should be required to pay "tyths and taxes" to the Crown, even if their religious convictions expressly forbade it.[523] Franklin took the side of the dissenters and gave an excellent analysis of the conflicting moral rights and obligations at play in the questions concerning the religious dissenters.

We have also shown that his lifelong dedication to the idea of religious toleration may be seen in his building of a non-denominational hall in Philadelphia for the use of "any preacher of any religious persuasion who may desire to say anything there." And that included even the "Mufti of Constantinople, who would find a pulpit at his service."

At the close of Chapter Five, we indicated that Franklin's defense of the Reverend Samuel Hemphill against the Presbyterian Synod of Philadelphia was one of the best of the American statesman's most eloquent expressions of his views on religious toleration in the eighteenth-century American context.

Additionally, we have shown that for the most part, Franklin was dramatically against the idea of any "religious test" that might be imposed by a colony, state or federal government, such as the notion that arose in the seventeenth century in New England, and again in his time that Jews should be expelled from certain colonies. He was always staunchly against such a religious test that often went on in the early colonies. Similar claims were made in some of the colonies to exclude Roman Catholics from residing in some places, and this particularly applied to the Catholic clergy.[524]

Ultimately, we have maintained that Franklin was in favor of citizens expressing their God-given right to worship the Divine anyway they wished to do so, while at the same time, was committed to the idea, which he appears to have held his entire life, that one has a moral obligation not to impinge upon, nor limit in any way, the exercise of other citizens to express their religious rights. In other words, he had a lifelong commitment to religious toleration.

This brings us to the sixth section of Chapter Ten, in which we will describe and discuss what Franklin had to say and write about the phenomena of ethics and the idea of moral virtue. It is to ethics, then, to which we move next.

Franklin on Morality, Ethics and Virtue

In the introduction to Chapter Six of this study of Benjamin Franklin's religion, we suggested that we would discuss the statesman's views on ethics and virtue in four separate sections, which can be summarized this way:

1. Background Information on Franklin's ethics.
2. Aristotle and Franklin on virtue.
3. Franklin's moral method.
4. Franklin's general observations and particular moral issues treated by him.

We began the first of these four sections of Chapter Six by describing the four major moral theories that were current in the statesman's time. These were Deontological Theory, the Teleological Perspective, also called Utilitarianism, Divine Command Theory, and Virtue Ethics. We also indicated in the background section that he occasionally mentioned Divine Command Theory but more often relied on the idea of virtue ethics.[525]

In the initial section of Chapter Six, we maintained that three of the sources that Franklin consulted in terms of cobbling together his idea of virtue were Cicero's cardinal virtues, Joseph Addison's characters Jubo and Cato in his drama *Cato: A Tragedy*, and the third chapter of the Biblical Book of Proverbs that mentions and discusses several moral and non-moral virtues.[526]

In the second section of Chapter Six on ethics and virtue, we began with a summary of the perspectives of ancient Greek philosopher Aristotle on the idea of virtue and his distinction between a moral virtue and a non-moral virtue. We followed this description with a summary of how his views on virtue both agreed and disagreed on the account given by the Greek philosopher.

Subsequently, our next task in this section was to provide a catalog of sorts of Franklin's thirteen virtues and short descriptions of what he had to say about each of them. We also pointed out that he originally planned to only include twelve virtues in his analysis but added a thirteenth when a Quaker friend pointed out that his list lacked any mention of humility, a virtue that, in the view of the friend, was something he sorely lacked.

At the close of section two, we pointed out that his account of ethics and virtue was not without its critics. Among those were Puritans, who said the list lacked any mention of God and doctrine. British critic D. H. Lawrence criticized Franklin's desire to achieve moral perfection and the American statesman's account of moral virtue.

The chief task of section three of Chapter Six on Franklin's ethics and views on virtue was to give a general summary of his moral method. We indicated that he devised a plan or method for cultivating his thirteen virtues, spending a week on each of them and recording in a notebook when he did, or did not, exemplify that particular virtue.

In the fourth and final section of Chapter Six, we set out two separate goals. The first was to supply some general observations of the American statesman's ideas on ethics and virtue. Indeed, we supplied an account of how he understood the relationship of religious belief to the phenomena of ethics and virtue.

We also included a summary of twelve personal moral characteristics for which Franklin was, and is, mostly known. Among these unique characteristics were that he was a champion of the common man, was the first great American "Networker," his being very good with people, his trustworthiness, and many other moral characteristics.

The other task of section four was identifying and discussing various moral issues about which Franklin was concerned over the years. Among these moral issues include his dedication to the poor, his treatment of the religious issues of Native Americans, and his being against the idea of expelling Jews and Catholics from some of the colonies.[527]

We also indicated that when the Presbyterian Synod of Philadelphia revoked the license of the Reverend Samuel Hemphill to preach from a Presbyterian pulpit that, in the mind of Franklin, that action was an entirely moral one because it created the conditions that, among other things, Samuel Hemphill could not make a living.

Indeed, we have suggested that his defense of the Reverend Hemphill was an example of a larger moral issue about how traditional religious figures in Europe and America generally treated religious dissenters. In fact, we showed how he defended dissenters in England where the Crown required the dissenters to pay "tyths and taxes."[528] For Franklin, this too was a moral issue, very much like the case of the Reverend Hemphill where the religious authorities were meddling into the ability of certain people to "make a living in the world."[529] This brings us to an analysis of Chapter Seven, "Franklin on Other Religions."

Franklin on Other Religions

The main purpose of Chapter Seven of this study of Benjamin Franklin's religion has been what the first American statesman said and wrote about other religions besides the conservative Christian faith in which he was raised. To that end, we began the chapter bSy speaking of the pervasive anti-Catholic attitudes among his family and Congregationalist and Presbyterian backgrounds.

Indeed, at times in his life, we have shown that Franklin appears to have exhibited some of these same religious sentiments regarding Catholicism. On the other hand, we have demonstrated that he embraced the Roman Church, such as when he nominated Father John Carroll in 1783 to become the head of the American Catholic Church to the Papal Nuncio in Paris. And that is precisely what happened a year later.

Before speaking of Franklin and Catholicism in the second section of Chapter Seven, we turned our scholarly attention to what he believed, wrote and acted upon with respect to Judaism. In that first section, we have shown that he supported the building fund of the Mikveh Israel Synagogue in Philadelphia in the same way he had supported rebuilding a bell and bell tower in Christian congregations in the same city.

We began the section by describing and discussing the state of Islam and Muslims in early America, including a catalog of many prominent Muslim slaves and Muslim members of the Continental Army in the time of the Founding Fathers.

We also pointed out, however, that in the seventeenth and eighteenth centuries, there was a strain in American politics that feared that the faith of Islam might be harmful to the new American union. Among those critics of Islam were Ludovico Marracci and the Reverend Cotton Mather. We also indicated in Chapter Seven that at the same time, in England and France, there were significant negative critiques of Islam in figures such as Voltaire, Montesquieu, and Englishman Edward Gibbon.

The bottom-line conclusion we have made in the third and final section of Chapter Seven is that, like the first great statesman's attitudes toward Judaism and Catholicism, his views on Islam, and those of other Founding Fathers as well, should be seen as being quite ambiguous.

Franklin on Immigration

In the eighth chapter of this study of Benjamin Franklin's religion, we organized it into four sections. In the first of these, we commented upon attitudes toward immigration in the history of the United States. In the second section, we turned our attention to a more specific treatment of immigration views in the period of the life of Franklin from 1706 until 1790.

The third section was a history of attitudes toward immigration in more modern times in America from the 1920s to the present. And in the fourth and final section, we examined the major views that Franklin had about the idea of immigration, particularly in relation to his colony/state of Pennsylvania.

In the fourth section, we indicated that the two main texts for determining what the first great American statesman believed about immigration were his 1751 essay "Observations Concerning the Increase of Mankind" and a May 9, 1753, letter to English statesman Peter Collinson.

What we have seen in these two sources was that he had an antipathy toward the immigration of German nationals into the colony/state of Pennsylvania and that he believed they were unable to adjust to American values and mores. We also showed that he was entirely correct about the number of Germans who had become residents of Philadelphia. Between 1749 and 1754, there were some estimates that as many as 100,000 residents in Philadelphia alone were of German descent.

Finally, at the close of Chapter Eight, we suggested that the twenty-first-century "crisis" at the southern border of the United States is much more significant than any previous periods of immigration in America, whereby various nationalities were looked down upon at various times in America, including the Chinese in the nineteenth century, the swarthy Italians and Greeks in the late nineteenth and early twentieth centuries, and the Japanese after World War II.

Franklin on Religious Tests

Chapter Nine concerns the phenomenon of religious tests in Great Britain and the United States in the seventeenth and eighteenth centuries. We began by describing a history of religious tests that existed in Scotland and England from the middle of the sixteenth century in Scotland to the late seventeenth century in England.

At the close of the first section, we discussed the "Popish Plot" or "Catholic Hysteria" led by Titus Oates, which had a grip on much of the population of Scotland and England from 1678 to 1681.

We devoted the second section of Chapter Nine to the phenomenon of religious tests in America and, in particular, to the proposal of delegate Charles Pinckney regarding the wording of Article VI, Clause 3 of the US Constitution that passed with a resounding affirmation among the other delegates, with the exception of Roger Sherman from Connecticut.

In the third section, we cataloged the views of ten other American Founding Fathers on the idea of a religious test requirement in the Constitution of the United States. We have seen that the overall consensus of these ten men was that they very much supported the proposal of Pinckney about there being "no religious test" in the new republic and its constitution.

In the fourth and final section of Chapter Nine, we turned our attention to what he specifically had to say and write about the phenomenon of religious tests in America. In that section, we indicated that Franklin was against the religious test contained in the first constitution of the state of Pennsylvania, particularly the stipulation that many Old Testament narratives were divinely inspired, for he could not understand how the story in the Book of Judges 4–5 could possibly have come from God.

We have also shown that regarding the idea of a religious test at the federal level, he voted for Pinckney's proposal for the wording of Article VI, Clause 3 of the US Constitution. We indicated in the same section that two letters of Franklin's, one to his anonymous friend in England and the other to his friend Richard Price on October 9, 1780, that the first great American statesman's views on religious tests in America were perfectly consistent with how he voted on the matter of Pinckney's proposal on May 31, 1787.

The bottom line of Franklin's views about the phenomenon of religious tests is perfectly clear in the available historical record. He was decidedly against the idea, whether it pertained to the colony/state of Pennsylvania or whether it was in regard to the United States Constitution. In short, he had deep reservations about any institution of a religious test for holding public offices in Pennsylvania or in the United States of America for that matter.

This brings us to eight appendices and an extensive bibliography.

Benjamin Franklin signing the
Declaration of Independence.
Courtesy of the Library of Congress.

Appendix A
Franklin on Happiness and Survival After Death

> Happiness is the meaning and the purpose of life, the whole aim and end of human existence.
> —Aristotle, *Ethics*

> We hold these truths to be self-evident, that all men are created equal, that they are endowed by their Creator with certain unalienable Rights, that among these are Life, Liberty, and the pursuit of Happiness.
> —Thomas Jefferson, "Declaration of Independence"

> Happiness consists more in the small conveniences of pleasures that occur every day, than in great pieces of good fortune that happen but seldom to a man in the course of his life.
> —Benjamin Franklin

Introduction

In this short appendix, we have two goals. First, to say something of what Benjamin Franklin wrote, believed and said about the idea of happiness. Our second goal in this document is to make some judgment about what the first great American statesman wrote and believed regarding the phenomenon of survival after death. As we shall see, he may have had ambiguous and conflicting views about what happens after physical death.

Franklin on Happiness

Among the many books in Franklin's home library was a thoroughly marked-up copy of ancient Greek philosopher Aristotle's tome on the *Nicomachean Ethics* that contains a lengthy description of what he called *Eudaimonia* or "human happiness." His scribblings in his copy are more thoroughly marked up in this section than in any other section of the book. These come at Book I, sections 1 to 7 of Aristotle's work.[530]

The best way to garner Franklin's views on happiness is an essay he wrote in 1785 called "On True Happiness." It was originally published in the *Pennsylvania Gazette* on November 20, 1735, but then later published as "On True Happiness" in a collection of essays named *On True Happiness and Other Essays*.[531]

He begins the essay by nodding in the direction of Aristotle when he observed:

> The desire for happiness in general is so natural to us that all the world are in pursuit of it. All have this one end, though they take such different methods to attain it, and are so much divided in their notions of it.

Franklin agreed then with Aristotle's moral dictum that "Happiness is the whole aim and end of human existence."[532] Next, in "On True Happiness," the first great American statesman turned his attention to the idea of evil when he observed:

> Evil, as evil, can never be chosen; and though evil is often the effect of our own choices, yet we never desire it but under the appearance of an imaginary good. Many things we engage ourselves in may be considered by us to be evils, and yet be desirable, but they are only considered as evils in their effects and consequences, not as evils at present and attended with immediate misery.[533]

In regard to this remark, he appears to be more indebted to Plato than to his student, Aristotle, in that Franklin seems to adhere to Plato's idea that evil is nothing more than "an absence of the good" or as a *privatio boni*, as Augustine defines "evil."[534] He also appears to be cognizant of the Utilitarian principle of Bentham and Mill that evil is more about outcomes and consequences than about moral principles.[535]

Next, in "On True Happiness," he turns his attention to the ideas of passion and reason and their relationships with each other. He suggests that the two ideas are often at odds with each other. He related:

> While there is a conflict betwixt the two principles of passion and reason, we must be miserable in proportion of the struggle, and when the victory is gained and reason is so far subdued as seldom to trouble us with its remonstrance, the happiness we have then is not the happiness of our rational nature, but only the happiness of an inferior nature and sensual part of us. Consequently, this is a very low variety and inferior version of happiness compared to what the other would have afforded us.[536]

Again, Franklin appears to base his view on the principles of passion and reason to be consistent with Plato's understanding of the soul in his famous work *The Republic*. Plato likens the soul and its parts to a chariot: a charioteer and two horses, a lighter and a darker horse. The darker horse, for Plato, is the passion. The lighter horse is the rules of society and the charioteer is reason, the element of the soul that should be in charge.[537] Franklin would concur that the happiness that arises in the darker horse is an inferior brand of happiness, a view of happiness that is often overruled by reason and or society's rules.

Sigmund Freud made the same point in his *Introductory Lectures in Psychoanalysis* and his ideas of Id (passions), Ego (reason) and superego (rules of society).[538]

Another source of Franklin's views on happiness is a letter to his sister Jane that appears in the same volume as "On True Happiness." The first great American statesman wrote to his sister:

> One's true happiness depends more upon one's judgment of one Self, on a Consciousness of Rectitude in Action and Intention, and in the Approbation of those few who judge impartially, than upon the Applause of the unthinking undiscerning Multitude, who are apt to cry Hosanna today, and tomorrow, Crucify him.[539]

In this letter, he again relies on the views of Aristotle and what the Greek philosopher believed about the idea of moral responsibility. Among the four elements that Aristotle claimed are necessary for full moral responsibility are the following:

1. Intention to do Right or Wrong
2. Knowledge of Right and Wrong
3. Knowledge of the Circumstances
4. And the Ability to Do Otherwise[540]

In his letter to his sister Jane, Franklin emphasizes the idea of intention in much the same way that Aristotle did many centuries before. His "consciousness of rectitude," of course, is nothing more than half of the "Knowledge of Right and Wrong." At the end of the letter, he turned his attention to two other items. First, the importance of the judgment of one or a few, as opposed to the multitude. And secondly, how quickly the standards for morality in society may change enough that in a short span, we may say Hosanna about an individual or group and crucify him or them a short time later.

Franklin also saw an important relationship between virtue and happiness. In an earlier chapter, we spoke of his thirteen virtues and personal experiments with those virtues and how to possess or exemplify them. At the same time, he, on many occasions, told us simply,

> Be in general virtuous, and you will be happy.[541]

Indeed, his autobiography is filled with observations about happiness. For example, he wrote,

> Marriage is the most natural state of man and the state in which you will find solid happiness.[542]

He also related in the same work,

> Wine is constant proof that God loves us and loves to see us happy.

Franklin made a similar remark about beer, to wit,

> Beer is proof that God loves us and wants us to be happy.

In another place in his autobiography, he again spoke of virtue and happiness when he claimed that they are "Mother and Daughter," meaning that happiness is spawned from virtue.[543] In several places of his written works, he made the claim that:

> It is the working man who is the happy man. It is the idle man who is the miserable man.[544]

Several times in his writing life, including in his letter to his sister Jane, Franklin related a view about the origin of happiness when he wrote,

> Happiness depends more on the inward dispositions of mind than on outward circumstances.

And about a famous line in the *Declaration of Independence*, he was fond of saying,

> You don't have a right to happiness but a right to pursue it. You have to catch it yourself.[545]

This brings us to the second part of this appendix, in which we will devote to Franklin's views concerning survival after death. As we shall see, this topic is not a simple matter when it comes to his views on the matter.

Franklin on Survival After Death

Scholar Thomas Kidd of Baylor University wrote an article entitled "The Complicated Religious Life of Ben Franklin" for *Baylor Magazine* in the Fall 2017 issue. In the article, Professor Kidd rehearsed many of the Franklin views on religion that we have outlined in the chapters of this book.[546]

Nevertheless, there are a few other observations about him and survival after death that are certain about his views. One of those is this: in the entire Franklin written corpus, there is no mention of the idea of resurrection of the body. This view, of course, is the most fundamental Christian perspective when it comes to survival after death. One way to see that is to remind ourselves that the resurrection of Jesus and the Christian feast to honor that Resurrection, or Easter, is absent from any discussion of metaphysics by Franklin.

This distinction between resurrection of the body and immortality of the soul can be seen in a pair of tombstones in the Grove Street Cemetery in New Haven, Connecticut. The burial markers of a nineteenth-century Presbyterian couple relate the following:

Ralph	**Edna**
Sleeping in the dust	*Gone to her*
But one day will meet	*Eternal Reward*
his Maker	

Ralph's tombstone is tied to the ancient Hebraic view of the resurrection of the body. Since his death, he is now "sleeping in the dust," but at the End of Time, he will "meet his Maker" and be judged.

The burial marker of his wife, Edna, however, is a decidedly different theological perspective. Her tombstone is akin to the Greek idea of the immortality of the soul, like the Greek philosopher Plato. At Edna's death, the soul separated from her body, and it went on to be judged immediately. And clearly, her soul was judged well because she is now experiencing her "Eternal Reward."

Nowhere in the corpus of the works of Franklin do the terms "resurrection" or "resurrection of the body" appear. This is peculiar because that view in the Christian faith is the more fundamental perspective. The closest that the statesman comes to the idea of resurrection is a comment he made in "A Defence of the Reverend Hemphill's Observations," in which he indicated that "by Christ's death and resurrection purchased for human faith and repentance."

Secondly, when he does refer to survival after death, it is always in the context of the immortality of the soul, the ancient Greek perspective. He mentions the soul's immortality in a consolation letter he wrote on February 22, 1756, to his niece Elizabeth Hubbard after her father's death. In that letter, he makes the following theological claims about this man's death:

1. We have lost a most dear and valuable relation.
2. But it is the Will of God and Nature that these mortal bodies be laid aside, when the soul is to enter into real life.

3. Tis rather an embryo state a preparation for living. A man is not completely born until he is dead.
4. Why then should we grieve that a new child is born among the immortal?
5. A new member has been added to the Happy Society.

From these five points that amount to a confirmation of Franklin's belief in the immortality of the soul, we see the use of words such as "the soul is to enter into real life," an "embryo state," and "born among the immortals," all seem to establish his belief in the immortality of the soul. This judgment is consistent with the letter he wrote to Madame Brillon on September 1, 1781, when the French noble lady asked for a summary of his religious beliefs.

In his missive back to Madame Brillon, he sent her a list of five beliefs of an overall belief system. The final two of those are directly related to our current issue at hand. These two religious beliefs were the following:

> Fourth, the human soul is immortal & fifth, that the future life is not I the present one, vice will be punished and Virtue will be rewarded.[547]

In a real way, as we have suggested earlier in this study of Franklin's religion, his September 1, 1781, letter to Madame Brillon, in these five assertions, there appears to be the great statesman's final word on survival after death. That is, he strongly assents to a belief in the immortality of the soul.

Benjamin Franklin.
Courtesy of the Library of Congress.

Appendix B
Foreign Words and Expressions

In the course of this study on Benjamin Franklin's religion, we have employed the following foreign words and expressions in the following languages:

        Classical Hebrew
        Classical Arabic
        Classical Greek
        German
        Latin
        French

Word or Phrase	Meaning	Language
Alah	curse	Classical Hebrew
Arar	vow or curse	Classical Hebrew
Bene ha Eohim	sons of God	Classical Hebrew
Bonifacius	Future tense of *bon*, thus "to be Good." It is also the Latin name for Cotton Mather's *Essays to do Good*.	Latin
Chorus	Dance	Classical Greek

Corpus	body or body of work	Latin
De Servo Arbitrio	On Free Will. It is also the name of a work by Martin Luther.	Latin
De Religionis Gentilium	The religion of the people. It is also the name of Herbert of Cherbury's book.	Latin
Deus	God	Classical Greek
Deus Absconditis	Hidden God	Classical Greek
Eudaimonia	happiness	Classical Greek
Euthyphro	Name of a dialogue of Plato's.	Classical Greek
Ha	"the" or definite article.	Classical Hebrew
Hippolytus	The name of the Greek hero and Euripides work *Hippolytus Veiled*.	Classical Greek
Kethuvim	Writings. It is also a part of the Hebrew Bible or Old Testament.	Classical Hebrew
Lahoo mu'aqqibaatum mim baini yadaihi wa min khafihee yahfazoonahoo min amril laah	Text from Al-Qur'an 13:11, which in English means, "For him are successive angels, before and behind him who protect him by the decree of Allah."	Classical Arabic
mikveh Israel	The Bath of Israel or The Hope of Israel. It is also the name of the synagogue in Philadelphia to which Franklin gave funds. There is also a settlement in Israel near Jerusalem named *Mikveh Israel*, founded in 1870.	Classical Hebrew

Nicomachus	The name of Aristotle's son in whose honor the *Nicomachean Ethics* was written.	Classical Greek
Memoir du Benjamin Franklin	Original title of Franklin's autobiography.	French
Middot	Virtue	Classical Hebrew
Nabiim	Prophets	Classical Hebrew
Philadelphische Zeitung	*Philadelphia Times*, the name of a German newspaper in Philadelphia.	German
Principia Mathematica	The Principles of Mathematics. It is also the name of Newton's most famous work.	Latin
Qui s'aaelant deistes	"Those who call themselves deists." It was an expression used by Pierre Viret.	French
Quinque Viae	Five ways for proving God's existence from the *Summa Theologica* by Thomas Aquinas.	Latin
Summa Theologica	The Summary of Theology or The Major Work of Theology. It is also the name of Thomas Aquinas' principal work.	Latin
Tam va yashar	Blameless and upright.	Classical Hebrew
Torah	Law. It is also the first five books of the Hebrew Bible or Old Testament.	Classical Hebrew

Tzedek	Justice	Classical Hebrew
Tusculan	Early Italian name for Tuscany.	Latin/Italian
De Veritate	On the Truth. It is also the name of the book by Herbert of Cherbury.	Latin
Virtus	Virtue. This word has connotations of valor and manliness.	Latin

Benjamin Franklin's warning to the British colonies in America "Join, or Die" exhorting them to unite against the French and the Natives.

Appendix C
Franklin as an Inventor and Scientist

> Franklin, in effect, launched the first American medical school. He devised an effective and flexible urethral catheter. He was aware of the placebo effect, and he identified lead poisoning as a cause of abdominal pain.
> —E. J. Huth, "Benjamin Franklin's place in the history of medicine"

> Benjamin Franklin's medical history shows that he suffered from repeated attacks of gout and a large bladder stone. These conditions caused him considerable pain and markedly decreased his mobility."
> —Stanley Finger, "Benjamin Franklin's Risk Factors for Gout and Stones"

> Science, for me, gives partial explanations for life. In so far as it goes, it is based on facts, experience, and experiment.
> —Benjamin Franklin, *The Autobiography of Benjamin Franklin*

Introduction

The purpose of this third appendix is to make some observations and judgments about the phenomena of Benjamin Franklin as inventor and scientist. We will see in these observations that, above all, the two aspects that both of these phenomena had in common were practicality and utility and the desire to make the world a better place.

We will begin Appendix C by discussing many of his inventions while pointing out the great American statesman's goals of utility and making the world a better place to live simply by making these inventions.

Next, in a separate section, we will give a short catalog of Franklin's scientific inventions and then make some observations and judgments about those scientific "discoveries." In the second section, we will discuss five medical inventions that the statesman was involved in and then five other scientific discoveries that he also had a hand in.

Franklin's Inventions

Among the many practical inventions of Franklin's, the following list gives a sense of their variety and practical utility, as well as his desire to make the world a better place to live. Among these inventions were the following:

1. The odometer
2. The glass armonica
3. The long-arm device
4. Bifocal eyeglasses
5. A three-wheel clock
6. Franklin stove
7. Swim fins for the hands
8. American political cartooning
9. Invention of vocabulary
10. American celebrity[548]

In our comments, we will discuss each of these inventions by Franklin, emphasizing their utility and how they made the world a much better place.

The odometer, a device for measuring the distance traveled by a person or a vehicle, was invented by him to solve a problem that the British government petitioned the statesman to help them solve. The problem was the slapdash postal system that had developed in the North American colonies.[549]

Franklin started on this task by first touring America's major postal centers, studying ways to standardize and streamline mail delivery. Along the way, he charted the distance between postal centers by attaching a geared device to the rear wheel of his horse and carriage. Every four hundred revolutions made by the wheel caused the device to "click" and to indicate the traveling of one mile, or 1.6 kilometers.[550]

By the end of his tour, he had gathered a stunningly accurate survey of early colonial roads. The ancient Romans had devices for recording distance. Inventors in Nova Scotia and the American Midwest would independently conceive of similar devices. But none of these devices would put the odometer to such a practical use as that of Franklin.[551]

Most modern automobile and truck odometers are electronic, but one can still view a slightly worn version of Franklin's odometer at the Phillips Museum of Art at Franklin & Marshall College in Lancaster, Pennsylvania.[552]

When Franklin lived in England in the 1750s, he attended a concert at Cambridge University by a professional wine-glass musician named Edmund Delaval. The artist arranged a collection of wine glasses on a table and then "tuned" them by filling each with different amounts of water. Delaval then carefully "played" them by rubbing the rims of the wine glasses.[553]

The first great American statesman was fascinated by the concert, while at the same time, he could not help but begin to think how Delaval's instrument might be improved. In fact, after two years of experimentation, he introduced his "Glass Armonica," a collection of different-sized glass bowls arranged on a rotating shaft. By spinning the shaft with a foot pedal and running wetted fingers over the rims of the bowls, Franklin discovered that he could coax out chords and melodies that Delaval could only dream of.[554]

The Franklin glass armonica was so successful that both Mozart and Beethoven penned music for the new instrument. Mozart wrote a 1791 piece for it, while Beethoven used the instrument in an 1814 melodrama called "Leonore Prohashka." At least another hundred composers and musicians penned musical pieces featuring the glass armonica.[555]

The "long-arm" device is another invention of Franklin. We know that his home in Philadelphia was packed with books and bookshelves from floor to ceiling. To reach the top shelves without using a step ladder, he devised a "long arm" in his workshop. This was nothing more than a piece of wood with two "fingers" mounted on the end. By pulling on a cable attached to the wood, he could bring the fingers together so that they could grip a book off the high shelf.[556]

One of Franklin's most popular inventions was the eyeglasses with bifocals. As he reached old age, he had difficulty seeing up close and at a distance. He reasoned that he needed a set of lenses enabling him to see distances and another separate set of lenses to examine things up close. Switching back and forth from one pair of glasses to another was cumbersome. So in his workshop, Franklin cut his lenses in half and mounted all four pieces in the same frame.[557]

In order to see long distance, he simply peered through the lenses mounted at the top of the frame. When reading, the statesman looked through the bottom lenses. Interestingly enough, both far-sighted and near-sighted glasses had been around since the High Middle Ages, but no one had ever thought of mounting the two of them in the same frame.

Aside from a few modern improvements, his original bi-focal design has remained unchanged until modern times. In 2006, a team of Arizona researchers announced that they had designed a pair of glasses with lenses that switch from far-sighted to near-sighted with the simple push of a button.

The three-wheel clock was invented and designed by the American diplomat in 1757. With three wheels, the clock could run for twenty-four hours, making it much simpler than other clock designs in the eighteenth century. An article called "The Three Wheel Clock" by James Ferguson stated:

> ...owned by the "Friends of Franklin" is a clock shewing the Hours, minutes, and seconds, having only three wheels and two pinions in the whole movement. Invented by Dr. Franklin of Philadelphia.[558]

The Franklin stove, our sixth invention on our list, was first developed by him in 1742. The chief practical purpose of this invention was to find a better way to heat Pennsylvania homes in the cold winters. The Franklin stove was a metal-lined fireplace designed to stand a few inches from the chimney. A hollow baffle at the rear let the heat from the fire mix with the air more rapidly, and an inverted siphon helped to extract more heat. Another important feature of the Franklin stove is that the invention produced far less smoke than a traditional fireplace, making it much more practical and desirable.[559]

Franklin's seventh invention on our list, swim fins for the hands, came from his devotion to life-long swimming. When he was eleven, he invented swimming fins for the hands. These were two oval pieces of wood equipped with leather bands so that one could move more swiftly through the water. He also tried out fins for the feet, but they were not as effective. When we use the expression "swim fins" today, we mean those for the feet. He wrote about his childhood invention in an essay later in his life that he called "The Art of Swimming."[560]

He also created the idea of the political cartoon. In 1752, the American colonies stood on the brink of war with France. As English-speaking settlers moved inland, they were constantly bumping into French settlers and territories. That year, Franklin, the owner of the *Pennsylvania Gazette*, published a drawing entitled "Join, or Die." In the drawing, he depicts a snake cut into eight pieces, one for each of the British colonies at that time.

With the publication of this cartoon, Franklin began the long American tradition—particularly among US newspapers—to have political cartoonists on their staffs, but very few of these people know that he was the father of this phenomenon.

Another invention of his that is not well known has to do with words and expressions used in many venues of American life. He coined much of the language still used in modern electronics and related to his experiments on electricity and medicine. These words include battery, charge, positive, negative, and conductor, for example.

Finally, it may be said quite rightly that Franklin was the first of many great American "celebrities." And like many American celebrities to follow him, he also had a charitable cause. In the years before his death, he freed his two slaves, George and King, and the statesman also became a vocal abolitionist, much like many of the other Founding Fathers.

In Franklin's final published work in 1789, an essay entitled "On Slavery" was introduced to the House of Representatives on February

12, 1790, and to the Senate three days later. It was denounced by pro-slavery congressmen and sparked a heated debate. This statement is from the essay:

> Slavery is such an atrocious abasement of human nature, that its very extirpation, if not performed with solicitous care, may sometimes open a source of serious evils.

Scientific Discoveries of Franklin

In addition to Franklin's many inventions, he made several scientific discoveries. We will list several of these and then speak of each of them separately and in the order they are given here. These scientific discoveries included three medical discoveries and at least seven other scientific discoveries.

The medical discoveries have to do with:

1. The urinary catheter
2. The common cold
3. Lead poisoning
4. Psoriasis
5. Advocate for vaccination[561]

The other scientific categories are:

1. The lightning rod and other discoveries in electricity
2. Chart gulf stream
3. Aurora Borealis
4. Meteorology[562]

We will begin our analysis of the five significant medical discoveries that may be attributed to Franklin. These will be followed by a discussion of the other five scientific phenomena with which he has been associated.

Regarding his medical discoveries, he was inspired to invent a better urinary catheter in 1752 when he saw what his kidney (or bladder) stone-stricken brother had to endure. Catheters at the time were simply rigid, metal tubes—none too pleasant. So, the statesman invented an alternative. His catheter was flexible. It was made of hinged segments of tubes. He had a silversmith make the design and then promptly mailed it off to his brother, complete with instructions for how to use it, as well as his best wishes.[563]

Another important medical discovery of his was discoveries that he made on the common cold. Specifically, he determined that colds have nothing to do with body temperature, as many people at the time believed, and that the common cold is most likely passed from person to person in indoor environments.

In Franklin's day, long before the discovery of germs and viruses, people believed colds were caused by wet clothing and dampness in the air. He observed that sailors usually wore wet clothes but did not appear susceptible to the common cold. So after years of experiments on the matter, he finally concluded that the common cold is transmitted from person to person when they are in close contact, such as in a small room.

For most of his life, Franklin suffered from psoriasis. He even conducted experiments to determine the cause of the scaly ailment that he called "scrufles." He was also very harsh about the ointments he was given to cure the condition.[564]

Finally, during the summer of 1721, half of the occupants of Boston were sick with a fever, aching bodies and painful skin rashes. Of the eleven thousand people in the city, fifty-nine hundred had smallpox. By the end of that summer, 844 people had died from the disease. Fifteen years later, he watched his four-year-old son Francis die of another outbreak of the disease.[565] Francis Folger Franklin was born on October 20, 1732, and died on November 21, 1736. The loss, accompanying grief and guilt Franklin felt changed his attitude toward inoculation. After that point, he championed the idea when, earlier in his life, he argued vociferously against it.

This brings us to comments and a discussion of five other scientific discoveries attributed to the mind of Franklin. The first of these is most likely his best-known discovery—the lightning rod. In 1752, he conducted his famous kite-flying experiments, proving that lightning is a form of electricity. He wanted his experiment to be practical, so he developed the lightning rod, which would be attached to the outside of a house. The top of the rod must extend higher than the roof and the chimney.[566] The other end is connected to a cable that stretches down the side of the house to the ground. The end of the cable was buried deep in the ground, at least ten feet or more. His wish originally was to keep homes and civic buildings from fire. And he did just that, as well as opening the first fire department in the United States.

The first great American statesman also made other discoveries in the field of electricity. One of those was his discovery that electricity sometimes resides in storm clouds. He also concluded that storms may move in the opposite direction of the wind. He also proposed one of the first correct explanations for the movement of storms in the Northern Hemisphere. Franklin also did the first mapping of the Gulf Stream. He became interested in the North Atlantic and water circulation on a voyage to England. He knew that trips from America to England took, on average, two weeks longer than voyages from England to America. The presence of the Gulf Stream was known as early as the Spanish voyages, but it was not mapped until he took an interest in it.[567]

During these trips in the North Atlantic, the statesman also observed the "Northern Lights," known as the Aurora Borealis. His explanation for the Northern Lights was that they were caused by a concentration of electrical charges in the North Pole that intensified the snow and moisture. As the area became overcharged with electricity released into the air, the illumination occurs.[568]

Finally, Franklin also made some discoveries related to barometric pressure. His discovery in this field is significant because he developed a means by which barometric pressure can be measured. And this device is still employed in weather stations around the world.[569]

Benjamin Franklin's close friend and preacher, George Whitefield.
Courtesy of the Library of Congress.

Appendix D
Franklin and George Whitefield

> He used to sometimes pray for my conversion but never
> had the satisfaction of believing that his prayers were heard.
> —Benjamin Franklin on George Whitefield

> Get a feeling of the possession of Christ, a kind
> of spiritual pangs, that is necessary for Salvation.
> —George Whitefield to Benjamin Franklin

Introduction

In Appendix D, we will say more about the relationship of the religion of Benjamin Franklin and how he was influenced by evangelical preacher George Whitefield. We will accomplish this task by looking at three separate areas in their relationship. The first of these is their meeting and the establishment of their friendship. The second area is what their letters can tell us about their relationship. And the third area is some issues where the two eighteenth-century thinkers appear to have disagreed. These are the purpose of education and the nature and importance of the Bible, particularly the Old Testament.

Meeting and Established Friendship

The Rev. George Whitefield met Franklin for the first time when Whitefield visited Philadelphia and preached to massive outdoor crowds from the steps of the city center. Franklin attended Rev. Whitefield's first sermon in Philadelphia and was attracted to the young, fiery revivalist nine years young than the first great American statesman.

That proved to be the beginning of a close and lasting friendship, which continued until Whitefield's death in Newburyport, Connecticut, on September 30, 1770.

They also became business partners when the former published the sermons and papers of the latter. When Whitefield passed away, Franklin was in London, and when he got the word, the American had a deep sense of loss in losing his British friend. At the time, he wrote:

> I knew him intimately for upwards of thirty years, his integrity, disinterestedness and indefatigable zeal in prosecuting every good work. I have never seen equalled, and I shall never see exceeded.[570]

The Rev. Whitefield was born in Gloucester, England, on December 16, 1714. In his school and college days at Oxford, Whitefield experienced a strong religious awakening that he called a "new birth." He also became friends with Methodist founders John and Charles Wesley and joined them in their missionary work in the Georgia Colony in America in 1738. A year later, the Rev. Whitefield was invited to preach in Philadelphia, and that is when Franklin and Whitefield met in 1739.

By that time, Whitefield was already known as a great evangelical preacher. He spent the remainder of his career between preaching in America from Georgia to Massachusetts and itinerate preaching in England, Scotland, Wales, and Ireland in the United Kingdom. The Rev. Whitefield believed that every person must experience a rebirth much like the one he experienced in his youth.

This brings us to the second section of Appendix D, in which we will discuss what we may glean about Franklin and Whitefield's relationship through their letters from 1739 until Whitefield's death in 1770.

Franklin-Whitefield Letters

In a letter dated July 2, 1756, Benjamin Franklin proposed to the Rev. George Whitefield that they partner together to establish a Christian colony "in the Ohio," which, at the time, was frontier country. In the letter, Franklin told the British evangelist:

I imagine we could do it effectively and without putting the nation at too much expense. What a glorious thing it would be, to settle in that fine country a large strong body of religious [Christians] and industrious people. What a security to the other colonies and an advantage to Britain.[571]

In this 1756 letter, he not only wanted to populate the Ohio River Valley with Christians but also to use this base for converting Native Americans to Christianity.

Franklin's first missive to Whitefield was written only days after meeting the preacher, on May 10, 1739. It was an open letter that he printed in *The Pennsylvania Gazette*. The publisher related this after Whitefield's Philadelphia sermon:

> It is not hyperbole to describe George Whitefield, the English clergyman who riveted colonists with his dramatic evangelical preaching, as a star celebrity.

The statesman's evaluation of the preaching of the Rev. Whitefield is very clear. It is riveting, dramatic, and has a star quality to it. This is a peculiar way to put the matter, for many historians believe that Franklin was the first American celebrity, particularly in England and France.

Another letter from July 6, 1749, written after Whitefield had returned to Britain in 1748, indicates that Franklin is working as Whitefield's agent in America. He tells the preacher, "I have received no money on your account from Franklin or from Boston." A few years later, on August 17, 1752, Whitefield wrote Franklin to tell him he had met an American named James Reed in London who had asked him to promote him with Franklin "to make a stand against vice and profaneness" and to promote "true religion and virtue." The Rev. Whitefield also told the great American statesman:

> You grow more and more famous in the learned world, as you have made considerable progress in the mysteries of electricity. I would now humbly recommend to your diligent unprejudiced pursuit and struggle and study of the mystery of rebirth.

Clearly Whitefield was very desirous of Franklin being "born again," but there is no evidence that the Boston-born patriot ever assented to that request. The preacher did sign the letter with "Your very affectionate friend, and obliged servant." However, in another letter to his British preacher-friend on August 17, 1752, Franklin thanks him for "Your repeated Wishes and prayers for my Eternal as well as temporal Happiness." This is followed by:

> I have myself no doubt that I shall enjoy myself of both as is proper for me, whose very chastisements have been Blessings to me. Can I doubt that He loves me. And if I doubt that He loves me can I also doubt that He will take care of me, not only here but hereafter? This may appear to some to be Presumption, but to me it appears to be the best grounded Hope, Hope of the future built on experience of the past.

Here Franklin expresses his optimism to the Rev. Whitefield about his fate in the present life and the next one, as well. But there is still no indication that the first great American statesman wished to number himself among the "born again." Although he and Whitefield remained good friends for over thirty years, they also had their disagreements on issues other than Franklin's soul. In the next section, we will speak of two of those disagreements.

Franklin-Whitefield Disagreements

Despite the many things we have said about the Franklin-Whitefield friendship and relationship, there were two issues, in addition to being born again, where the two eighteenth-century worthies disagreed. These two issues were about the Old Testament and the purposes of a good education.

In our chapter on Franklin and the Bible regarding the Old Testament or Hebrew Bible, we indicated two elements he believed about the ancient Jewish Bible. The first was that he had difficulty believing that God sanctioned certain Old Testament narratives. These narratives tended to be violent episodes that could not be associated with an All-Good God.

Another disagreement between the two men regarding the text of the Old Testament has to do with what the New Testament calls the "spirit" as opposed to the "Letter." The Rev. Whitefield preferred that a text is best understood by the literal or the "Letter" understanding. Whitefield was a literalist, while Franklin preferred the "Spirit" and sometimes even "allegorical" comprehension of the text.[572]

The other dispute had to do with the nature of the curriculum in a college or university education. This disagreement first became an issue between the two when Franklin was envisioning the opening of an "Academy" in Philadelphia.

In 1750, Franklin sent Whitefield a document he called "A Proposal Relating to the Education of Youth in Pennsylvania."[573] In this proposal, he made a strong case that the curriculum for the Academy be based on a Liberal Arts education, in a time in America where there were only four colleges—Harvard, Yale, Princeton, and William & Mary. The site of the new Academy, which later became the University of Pennsylvania, was the "New Building," a spacious venue that Whitefield's supporters had erected when the itinerate preacher first came to Philadelphia.

Although Whitefield was initially keen on the idea of the curriculum for the Academy, on second thought, he had some new ideas. Some of his supporters pointed out to him that "Christianity seemed to be an afterthought." Franklin, on the other hand, was more concerned about the Academy being nonsectarian than evangelical.

Franklin also believed that virtue should be the main emphasis in the Academy. Whitefield was aghast at this idea and wrote, "Virtue cannot be the main idea of education in this life or in the life beyond."[574] Thus, the two great eighteenth-century thinkers had deep disagreements about three things, all of which are related to religion.

Whether Franklin agreed that he should be "born again" in the Great Awakening tradition, whether the Old Testament is divinely inspired and whether it is to be understood literally, and whether the curriculum of the Philadelphia Academy should be based on Liberal Arts or more Jesus-centered.

Thomas Paine (1737–1809) was an English-born American Founding Father, political activist, philosopher, political theorist and revolutionary. Courtesy of the New York Public Library.

Appendix E
More on Deism and Franklin

> Bolingbroke gave Jefferson his heterodox views, which
> emphasized a deistic, universal, impartial God.
> —Allen Jayne, *Jefferson's Declaration of Independence*

> The deists, those who dropped their Christian
> faiths and became proponents of deism.
> —David Holmes, *The Faiths of the Founding Fathers*

> And so, in short, I soon became a thorough deist.
> —Benjamin Franklin, *The Autobiography of Benjamin Franklin*

Introduction

In this fifth appendix on the religious thought of Benjamin Franklin, we will say more about the movement in the seventeenth and eighteenth centuries known as deism, what it was and is, the origin and history of the movement, which of the American Founding Fathers considered themselves deists, and finally, as best we can tell, the development of Franklin's ideas on deism from his youth until his religious view in his later life.

We will begin with the nature and origins of the theological movement known as deism. This will be followed by a second section of Appendix E on which of the American Founding Fathers can more probably be identified as deists. Finally, in the third section of the appendix, we will make some further observations—beyond those we have made in Chapter Four of this work on what Franklin said, wrote and believed in regard to the movement known as deism.

Nature and Origins of the Word Deism

The English word "deism" comes from the Classical Greek noun *Deus*. It began to be used in English in the seventeenth century, primarily to distinguish it from the English theism that comes from the Latin, *Theos*. Thus, the early seventeenth-century deists wanted to distinguish themselves from traditional theism.

In traditional theism, God is seen as being All-Good, All-Knowing, and All-Powerful, as well as being the Creation of the Universe, *ex nihilo*, or "out of nothing." In traditional theism held by Judaism, Christianity and Islam, God is believed to answer prayers, as well as act in the affairs of people, such as performing miracles.

As we indicated in Chapter Four of this work, the deists had some beliefs in common with the theists, and they also, in the seventeenth and eighteenth centuries, had some disagreements with those who believed in theism.

The deists were monotheists; that is, they believed in only one God. They also believed that God created the universe, as well as the laws that it works by. Specifically, those laws discovered by Sir Isaac Newton that defined gravitational pull, the movements of heavenly bodies, and explanation for falling bodies. Newton was the first to propose that the same forces or laws were responsible for the movements of bodies on Earth, as well as planetary motions.

Earlier, Galileo, Robert Hooke and Christopher Wren also made some progress in understanding gravitation, but Newton put it all together in his principal work, *Principia Mathematica*.[575]

One way that the deists were different from the theists, however, is that the deists thought that once God had made the universe and the scientific rules it runs by, then He no longer has any contact with the world, so He does not bring miracles to humans, nor does He answer their prayers. As we have indicated in Chapter Four, for the deist God is a *Deus Absconditis*, that is, a "God who absconds" after His creation.[576]

We also indicated in Chapter Four that the English term "deism" appeared in the writing of an English Lord, Edward Herbert, in his book, *De Veritate*, or "On Truth." This was to distinguish it from "Revelation," or the form of knowledge found in the Bible.

Herbert outlined a belief system that he thought was based on Reason and was a way of reconciling the religious strife and violence that had stormed through Europe as a result of the Protestant Reformation.

Lord Herbert outlined five major tenets of the belief in deism. These were what he called:

1. Belief in one Supreme God.
2. That God is to be Worshipped.
3. Virtue and Piety are the nature of that Worship.
4. People should be remorseful and repent their sins.
5. There is punishment in this world as well as in the next.[577]

Lord Herbert postulated that these ideas were innate in human beings, planted by God in human souls and that these are the core tenets of the religions he knew about—Judaism, Christianity and Islam, and even, he thought, in the paganism of Rome. Herbert believed that religion became barbarous when it started to get too far from his five-belief core. And the results, in his view, are the reasons for destroying other religious views, such as in the Reformation or competing sects in the eighteenth and nineteenth centuries in America.[578]

With the establishment of the British colonies in the New World in the seventeenth and eighteenth centuries, in his book *The Faiths of the Founding Fathers*, American historian David Holmes outlines three categories as a way to roughly describe the religious faiths of the individuals who founded the United States.[579]

These religious categories were the following:

1. The deists, those who dropped their Christian faiths and began proponents of deism. This is Holmes smallest category.
2. Practicing Christians such as Alexander Hamilton, John Jay, and Patrick Henry, for example.
3. Christians influenced by deism, those who rejected many metaphysical and supernatural aspects of the Christian religion such as the Divinity of Jesus, the Virgin Birth, the Trinity, and many other fundamental ideas that come not from Reason but from Revelation.[580] Holmes believed this was the largest category by far in his scheme.

This brings us to the second section of Appendix E, in which we will discuss those Founding Fathers found in Professor Holmes's first category, the deists. As we shall see, some of these men explicitly identified as deists, while others did not.

Deists Among the Founding Fathers

There has been much debate in American scholarly circles since the second half of the twentieth century to the present about which of the many Founding Fathers of the United States thought of themselves or should be considered believers in the theological movement known as deism.

As we have shown in Chapters Two and Three of this work, Franklin declared himself a deist and did not hold that view by the close of his life. But what other of the Founding Fathers also considered themselves to be deists? Among those considered deists were Ethan Allen, Thomas Paine and Thomas Jefferson, but for vastly different reasons.

Ethan Allen (1738–1789), the leader of the Green Mountain Boys of Vermont, the hero of Fort Ticonderoga and the best advocate that Vermont become a state, along with his friend Thomas Young (1731–1777), published the first American book that advocated deism in 1784. The book was entitled *Reason: The Only Oracle of Man*.[581] With this text, the American population was formally introduced to the ideas of deism. In their work, they systematically dismantle the ecclesiastical foundations of New England's Congregationalism, Anglicanism, the Congregationalists and Presbyterians.

The book only sold a few hundred copies, and after its publication, Allen did not play a crucial role in American politics. Even modern writers on Ethan Allen agree that he was "disorganized and clumsy as a writer." What is significant about *Reason* is that he identified himself several times as being a deist.[582]

The duo also focused upon many topics central to the European Enlightenment, such as substance and matter, formation versus creation, immortality, the soul, the nature and motives of prophecy and time versus eternity. Thomas Young, a student of deism, mentioned to Allen the philosophical movement and instilled in his friend a theology based on the writings of Charles Blount and John Locke, and then collaborated on their anti-Calvinist, American premiere deist text.

A decade later, Thomas Paine published his famous defense of deism called *The Age of Reason*.[583] Paine was born and raised in England. He only spent twenty of his seventy-two years in America, so some critics asked if he should reasonably be considered an American. Added to this is the fact that the book was written and completed in Europe. Nevertheless, there is an essay in the *Age of Reason* that Thomas Paine called "The Religion of Deism Compared with the Christian Religion."[584]

In that essay, Paine points out that one difference between Christian views and his deist-leanings is that the latter does not accept many of the miracles related to the life of Jesus. In fact, Paine even gives alternative explanations for some of the episodes in the New Testament. For example, Paine thought that Mary, the mother of Jesus, had been impregnated by a Roman soldier, and when she married Joseph, he could not understand how she could be pregnant, for they had not had sexual relations.[585] The belief of the Redemption of Jesus Christ is not the doctrine of the New Testament. Paine remarks in the same essay, "It is an all together invention of the Church of Rome."[586]

Then Paine adds:

> What the writers of the New Testament attempted to prove by the story of Jesus and his resurrection of the same body from the grave which was the belief of the Pharisees, in opposition to the Sadducees, a sect of Jews who denied it.[587]

In the same essay, Thomas Paine disparages St. Paul and his letters that proclaim the resurrection of Jesus, as well as the life to come for Christians. As Paine puts it, "By his [Jesus] death, he rubs off all and pays his passage to Heaven gratis."[588] Because of these and many other examples, Thomas Paine concludes in the essay in question:

> Here it is then that the Religion of deism is superior to the Christian Religion. It is free from all those invented and torturing articles that shock our Reason or injure our humanity, and with which the Christian Religion abounds. Its creeds is pure and sublimely simple. It believes in God and there it rests.[589]

In his widely read *Age of Reason*, Thomas Paine, the principal American proponent of deism, called Christianity "a fable." Paine, a protégé of Franklin, denied that "The Almighty God ever communicates anything to people, by speech, language or vision."[590] Instead, he postulated a distant deity whom he called "Nature's God."

As Father James V. Schall reports in his essay, "The God of the Founding Fathers: Nature's God," meant:

> Nature's God, as Jefferson and other founders conceived Him, was the cause or the source of a natural order that included a human order, a law of nature that applied to human affairs. Many of the founding fathers were learned men, good men... But they were worried about theological differences, but paradoxically they did not think this "living together." was possible without an ethic that looked very much like the Christian ethic of the New Testament.[591]

The case of Thomas Jefferson and his deism is an entirely different matter. Our third president rejected Orthodox Christianity, but he went to great lengths to keep his religious views far from the public.

Nearly all the examples in Jefferson's writings that reveal his true religious beliefs can be found in his letters written to family members and close friends. And he often asked in those letters that these beliefs of his be kept private. In an 1819 letter to his friend William Short, for example, Jefferson rejected doctrines "invented by ultra-Christian Sects," such as the Immaculate Conception of Jesus, his deification, the creation of the world by Him, and his miraculous powers."[592]

In the same letter to William Short, Jefferson also indicated to his friend his rejection of "his resurrection and visible Ascension, his corporeal presence in the Eucharist, the Trinity, Original Sin, the Atonement, what Jefferson called "Regeneration." Election and the orders of the Hierarchy."[593]

Thomas Jefferson was a philosophical skeptic, but he realized he could not publicly advocate his religious views because that would be a form of political suicide. But two other texts from the pen of Thomas Jefferson give us a better insight into his authentic religious views. These texts are his 1784 *Notes on the State of Virginia*, in which the third president said boldly, "It does me no injury for my neighbor to say there are twenty gods, or no gods. It neither picks my pocket nor breaks my leg."[594]

The other written text of Jefferson's that is relevant to our discussion is the "Jefferson Bible," whose official title is *The Life and Morals of Jesus of Nazareth*.[595] The work was completed in 1804. When Jefferson was a young man, he wrote to a Philadelphia publisher to get copies of the four gospels in Greek, Latin, French and in English. He then arranged the gospels in columns, and with a razor, he cut out the theological things he did not believe in and then pasted back together what he had left.

In short, what he cut out were any references to the metaphysical episodes of the life of Jesus, his Divinity, his miracles, etc. What he pasted back together, more or less, was any reference to Jesus' moral point of view. For Jefferson—as for Ethan Allen and Thomas Paine—the original teachings of Jesus were what he had to say about ethical matters.[596]

This brings us to the third and final section of Appendix G on the first great American statesman, Benjamin Franklin, and his views on the phenomenon of the religious movement known in his time as deism.

Franklin on deism

Already in this study of Franklin's religion, we have indicated that in his adolescence, the great statesman began to give up his parents Calvinism in favor of what he called deism. We know he was a deist because in his autobiography, in discussing his religion in his youth he simply wrote about that period, "And so, in short I soon became a thorough deist."[597]

We also have shown in this work that throughout his adult life, Franklin constantly did and said things that did not seem very deistic. His speeches and letters made constant references to allusions in the Bible, and he once predicted that God would bring judgment on the British during the American War of Revolution. Most famously, at the Continental Congress in 1787, Franklin proposed that the convention open its meetings with prayer.[598]

In the midst of a discussion about his proposal at the convention, Franklin asked, "How has it happened that we have not hitherto once thought of humbly applying to the Father of Lights to illuminate our understandings?"

This would appear to be an odd request for a deist to make. Did deists not believe that God was unconcerned about the matters of humans? Even more peculiar was the fact that, besides Franklin, only three other delegates voted for his prayer proposal. Thus, the motion was tabled, and Franklin should real consternation about that fact.

But reading up on deism as a teenager was not enough to eradicate from his soul the Congregationalism of his mother and the Presbyterianism of his father. In his later adult life, Franklin had a tension between his intellectual skepticism, and the enduring influence of the faith of people who had fostered his religious life, like his mother and father, sister Jane, Uncle Ben, and theologian George Whitefield.

At the end of his life, Franklin was asked on two separate occasions—as we have indicated earlier in this study—with Madame Brillon and Yale University President, Ezra Stiles, the great statesman was asked for a short summary of his theological beliefs. In his response to both of these letters, Franklin provided a set of propositions that the Boston native truly believed in.

What was most interesting, we believe, about Franklin's letters to Madame Brillon and to President Stiles is the set of beliefs that the great statesman set forth were much closer to the Calvinism of his parents and friends than it was to the belief systems of men like Ethan Allen, Thomas Paine, or his friend, Thomas Jefferson.[599]

Benjamin Franklin playing chess with Lady Caroline Howe, showing Franklin being placed in checkmate by Lady Howe while Admiral Lord Richard Howe stands in the background. The chess games were the pretense under which Franklin met with the admiral. Courtesy of the New York Public Library.

Appendix F
Franklin and Diplomacy

I would feel the loss of America like the loss of a brother.
—Admiral Richard Howe

I played with Dr. Franklin at Chess and was equal to him at the game.
—Thomas Jefferson, quoted in John French,
"Travels in the US and Canada" (1833)

The greatest of Benjamin Franklin's diplomatic accomplishments was the signing of the Treaty of Alliance of 1778 between France and the new United States.
—Walter Isaacson, *Benjamin Franklin: An American Life*

Introduction

The main purpose of this appendix is to make some observations about Benjamin Franklin's participation in American diplomacy, as well as his accomplishments in that field that stretched back at least to the year 1757 when the Pennsylvania Colonial Assembly commissioned him to represent the colony in London in a taxation dispute with the government of King James II.[600]

This was followed beginning in 1776 when the newly formed United States made Franklin the first important American diplomat. The purpose of his visit to France was to negotiate and secure a formal alliance and treaty between the United States and France. He was named as a diplomatic agent of the Continental Congress. Exactly one month to the day of being named the Congress' representative on October 26, 1776, Franklin set sail from Philadelphia to Paris.

Two years later, on February 6, 1778, he officially declared an alliance between the US and France by signing what was known as the "Treaty of Amity and Commerce and Alliance."[601] The French aid that these agreements guaranteed was crucial to the eventual American victory over the British in the American War of Independence.

In Appendix F, we will provide two main sections, one on Franklin in Britain, the other on the statesman's time in France. Along the way—particularly in the second section of the appendix—we will make some comments on his negotiating techniques and strategies that were best described in an essay he called "The Morals of Chess," written and published on June 28, 1779.[602]

Franklin as a Diplomat in Britain

Benjamin Franklin made three separate trips to London, the first time at the age of eighteen in 1724, and the other two times as serving diplomatic missions in 1757 and again in 1764. In all three of these trips, he spent many months, or even years, on the "other side of the pond."

The purpose of his first trip to London was to purchase printing equipment so he could open his own print shop back in the States and also possibly to open his own newspaper in his adopted city of Philadelphia. He visited Sir William Keith, the Royal Governor of Pennsylvania, who promised to pay for the equipment. Governor Keith promised to send a letter of credit to officials in London, so Franklin would have the money when he got there.[603]

Unfortunately, when Franklin arrived in London on Christmas Eve 1724, he realized that Governor Keith had not followed through on his promise and likely had no intention of paying for the printing equipment.[604] This left the soon-to-be American statesman stranded in London at the age of eighteen. He went directly to the printing establishment of Samuel Palmer, a famous and prestigious British printer at the time.

In fact, Palmer (died 1732) gave Franklin a job a few days later. He stayed in London for the next eighteen months, working for the funds to pay for his trip back to Philadelphia. During this time, he also worked for another famous London printer, a man named James Watt, who was famous for his invention of what was called the "Copying Press" that he patented in 1780.[605]

Franklin finally left London on July 22, 1772. He was accompanied by a Philadelphia merchant named Thomas Denham, a shopkeeper for whom Franklin worked when they returned to Philadelphia. The voyage back from London arrived in Philadelphia on October 11, 1726.[606]

The second time he went to London was in 1757. Over the years, he became more and more involved in Pennsylvania politics, serving, for example, as a councilman in the Pennsylvania Assembly and also as postmaster general, as well as other positions in Philadelphia political circles. We have spoken of many of these civic positions earlier in this study.

Technically, the colony of Pennsylvania was "owned" by the William Penn family. King Charles II gave the Royal Charter for the land to the Penn family in 1681. This made the members of the Penn family the arbiter and final word concerning any decisions in the colony. Because of this "final say" of the Penn family, this caused many conflicts over the years between the Penns and the colonist.

By 1757, the colony had hired Franklin to travel to England to represent the colonists' concerns about the Penn family. The statesman's mission was to get the king to end the Penn family's right to overturn decisions of the Pennsylvania Legislation. He also wanted to eliminate the Penn family's exemption from paying taxes.[607]

The first great American statesman was in England this time for five years. Ultimately, he was unsuccessful in persuading the king to limit the authority of the Penn family in the Pennsylvania Colony, so he left London in August of 1762 and arrived back in Philadelphia on November 1 of that same year.[608]

By 1764, the thirteen colonies were in an uproar over what was called the "Sugar Act," the proposed "Stamp Act," and other activities imposed by the British Parliament and King Georg III.

The Sugar Act, also called the Plantations Act of Revenue of 1764, was a British legislation aimed at ending the smuggling trade in sugar and molasses from the French and Dutch West Indies. The Stamp

Act of 1765 was also called the Duties in American Colonies Act. The purpose of the act was to raise funds to finance British military forces in America after the French and Indian Wars.

In 1764, amid the controversies of the Sugar and Stamp Acts, the Pennsylvania Assembly once again appointed Franklin to represent the colony's interests to the king. This time, he sailed to London on November 7, 1764, and arrived there on December 10, 1764.[609] He stayed in England for eleven years. During that time, he represented the colonists of Pennsylvania before the king and later represented Massachusetts, Georgia and New Jersey, as well.[610]

During his third trip to Britain, Franklin saw that King George and Parliament continued to deny the American colonies their basic rights concerning taxation, law-making and various other issues like trade. In England, he saw first-hand the belligerence of the British lawmakers and eventually realized that diplomacy was not going to solve the differences between the two sides.[611]

So, he left London on March 20, 1775, and arrived in Philadelphia on May 5, 1775. The very next day, the Pennsylvania Assembly elected him as a delegate to the Second Continental Congress. But Franklin had no diplomatic accomplishments on his third voyage to London, and overall, his time in Britain—at least in terms of diplomacy—was not very successful. He did, however, have more success in France, as we shall see in the second section of this appendix.

Franklin and Diplomacy in France

As we indicated earlier in this appendix, the Continental Congress sent Franklin to France in 1776 as a commissioner for the colonies during the American Revolution. Later, the statesman was elevated to the title of Minister of Plenipotentiary in 1778 after two years in France. When he presented his credentials to the French Court in 1779, he became the first American minister, the equivalent of a modern ambassador.

Several weeks before the Treaty of Paris, Franklin arranged for the translation and publication of the thirteen state constitutions along with other founding documents and treaties of commerce and alliance. He believed that presenting these to the French would aid America in securing help from the French.

Franklin had these volumes sumptuously bound in leather with fine paper and presented them to the king and queen, as well as the French foreign ministers. The Great Seal of the United States, which Congress approved in June of 1782, made its first appearance in print in a personally inscribed copy to the translator.

His popularity in France bolstered the American cause there. The French people viewed him as a representative of Republican simplicity and honesty, an image that he was only too quick to cultivate.

In his time in France, the statesman skillfully employed his negotiation techniques and art of persuasion. He made friends with influential officials throughout the country while continuing to push for a formal alliance. France secretly gave support to the American patriots with shipments of war supplies, but it was not until the Battle of Saratoga that the French began to believe that the Americans might win the American Revolutionary War.[612]

From September 19 to October 7, 1777, the Battle of Saratoga marked the climax of what was called the Saratoga Campaign by the British, and it gave a decisive victory to the United States over the British in the American Revolutionary War. British General John Burgoyne led an invasion army of seven to eight thousand soldiers southward from Canada, in the Chaplain Valley, hoping to meet similar British forces marching north from New York City and a third from Ontario marching east. The goal was to take the city of Albany, but the southern and western British contingents never arrived, so the Americans won the battle.[613]

A few months after the Battle of Saratoga, representatives of the United States and France met in Paris, including Franklin. What followed was the Treaty of Paris, also known as the "Treaty of Alliance" that he persuaded the French to sign after two years on the job. The treaty was signed on February 6, 1778. It formalized France's financial and military support for the Revolutionary government in America.[614] According to this first peace treaty signed by the new United States, America also agreed to aid France if Britain should attack them from the west.

The Treaty of Alliance of 1778 was negotiated by American diplomats Silas Deane, Arthur Lee and, above all, Benjamin Franklin.

The Treaty of Alliance was written in French and English. At this time, the French government officially recognized the independence of the United States of America.

The end of the Treaty of Alliance stipulates that:

> The essential and direct End of the present defensive alliance is to maintain effectually the liberty, Sovereignty and independence absolute and unlimited of the said United States, as well as in Matters of Gouvernement as of commerce.

The Treaty of the Alliance also stipulated that the Americans and French would not lay down their arms "until the independence of the United States shall have been formally or tacitly assured by the Treaty of Treaties that shall terminate the war."

The vast majority of the work, as well as the language of the treaty, was accomplished by Franklin. There can be little doubt that his most important and long-lasting diplomatic accomplishment was the signing of the 1778 Treaty of Alliance between France and the United States.

One interesting essay of Franklin's was an attempt at explaining his power of persuasion and views on war. The essay was entitled *la morale des Echcs*, or in English, "The Morals of Chess." published in June of 1779.[615] At one point, the statesman likens chess to life itself with winners and losers, particularly in the context of war. He also speaks of strategy in chess and how it is like or should be war play.[616]

In the opening of the essay, he told us this:

> The game of chess is not merely an idle amusement. Several valuable qualities of mind, useful in the course of human life, are to be acquired or strengthened by it so as to become habits, ready on all occasions. For life is a kind of chess match in which we often have points to gain, and competitors and adversaries to contend with, and in which there is a vast variety of good and ill events, that are, in some degree, the effects of prudence or the want of it. By playing at chess then we may learn.[617]

At this point in the essay on chess, Franklin describes four essential characteristics for a game of chess, as well as an encounter in diplomacy, or even an episode in battle. These four characteristics are the following:

1. Foresight
2. Circumspection
3. Caution
4. Not being discouraged[618]

In his autobiography, Franklin wrote about his time as a diplomat in Britain and France during the 1760s and 1770s. He noted that while negotiating the Treaty of Alliance in 1778, he frequently engaged in chess matches with British and French officials. Among these were Admiral Howe of the United Kingdom and several French government officials.

The chess match with Richard Howe came at the end of what is called the "Staten Island Peace Conference," a diplomatic conference held between officials of the British Crown—represented by Richard Howe and members of the American Second Continental Congress that included John Adams, Edward Rutledge, and as the group's head, Benjamin Franklin. After two hours of negotiating, there was no progress made, so Franklin suggested a game of chess to which Admiral Howe agreed. The meeting took place on September 11, 1776, a few days after the British had captured Long Island.[619]

Ironically, perhaps, an acquaintance of Franklin named Caroline Howe was the sister of Admiral Richard Howe and General William Howe, the two eventual commanders of the British on land and at sea. Caroline Howe met Franklin when she invited the diplomat to a "game of Chess." There is also evidence that they played each other in another match on Christmas Day, 1774.[620]

In fact, Caroline Howe had initiated a three-month series of chess matches in her Grafton Street townhouse in London. She became a conduit for the last-gasp British government to remain in control of the American colonies. Nothing came of the games or her effort at diplomacy. So, he soon returned home to join his fellow revolutionaries.

Later, in France, during Franklin's ambassador days, his center for chess in Paris was the Café de la Regence, where he reportedly met and played a match with world champion Francois Andre Philidor, who reportedly beat him in nine minutes.[621] Again, ironically, Philidor had no idea who Franklin was.

There is also abundant evidence that the first great American statesman played chess against several other French officials, and many of these appear to have been arranged by Madame Brillon, including one that supposedly took place in her bathroom while Franklin and his opponent played chess while she took a bath.[622]

Regarding that particular occasion, Walter Isaacson wrote about Franklin and Madame Brillon:

> They flirted over the chessboard. She was still a little miffed, Madame Brillon teasingly wrote of herself about the six games of Chess he won so inhumanely, and she warns him she will spare nothing to get her revenge.[623]

The most famous defeat of Franklin at chess was not even against a human. It happened in 1783 while negotiating the terms of independence from Great Britain when the ambassador played a round of chess with what was known as the "Mechanical Turk." This was an amazing specimen of an automaton that was then touring Europe. Anticipating the super-intelligence of artificial intelligence and modern chess machines, the Turk was—as Franklin deduced—an elaborate hoax.

In the base of the device was hidden a talented chess player. He used a complex array of pulleys and magnets to manipulate the pieces on the board above him. The device was invented by an Austrian named Wolfgang von Kempelen, and it fooled many people in the late eighteenth century in Europe.[624]

Perhaps in some of these arranged chess matches, Franklin made some progress toward the Treaty of Alliance. If he did, the American diplomat certainly employed the characteristic of foresight, circumspection and caution while refusing to be discouraged.

Benjamin Franklin working in his print shop.
Courtesy of the Library of Congress.

Appendix G
Franklin on Separation of Church and State

> Congress shall make no law respecting an establishment of religion or prohibiting the free exercise thereof.
> —Establishment Claus of the First
> Amendment to the US Constitution

> I contemplate with solemn reverence that act of the whole American people which declared that their legislature should 'make no law respecting an establishment of religion, or prohibiting the free exercise thereof,' thus building a wall of separation between Church and State.
> —Thomas Jefferson, Letter to Danbury Baptists, January 1, 1802

> The Church, the State and the Poor are three daughters which we should maintain but not portion off.
> —Benjamin Franklin, *The Autobiography of Benjamin Franklin*

Introduction

The principal goal of this appendix is to make some observations about what the first great American statesman had to say and to write about the phenomenon of the separation of church and state in the United States.

We will accomplish this primary goal by providing three separate sections. In the first of these, we shall make some observations and comments on the history of the idea of church and state in America. In the second section, we will explore and comment upon what other Founding Fathers said about the issue.

And in the third and final section of Appendix G, we will write specifically about what Franklin had to say and wrote about the phenomenon of the separation of church and state in his native United States of America.

History of Church and State in America

As one of the epigrams for this appendix indicates, on January 1, 1802, President Thomas Jefferson wrote a letter to the Danbury Baptist Association in Connecticut in answer to a correspondence written to the president on December 19, 1801, that the Baptists had heard that a "national religion was about to be established."

In President Jefferson's response, he coined the term "Separation of Church and State," and the Baptists appear to have been satisfied with that theological response.

It is important to point out, however, that Jefferson's letter and his invention of the phrase are not a part of the First Amendment of the US Constitution. It appears to have been what some have called "far-fetched legal reasoning" to give the idea some sort of legal standing and perhaps to infer the delegates' intent at the Constitutional Convention of 1787.

The Jefferson letter to the Danbury Baptists remained in relative obscurity until 1878, when the US Supreme Court, in the case of *Reynolds v. the United States*, cited the entire letter and suggested that the separation of church and state meant the following:

> Congress was deprived of all legislative power over mere religious opinions but was left free to reach only those religious actions which were in violation of social duties or subversive of good order.

Nearly seventy years later, in the 1947 Supreme Court decision of *Everson v. Board of Education*, a major conceptual change about the matter at hand can be seen.[625] The court at that time only cited Jefferson's six words, "a separation of church and state," and not the precedents of the Supreme Court decisions since his time.

Then in 1962, in the case of *Engel v. Vitale*, the Supreme Court chose to redefine the word "church" to mean "any religious activity in public."[626] This would appear to turn the original intent of his comment in his letter. Originally, it was to protect the church from the state, but now, in *Engel*, it is to protect the state from the church.

Since 1962, more than six thousand court cases have challenged religious expressions in public institutions and in public life. For example, numerous court cases have ruled that verbal prayers in public schools—even if voluntary and denominationally neutral—were unconstitutional. In 1980, for example, it was ruled that it was unconstitutional to hang the Ten Commandments on the walls of a public school classroom.[627] One of the great ironies is that the Ten Commandments are engraved on the chamber walls of the US Supreme Court.[628]

To cite another example, in Virginia, a federal court ruled that a homosexual newspaper may be distributed on a high school campus, but religious newspapers may not. This decision is evidence that church-state separation is now part of the culture wars now taking place in contemporary America.[629]

Another interesting element of this history is that since the 1990s, the tide of the separation of church and state has begun to change. In recent court decisions, more have favored religion. In 1990, for example, the Supreme Court ruled it is permissible to have prayer and Bible clubs at public high schools.[630] The Court also decided on another case at the time that premarital sexual abstinence programs, while religious in nature, can be taught in public schools.[631]

Regarding the Roberts Court in 2019, Justice Brett Kavanaugh, writing for himself alone, insisted that the "Lemon test" the court had been using for decades is not good law.[632] In fact, in 2022, the court abandoned the Lemon Test by a 6 to 3 vote, when the court said in *Kennedy v. Bremerton School District* that the school district was wrong for firing a football coach who led prayer vigils at the fifty-yard line after games.[633]

This brings us to the second section of Appendix G on Franklin and the separation of church and state, where we will comment on what several of the other American Founding Fathers have said and written about the matter at hand.

Separation and Other Founding Fathers

In addition to Benjamin Franklin, who spoke about the separation of church and state, at least another seven or eight Founding Fathers also made comments about the issue at hand, including Georg Washington, John Adams and Thomas Jefferson, as we have seen, as well as Alexander Hamilton, Thomas Paine, Roger Williams, James Madison and many others.

George Washington, our first president, did not explicitly comment on the issue at hand, but he did say this about religion in the spirit of the Enlightenment:

> We have abundant reason to rejoice that, in this land, the light and truth of reason has triumphed over the power of bigotry and superstition, and that every person may here worship God according to the dictates of his own heart.[634]

One may quibble about what the gentleman at Mount Vernon meant by many of the words of this statement, but he seems to be against the idea of a state religion and in favor of using reason rather than superstition in religious pursuits in the new United States of America.

John Adams, our second president, was more direct about his view of the matter at hand. He observed:

> The Government of the United States of America is not, in any sense, founded on the Christian Religion.[635]

Adams' friend, Alexander Hamilton, agreed in regard to this issue. Hamilton related:

> In politics as in religion, it is equally absurd to aim at making proselytes by fire and sword. Heresies in either can rarely be cured by persecution.[636]

Hamilton does not speak about separation of church and state; rather, he relates how the two realms are similar and how there are heresies in both realms.

Thomas Paine took a much more direct view of religion, which we might call Neo-Marxist today. He wrote:

> All national institutions of Churches, whether
> Jewish, Christian, or Turkish appear to me to be nothing
> more than human inventions, set up to terrify and enslave
> mankind, and monopolize power and profit.[637]

This remark from his "Common Sense" pamphlet reminds us of the Marxist dictum, "Religion is the opiate of the masses." And "the heart of a heartless world."[638] Marx first employed the expression in German, *Opium des Volkes*, or "Opium of the masses," in 1843 in his *Critique of Hegel's Philosophy of Right*.

In 1774, James Madison, the author of the American Bill of Rights and a Founding Father, stated the following in a letter to his friend, William Bradford:

> If the Church of England had been the established and general religion in all the northern colonies as it has been among us here, and uninterrupted tranquility had prevailed throughout the continent, it is clear to me that slavery and subjection might and will have been gradually insinuated among us. Union of religious sentiments begets a surprising confidence and ecclesiastical establishments tend to great ignorance and corruption., all of which facilitates the execution of mischievous projects.[639]

From this comment, we may make the following conclusions. First, Madison was against the idea of a national church. Second, he was decidedly against the idea of the Church of England as the established church in the colonies. And finally, like Paine, Adams and Hamilton, Madison believed that not all that is associated with religion in America are morally good things.

The founder of the Rhode Island Colony, Roger Williams, used the expression "a hedge or wall of separation" between the "Garden of the Church and the Wilderness of the world." Williams said he did this to keep religion pure. Roger Williams is also credited with helping to shape the church and state debate in Britain and influencing thinkers like John Milton and John Locke on the issue at hand.[640]

This brings us to the third and central section of Appendix G, in which we will describe and discuss what the first great American statesman Benjamin Franklin has said and written about the issue.

Franklin on Church and State Separation

The only place in the speeches and writings of Franklin where he speaks specifically about church and state is in an entry in *Poor Richard's Almanac* where he stated the following:

> The Church, the State, and the Poor, are three daughters which we should maintain, but not portion off.[641]

We presume that Franklin meant that the three realms he identified, church, state and the poor, have no real relationships among the three, and thus, they were to be kept separate from each other. But that still leaves the question of why the great statesman included the "Poor," with the other two realms.

He did a great deal for the poor in his many charitable actions for the city of Philadelphia. He even wrote an essay entitled "On Doing Good to the Poor," in which he boldly proclaimed:

> The best way to help the poor is to make them uncomfortable in their own poverty.[642]

One only thinks about the poor in twenty-first-century America and whether the first great American statesman was prescient and predictive of how the poor will be treated later in American history. In the same essay, Franklin also commented,

> I think the best way of doing good to the poor is not making it easy in their poverty, but leading or driving them out of it.[643]

Franklin also observed that,

> Government welfare programs effectively subsidize poverty and ultimately make things worse.[644]

Nevertheless, most of what we can glean about Franklin's views on the separation of church and state are implied from other things he said and wrote about religion, particularly Christianity. Like Jefferson, for example, he believed that the modern forms of Christianity and the medieval forms ruined the pristine nature of the original Christian faith. He wrote:

> Whoever shall introduce into public affairs the principles of primitive Christianity will change the face of the world.[645]

Or consider Franklin's observation that, "A lighthouse is far more valuable than any church."[646] He also told us that, "The primitive Christians thought that persecutions were extremely wrong in the Pagans, but they practiced it on one another," continuing into the sects of his own time.[647]

In summary, then, most contemporary scholars of Franklin believe that he had a view of the separation of church and state much like that of Thomas Jefferson or Roger Williams, who both spoke of a "wall" or a "hedge" that should separate the two realms.

A statue of Benjamin Franklin, located at Printing House Square, the corner of Park Row and Spruce Street, New York. Courtesy of the Library of Congress.

Appendix H
Franklin and Abortion

> For if a woman is quick with child, and by a potion or otherwise, kills it in her womb or if anyone beat her, whereupon the child dies in her body and she delivers a dead child, this, though not murder, was by the ancient law homicide or manslaughter.
> —Sir William Blackstone, *Commentaries on the Laws of England*

> This ruling took an extreme and dangerous path. It is a sad day for the Court and for the Country as well.
> —President Joe Biden responding to *Dobbs v. Jackson* decision

> Now I am upon Female infirmities. It will not be unreasonable to touch upon a common Complaint among unmarried women, namely the "Suppression of the Courses."
> —Benjamin Franklin, "Suppression of the Courses"

Introduction

The purpose of Appendix H is to do the following things. First, to make some comments on the foundations of American law on general issues related to women's rights and specifically to abortion rights. The legal foundation comes mostly from eighteenth-century British scholar Sir William Blackstone and his *Commentaries on the Laws of England*.[648]

In the second section of this appendix, we will make some general comments about how the American Founding Fathers and American law dealt with the issue of abortion in the seventeenth and eighteenth centuries.

In the third and final section of this appendix, we will make some observations about how the issue of abortion entered into Franklin's life. As we shall see, these tangents on abortion are found in his autobiography and some pseudonymous letters he wrote in his newspaper. Interestingly enough, these comments are attributed to two women, written anonymously by Franklin.

Legal Foundations of American Women's Rights

As indicated above, the major philosophical foundation for American women's rights is the work of Sir William Blackstone, *Commentaries on the Laws of England*. The British jurist, writing about the right to life, wrote the following:

> For if a woman is quick with child, and by a potion or otherwise, kills it in her womb; or if anyone beat her, whereby the child dies in her body, and she delivered a dead child, this though not murder was by the ancient law, homicide or manslaughter. But at present, it is not looked upon in quite so atrocious a light, though it remains a very heinous misdemeanor.[649]

In the same section of his *Commentaries,* Blackstone also explains that a "fetus in the mother's womb" is legally considered "to have been born." Thus, the law considered a quickened fetus to be his or her own person, independent of the mother.[650] In early America, then, any abortion perpetrated after the stirring or "quickening" of the infant in the mother's womb was, at the least, a "heinous misdemeanor."[651]

In fact, early American courts upheld this traditional common law approach in characterizing an abortion as either a "heinous misdemeanor" or murder. From the beginning, laws in American states criminalized abortion. The State of Virginia, for example, outlawed the practice of using a "potion" to unlawfully destroy the child within her [womb] and even classified the practice as "murder."[652] Many of these state laws were crafted by the very same men who wrote the US Constitution.

It seems inconceivable that the framers intended constitutional protection for abortion as a "fundamental right." An examination of early American law reveals that the framers believed just the opposite.

From these seventeenth- and eighteenth-century thinkers, the unborn child had a fundamental "right to life" that would be infringed upon by an abortion that ends the fetus' life.

For the framers in the late eighteenth century, a constitutional right to an abortion would have been seen as a misnomer. It would appear very dishonest to claim that the framers intended to protect abortion under some vague and unwritten "right to privacy" when they had criminalized the practice of abortion. Since 1973 and *Roe v. Wade*, many courts and judges—often on the American Left—have long upheld a legal doctrine at odds with the Constitution, perhaps revealing the rogue nature of the modern judiciary in the United States. The time was ripe for the Supreme Court to correct this error in the recent Supreme Court decision on abortion called *Dobbs v. Jackson*.[653]

In the *Dobbs* case, in June of 2022, the US Supreme Court overturned the 1973 landmark *Roe v. Wade* decision recognizing a woman's constitutional right to an abortion. The *Dobbs* 6 to 3 decision was condemned by President Biden. He said that the ruling took "an extreme and dangerous path. It is a sad day for the Court and for the country, as well."

This brings us to the second section of this appendix on Franklin and abortion, in which we will make some observations about other American Founding Fathers who commented on the abortion issue.

Founding Fathers on Abortion

For the most part, the founding fathers in the eighteenth century took an approach to the abortion issue much like the quickening perspective alluded to earlier in his appendix. James Wilson (1742–1798), for example, a Scottish-born American founding father and legal scholar, jurist and statesman, gave us a clear embodiment of this view when he wrote:

> Human life from its commencement to its close is protected by the Common Law. In the contemplation of the law, life begins when the infant first is able to stir in the womb and by the law is protected.[654]

Wilson suggests, as most of the founding fathers did, that as soon as the mother feels there is life in her womb, that life is protected by the law. Of course, there have been significant technological advancements to know much earlier when there is life in the womb than in Wilson's time. But the point is still the same: As soon as the mother knows there is life in her womb, the life there is protected.

Medical doctor Benjamin Rush (1749–1813), often called the "Father of American Psychiatry," wrote the first systematic book on mental diseases and disorders called *Medical Inquiries and Observations Upon Diseases of the Mind*, published in Philadelphia in 1812.[655]

In a discussion of blood-letting, Dr. Rush maintained that the procedure is a possible treatment for preventing miscarriage during the third month of pregnancy when he thought there was a particular tendency to spontaneous abortion Rush asks the question, "What is an abortion but a haemoptysis?"[656] This is a medical term that refers to the coughing up of blood.

A third American founding father who also took the quickening view about when abortion is no longer permitted was St. George Tucker (1752–1827). A native of Bermuda, lawyer, military officer, and faculty member at the College of William & Mary, he made some observations on abortion, as well. He was a James Madison judicial appointment.

He explained in one of his celebrated legal treatises on American law that abortion "is a great misprision [misdemeanor] to kill a child in its mother's womb."[657] Presumably, Tucker meant after the mother feels the child in its womb for the first time.

Another Founding Father-era thinker who commented on the issue of abortion was English-born printer and emigrant Samuel Keimer (1689–1742). He was also the original owner of the *Pennsylvania Gazette*. On October 2, 1729, Franklin bought the newspaper from Keimer.

Keimer appears many times in Franklin's autobiography. In one of those entries, Franklin refers to an incident in 1729 when his former employer, Samuel Keimer of Philadelphia, published an encyclopedia whose first volume included a detailed article on abortion, including directions for ending an unwanted pregnancy. As Keimer's article explained it:

> We mean immoderate Evacuations, violent motions,
> sudden passions, Frights... violent Purgatives and in
> general anything that tends to promote the Menses.

Franklin responded to the Keimer article on abortion through the satiric voices of two fictional characters, who expressed outrage for exploring the "secrets of our sex which ought to be reserved for the repository of the learned." We will say more about these two fictional female characters at the beginning of the third section of this appendix, which we will discuss next.

Franklin on Abortion

The names of the two female fictional characters who responded to Samuel Keimer's essay on abortion were Celia Shortface and Martha Careful. In the first of these letters from Martha Careful, dated January 24, 1728, she tells Andrew Bradford that she wishes to insert an essay in his newspaper, *The Mercury*, in response to Keimer's article on abortion. She also relates that if she were to meet Keimer on the street, she would "run the Hazard of taking him by the Beard."[658]

On November 27, 1728, Celia Shortface tells Bradford:

> I desire Thee to insert in the next Mercury the following letter
> to Samuel Keimer, for by doing it Thou may perhaps save Keimer
> his Ears, and very much Oblige our Sex in general, but in a more
> Particular manner, thy modest friend. Celia Shortface.[659]

It is not entirely clear why Franklin thought it was prudent to invent these fictions of Celia Shortface and Martha Careful. We do know that by the beginning of 1728, Keimer and Franklin were no longer friendly. It is clear that something piqued the sensibilities of Franklin regarding what Keimer wrote in his essay on abortion, but we cannot be sure about what that thing, or things, was or were.

At any rate, twenty years later, in 1748, Franklin's printing house published a manual titled *The American Instructor or Young Man's Best Companion*, a text that provided all kinds of information and advice on arithmetic, writing and spelling, bookkeeping, and many other topics. The book had first been published in London a few decades earlier.

This 1748 edition published by him and his printing partner, David Hall, was essentially a reprint of the London edition, with some new sections added to the work.[660]

Among the additions was John Tennent's *The Poor Planter's Physician*, employed as a preface to the new edition. This preface related:

> In the British edition of this Book, there were many Things of little or no Use in these parts of the world. In this edition those Things are omitted, and in their Room many other Matters inserted, most immediately useful to us Americans.[661]

The tenth edition of the *American Instructor*, published by Franklin and Hall in 1758, carried nearly the same material as the earlier editions. However, two paragraphs were added to the *The Poor Planter's Physician* preface under the heading "The Suppression of the Courses."

The first and longer of the two paragraphs tells us the following:

> Now I am upon Female Infirmities, it will not be unreasonable to touch upon a common Complaint among unmarried women, namely, the Suppression of the Courses. This don't only disparage their Complexions, but fills them, besides, with sundry Disorders. For this Misfortune, you must purge with Highland Flagg, (commonly called Belly-ach Root) a Week before you expect to be out of Order; and repeat the same 2 Days after: the next Morning, drink a Quarter of a Pint of Pennyroyal Water, or Decoction, with 12 Drops of Spirits of Harts-horn, and as much again at night when you go to Bed. Continue this 9 Days running; and after Resting 3 Days, go on with it for 9 more. Ride out every fair Day, stir nimbly about your Affairs, and breathe as much as possible in the open Air...

The "Suppression of the Courses" may apply to many medical conditions, but the entry refers specifically to "unmarried women." For this "misfortune," it recommends several known abortifacients from that era, such as pennyroyal water and belly-ache root, also known as Angelica. There is substantial evidence that these same substances were used among the ancient Greeks as a way of inducing abortion or to hinder pregnancy.[662]

More recently, *Slate* magazine reprinted the ninth edition of the "Suppression of Courses." The contemporary article also recommends the use of "Hartshorn," which Merriam-Webster relates is "an American pasqueflower." Gregory L. Tilford, in his *Edible and Medicinal Plants of the West*, were employed by Native Americans to induce abortions or hasten the course of childbirth.[663]

The *Slate* article warns people that "taking opiates too often, or Jesuits-Bark must be avoided. Jesuits-Bark was also known as Quinine and was an important anti-Malaria drug and was mistakenly believed to have been an abortifacient."[664]

So, what are we to conclude about Franklin's views on abortion? In his book *Benjamin Franklin: An American Life,* Walter Isaacson suggests that the first great American statesman "manufactured an abortion debate," largely because he wanted to crush his rival and former employer, Samuel Keimer.[665]

Franklin's personal views on abortion are unknown, but we suspect that Walter Isaacson is correct when he wrote that "Benjamin Franklin 'manufactured' the first great abortion debate in the United States of America." And it certainly will not be the last of those controversies.

Stephen Vicchio was educated at the University of Maryland, Yale, Oxford, and Saint Andrews University in Fife, Scotland, where he received his Ph.D. He is the author of forty books that include works in drama, stories, essays, religion, philosophy, and books about the Bible. He retired from full-time teaching after having taught at several universities in the United States, Britain, Syria, Egypt, and Portugal, among other places.

Bibliography

We have divided this bibliography into several parts. These include:

    I. Primary Sources Written by Benjamin Franklin
    II. Secondary Sources on Benjamin Franklin
    III. Historical Sources of the Life of Benjamin Franklin
    IV. Sources from the History of Philosophy
    V. Sources from Literature and Drama
    VI. Legal Documents and Court Cases
    VII. Biblical Sources
    VIII. The Great Awakening Sources
    IX. Statistics and Demographics
    X. Inventions and Discoveries

We will use this rubric in offering the bibliography to follow, beginning with materials written by Benjamin Franklin.

I. Primary Sources Written by Benjamin Franklin

Franklin, Benjamin. *Papers of Benjamin Franklin*. Philadelphia: Madison and Adams Press, 2017. The papers are held by the University of Pennsylvania Library, Manuscript Collection 900, and have been the most helpful of the collection.

———, and Francis Dashwood. New Version of the Anglican Book of Common Prayer. *Papers of Benjamin Franklin* (1782): 510–516.

———, and Francis Dashwood. *The Anglican Book of Common Prayer*. Philadelphia: Franklin Publishing, 1743.

———. "A Defence of the Reverend Hemphill's Observations." *Papers of Benjamin Franklin*, 432–443.

———. "A Dissertation on Liberty and Necessity." *Papers of Benjamin Franklin*.

———. "A Narrative of Great Massacres." *Pennsylvania Gazette*, January 30, 1764.

———. "A Witch Trial at Mount Holly." *Pennsylvania Gazette*, October 22, 1730.

———. "Appeal for the Hospital." *Pennsylvania Gazette*, March 1, 1751.

———. "Dialogue Between Two Presbyterians." *The Complete Works of Benjamin Franklin*, 277–283.

———. "Doctrine to be Preached," National Archives, Founders Online, https://bit.ly/3D3O7jL.

———. "Franklin on George Whitehead." National Humanities Center, The Library of Congress, 1956.

———. "Genesis Fifty-One." *The Ortago Witness*, December 2, 1887.

———. "On the Prices of Corn and the Management of the Poor." *Papers of Benjamin Franklin*. New York: Library of America, 1987, 387–388.

———. "Proposals Relating to the Education of the Youth of Pennsylvania," 1741.

———. "Religious Toleration in Old and New England." *The London Packet*, June 3, 1772.

———. "Self-Denial is Not the Essence of Virtue." *Pennsylvania Gazette*, February 18, 1735.

———. *Articles of Belief*. New York: New York State Printing House, 1966.

———. New Version of the Bible. *Papers of Benjamin Franklin*. 1782,

499–510.

———. *On the Providence of God in the Government of the World* with illustrations by John De Pol. Washington: Kitab Hola, 1967.

———. *Poor Richard's Almanac*. New York: Dover Books, 2013.

———. *The Autobiography of Benjamin Franklin.* Three Volumes. New York: Independent Publishing, 2020.

———. *The Autobiography of Benjamin Franklin: with Related Documents*. Edited by Louis P. Masur. Boston: Bedford Books, 1993.

———. *The Silence Dogood Letters*. Edited by Carl Van Dora. New York: Penguin Books, 1938.

———. *The Way of Wealth*. New York: Applewood Books, 1986.

———. *The Wit and Wisdom of Benjamin Franklin*. New York: Peter Pauper Press, 1998.

Letters

Among the letters of Benjamin Franklin we have used in this study are the following:

Franklin to Josiah Franklin, March 19, 1727.

Franklin to Philadelphia Presbyterian Synod, July 17, 1735.

Franklin to Peter Collinson, May 9, 1753.

Franklin to an English friend, October 21, 1755.

Franklin to Polly Stevenson Henson, August 20, 1757.

Franklin to T. H., December 13, 1757.

Franklin to Lord Kames, February 25, 1767.

Franklin to Jane Mecom, December 28, 1757.

Franklin to John Adams, March 17, 1776.

Franklin to Polly Stevenson Henson, September 8, 1776.

Franklin to French Minister, March 19, 1778.

Franklin to Richard Price, October 9, 1780.

Franklin to Madam Brillon, April 13, 1781.

Franklin to Benjamin Vaughan, November 2, 1789.

Franklin to Ezra Stiles, February 29, 1790.

II. Secondary Sources on Benjamin Franklin

Anderson, Shannon. *The Story of Benjamin Franklin*. Chicago: Rockridge Press, 2020.

Anonymous. "The Founders' Toleration." The Lehrman Institute. https://bit.ly/3Ek9hfV.

Aquinas, Thomas. *Summa Theologica*. First part, question 2.

Aristotle. *Metaphysics*. Book 8, 4–6.

Barry, John. "God, Government, and Roger Williams' Big Idea." *Smithsonian* (January 2012).

Bax, Gavin. *Cultivating Greatness: Building Virtues with Benjamin Franklin's Virtue*. New York: GF Books, 2021.

Behuukkotai, Behar. "A Little Black Mark." https://bit.ly/3YY2ge9.

Bentham, Jeremy. An Introduction to the Principles of Morals and Legislation. New York: Create Space, 2017.

Brands, W. The First American: The Life and Times of Benjamin Franklin. New York: Anchor Books, 2002.

Bunyan, John. Pilgrim's Progress. New York: Dover Books, 2003.

Campbell, James. Recovering Benjamin Franklin. New York: Open Court Press, 1999.

Chavez, Pamela Hernandez. "Benjamin Franklin: Deist or Not?" https://bit.ly/3MJrl77.

Chernow, Ron. Washington: A Life. New York: Penguin Books, 2011.

Cousins, Margaret. Ben Franklin of Old Philadelphia. New York: Random House, 2004.

Craighead, Alexander. *Renewal of the Covenants*. Philadelphia: Franklin Press, 1743.

———. *The Covenant*. Philadelphia: Franklin Press, 1748.

———. *The Solemn League*. Philadelphia: Franklin Press, 1744.

Dallimore, Arnold. *The Biography of George Whitefield*. New York: Crossway Books, 2010.

de Ricci, Scipione. Female Convents: Secrets of Nunneries Exposed. Nabu Press, September 2, 2011.

Euripides. *Euripides Unveiled*. Four Plays by Euripides. New York: Peter Laing, 2008.

Franz, John. "Franklin and the Pennsylvania Germans." *Pennsylvania History* 65, no. 1 (Winter 1987): 21–34.

Gavin, Anthony. Master Key to Popery, 1841.

Gregory, T. Ryan. "The Argument from Design." *Evolution, Education and Outreach* 2 (2009): 602–611.

Hall, Mark David, and Emily Lynn Warren. "The Fiery Patrick Henry." *Law and Liberty*. August 23, 2017. https://bit.ly/3PknboK.

Hamilton, Alexander. *Papers*. Library of Congress, Washington, DC.

———, James Madison and John Jay. *The Federalist Papers* (1788).

Heyman Christine, Leigh. "What is the First Great Awakening?" https://bit.ly/3oONg4D.

Hume, David. *Natural History of Religion*. Edinburgh, 1751. Reprinted by Crate Space in 2015.

———. *The Dialogues Concerning Natural Religion.* Edinburgh, 1776. Reprinted by Hackett Books in 1998.

———. "Of Miracles," in *An Inquiring Concerning Human Understanding.* New York: Hackett Books, 1993.

Isaacson, Walter. "Citizen Ben." *Time* (June 7, 2003).

———. *Benjamin Franklin: An American Life.* New York: Simon and Schuster, 2004.

Kidd, Thomas. *Benjamin Franklin: The Religious Life of a Founding Father.* New Haven: Yale University Press, 2017.

Kleet, Carmella. *Benjamin Franklin: Inventor.* New York: Nomad Books, 2007.

Krull, Kathleen. *Benjamin Franklin: Giant of Science.* New York: Puffin Books, 2014.

Larson, Edward J. *Franklin & Washington.* New York: Custom House, 2021.

Lawson, Robert. *Ben and Me: An Astonishing Life of Benjamin Franklin by His Friend, Mouse Amos.* Boston: Little Brown, 1988.

Mill, John Stuart. *Utilitarianism and Other Essays.* New York: Penguin Books, 1987.

Miller, Brandon Marie. *Benjamin Franklin: American Genius.* Chicago: Chicago Review Press, 2009.

Paine, Thomas. *Common Sense.* Washington: Coventry House Press, 2018.

———. *Age of Reason.* Anne Arbor: Michigan Legal Publishing, 2014.

Paley, William. *Natural Theology.* London, 1802.

Reed, Rebecca Theresa. *Six Months in a Convent.* 1835.

Reeves, Richard. *Infamy: The Shocking Story of Japanese American*

Internment in World War II. New York: Picador Press, 2016.

Rosenstock, Barb. *Ben Franklin's Big Splash*. New York: Calkins Creek Press, 2001.

Rousseau, Jean-Jacques. *The Social Contract*. New York: Hackett Books, 2019.

Rudberg, E. G. "Benjamin Franklin as Scientist." Quoted in his acceptance speech for the Noble Prize for physics in 1956.

Rutland, Robert A., Editor. "George Mason on Religious Freedom." *The Papers of George Mason* 3:1071 and 1119.

Schiff, Stacy. *Great Improvisation: Franklin, France, and the Birth of America*. New York: Holt, 2006.

Tindal, William. *Christianity as Old as Creation*. London: Forgotten Books, 2012.

Trenchard, John and Thomas Gordon. *Cato's Letters*. Edited by Ronald Hamory. Washington: Liberty Fund, 1995.

Vicchio, Stephen J. and Sister Virgina Geiger. "The Origins and Development of Anti-Catholicism in America. *Perspectives on the American Catholic Church*. Westminster: Christian Classics, 1989, 84–183.

———. *Muslim Slaves in the Chesapeake: 1634 to 1865*. Minneapolis: Wisdom Editions, 2019.

Viret, Pierre. *The Christian and the Magistrate*. London: Psalm 78 Ministries, 2015.

Wood, Gordon. *The Americanization of Benjamin Franklin*. New York: Penguin Books, 2005.

Whitefield, George. *A Travelogue of the Voyages of George Whitefield*. Philadelphia: Franklin Press, 1740.

———. *Sermons*. Philadelphia: Franklin Press, 1746.

III. Historical Sources of the Life of Benjamin Franklin

In this study we have made use of materials related to several key events in the life of Benjamin Franklin. These events and their years are the following:

    The Franklin residence, 17 Milk Street, Boston. (Early eighteenth century)
    Franklin was born. (January 1706)
    Attends the Boys Latin School in Boston. (1715–1716)
    Begins to read Plutarch, Defoe and Cotton Mather. (1717)
    Starts apprenticeship with Brother James. (1718)
    Attends George Brownell English School. (1716–1717)
    Becomes a vegetarian and a "thorough deist." (1721)
    Writes the first Silence Dogood letter. (1722)
    Publishes the first pamphlet in London. (1725)
    Establishes the Junto Club. (1727)
    Has an affair resulting in the birth of his son William. (1728)
    Buys the *Pennsylvania Gazette*. (1729)
    Marries Deborah in a common law marriage. (1730)
    Lodges with John Read's family. (1730)
    Joins the Mason Lodge. (1731)
    Establishes the Library Company. (1731)
    Publishes the first edition of *Poor Richard's Almanack*. (1732)
    Is elected Grand Master of Masonic Lodge. (1734)
    Organizes fire department of Philadelphia. (1736)
    Appointed Postmaster. (1737)
    George Whitefield comes to Philadelphia to visit Franklin. (1739)
    Organizes the Pennsylvania Academy. (1749) Later becomes University of Pennsylvania.
    Establishes Pennsylvania Hospital. (1751)
    Establishes insurance against loss by fire. (1756)
    Establishes printing offices in five American cities. (1757)
    Paves the streets of Philadelphia. (1757)

Receives Honorary Degree from Oxford University. (1762)
Starts the American Philosophical Society. (1769)
Begins his autobiography. (1771)
Deborah Franklin dies. (1774)
Signs the Declaration of Independence. (July 1776)
Elected President of Pennsylvania Abolition Society. (1789)
Franklin's anti-slavery treatise. (February 3, 1790)
Franklin died. (April 17, 1790)

IV. Sources from the History of Philosophy

Plato. "The Euthyphro." *The Dialogues of Plato in Five Volumes*. New York: Hackett Books, 2002.

Aristotle. *Nicomachean Ethics*. New York: Create Space, 2016.

Cicero. *Tusculan Disputations*. London: Kessinger Books, 2010.

Thomas Aquinas. *Summa Theologica*. Part One, questions 2 to 27. Billings: Coyote Canyon Press, 2018.

Bayle, Pierre. *Historical and Critical Dictionary*. New York: Hackett, 1991.

Buchanan, George. *Antislavery Treatise*. Cincinnati: Cincinnati Literary Club, 1878. This text was originally written in 1572.

Calvin, John. *Institutes of the Christian Religion*. New York: Create Space, 2017.

Doddridge, Philip. *The Rise and Progress of Religion in the Soul*. New York: Palala Press, 2015.

Butler, Joseph. *The Analogy of Religion*. New York: Palala Press, 2016.

Locke, John. *A Letter Concerning Toleration*. New York: Hackett Books, 1983.

Mather, Cotton. *Essays to Do Good*. London: Forgotten Books, 2018.

Paley, William. *Natural Religion*. New York: Independent Press, 2019.

Voltaire. *Treatise on Toleration*. New York: Penguin Books, 2017.

_____. *Toleration and Other Essays*. New York: Penguin Books, 1998.

Hume, David. *Dialogues Concerning Natural Religion*. New York: Hackett Books, 1998.

_____. The Natural History of Religion. New York: Create Space, 2015.

Kant, Immanuel. Lectures on Ethics. New York: Hackett Books, 1980.

Bentham, Jeremy. An Introduction to the Principles of Morals and Legislation. New York: Create Space, 2017.

Mill, John Stuart. Utilitarianism. New York: Independent Publishing, 2020.

V. Sources from Literature and Drama

Addison, Joseph. *Cato: A Tragedy*. Washington: Liberty Fund, 2004.

John Bunyan. *Pilgrim's Progress*. New York: Dover Books, 2003.

Dostoevsky, Fyodor. *The Brothers Karamazov*. New York: Penguin Books, 2003.

Lawrence, D. H. "Benjamin Franklin on Virtue and Moral Perfection." Biblioklept, https://bit.ly/3Z1Mhfb.

Sewall, Samuel. *The Selling of Joseph*. Jerusalem: Gehenna Press, 1966.

Legal Documents and Court Cases

    Corporation Act, 1661
    Scottish Test Act, 1681

Test Act of 1673
The Sugar and Molasses Act, 1733 (British)
Pennsylvania act to Forbid the Importation of Convicts, 1749
The Sugar Act, 1764 (British)
The Treaty of Paris, 1783
Reynolds v. United States, 1878
Employment Division v. Smith, 1990
Rosenberg v. Rector and Visitors of the Univ. of VA, 1995
Cakeshop v. Colorado Civil Rights Commission, 2017
The Stamp Act, 1765 (British)
Declaration of Independence, 1776
The Constitution of the United States, 1776
Asiatic Barred Zone Act, 1917
Yasamashiti v. US, 1922
Ozawa v. US, 1922
Bhagat Singh Thind v. US, 1923
Treaty of Amity and Commerce, 1778
Treaty of Alliance, February 6, 1778

Biblical Sources

In this study we have used the following editions of the Biblical text:

The King James Version (KJV)
The Revised Standard Version. (RSV)
The New International Version, (NIV)
The New Revised Standard Version. (NRSV)
The New Testament. Philadelphia: Franklin Press, 1740. This is the Baskett Bible.
The Holy Bible. Cambridge: Cambridge University Press, 1763. Franklin family Bible.
Franklin's New Version of the Bible. 1743.
Franklin's Bible Hoaxes: Genesis 51 and Hezekiah 6:1

We have also quoted the following Bible passages in this study:

> 2 Corinthians 5:14
> 2Peter 1:3
> Book of Daniel 4:27
> Book of Job 1:6–11
> Deuteronomy 15:7 and 8
> Deuteronomy 27:23
> Exodus 4 and 5
> Judges 4 and 5
> Mark 12:30 and 31
> Matthew 11:16 and 17
> Philippians 4:8
> Proverbs 11:3
> Proverbs 14:21
> Proverbs 19:1
> Proverbs 22:22 and 23
> Proverbs 8:18
> Psalm 106:34–36
> Psalm 127:1
> Psalm 8:3–5
> Psalm 82:1
> Psalm 94:8

We have also consulted the Al-Qur'an. Edited by Ahmed Ali. Princeton: Princeton University Press, 1993, for its translation of Surah 13:11 of the Muslim Holy Book.

The Great Awakening Sources

Dallimore, Arnold. *George Whitefield*. New York: Crossways Books, 2010.

Franklin published Whitefield's *Travelogue* in his printshop in 1740 and his *Sermons* in 1746. Franklin also published an anonymous work on the Great Awakening, most likely written by George Whitefield in 1741.

Franklin wrote an article in 1739 about the first time he saw George Whitefield. Franklin discussing the same scene in Part Two of *The Autobiography of Benjamin Franklin*, 99–101. The statesman also discusses Whitefield's note that Franklin's hospitality in his Philadelphia home was for "Christ's sake."

Heyman, Christine Leigh. "What is the First Great Awakening?" Docest, https://docest.com/the-first-great-awakening.

Kidd, Thomas. *The Great Awakening*. New York: St. Martin's Press, 2007.

Lambert, Frank. *The Great Awakening*. Princeton: Princeton University Press,1999.

Mather, Cotton. *Essays to do Good*. London: Forgotten Books, 2018. Another manifestation of the Great Awakening in the study, as were Jonathan Edwards and Alexander Craighead.

Severance, Diane. "The Second Great Awakening: Its Story and Impact." Christianity, https://bit.ly/3PnABAh.

Tracy, John. *The Great Awakening*. New York: Independent Publishing, 2019.

Statistics and Demographics

Population statistics for Colonial America and other demographics, The Growth of the Colonies. Course Hero, https://bit.ly/3N94bbt.

Alexander, John. "The Philadelphia Numbers Game," *Pennsylvania Magazine of History and Biography*. Vol. 108, 1974, 314–324, https://bit.ly/3Z3zZTF.

Smith, Billy G. "Death and Life in a Colonial Immigrant City: A Demographic Analysis of Philadelphia." The *Journal of Economic History*. Vol. 37, no. 4, December 1976.

Inventions and Discoveries

    Invents swim fins for hands (1717)
    Organizes environmental protest (1739)
    Franklin Stove (1741)
    Designs catheter (1752)
    Conducts experiments on electrical charges (1752)
    Invented glass armonica (1762)
    Established postal routes to colonies (1762)
    Invented faylight savings time (1782)
    Invented bifocals (1785)

Other Inventions and Discoveries

    The Odometer
    The Longarm
    Mapping the Gulf Stream
    Streetlamps
    Street sweeping machines

Endnotes

1 The Boys Latin School of Boston opened its doors to students in April of 1635. Harvard College was established six months later, in 1636. Yet, Harvard calls itself "The oldest school in America."
2 Benjamin Franklin, *The Autobiography of Benjamin Franklin* (New York: Independent Publishing, 2020), 1:17.
3 The George Brownell English School was established by George Brownell (1702–1779). He began his school in 1716 with his father's financial help. Brownell was only fifteen years old. Benjamin Franklin attended the school as one of its first students. He was only a student there for one year, and he left in 1716 when the statesman was ten years old. This was the second of Franklin's only two years of formal schooling.
4 The edition of the Mrs. Silence Dogood letters used in this study is Carl Van Doran, *Benjamin Franklin* (New York: Penguin Books, 1938). There are fourteen Mrs. Dogood letters, all written when Franklin was sixteen years old.
5 Ibid., 27.
6 Samuel Keimer (1689–1742) was an emigrant printer for whom Benjamin Franklin worked for a short while. John Read was where the statesman took in lodging during that time. Later, in 1730, Franklin married Read's daughter Deborah (1708–1774). John and Sarah Read were Quakers. John Read was a moderately prosperous builder and carpenter. Deborah Read and Benjamin Franklin met in October of 1723 after the statesman moved to Philadelphia. Franklin lodged with the Reads in that same year. They married seven years later.
7 The Philadelphia population statistics come from John K. Alexander, "The Philadelphia Numbers Game," *Pennsylvania Magazine of History and Biography*, 108 (1974): 314–324.
8 Franklin, *Autobiography*, 33.
9 Benjamin Franklin bought the *Pennsylvania Gazette* with his partner, Hugh Meredith, on October 2, 1729. Franklin's final edition of the paper was on

March 9, 1754. After that, he retired from business.

10 The Junto Club was established in the Fall of 1727. The original club had twelve founding members. The Junto Club was also known as the "Leather Apron Club," for many of its members wore leather aprons or working-class attire on their jobs. Franklin was only twenty-one years old when he organized the Junto Club.

11 Benjamin Franklin was initiated into the Masons in the February meeting of 1731. He died in April of 1790, making him a Mason for sixty years. Many of the most prominent citizens of Philadelphia were also Masons in Franklin's day, including Franklin William Bradford, Henry Price, J. E. Burnett, and M. W. Melvin. These men were also some of the first officers of the Saint John's Lodge in Philadelphia that began in 1730.

12 What is now known as the Library Company of Philadelphia was begun by Benjamin Franklin in 1731. It was the first subscription library in the United States. Later it became a free public library as it is today.

13 The American Philosophical Society was founded in Philadelphia in 1743 by Benjamin Franklin and his friends. Franklin was thirty-seven years old at the time. The society is still at its original location at 104 South Fifth Street. It is dedicated to the advancement of the sciences and humanities.

14 The Pennsylvania Hospital was established in 1751 by Dr. Thomas Bond and Benjamin Franklin when the statesman was forty-nine years old. The main building was erected in 1756. Today, it is a 550-bed teaching hospital.

15 The Philadelphia Contribution for Insurance Against Loss by Fire was established in 1752 by Benjamin Franklin. The first Philadelphia Fire Department was also formed in the same year.

16 Franklin set up printing shops in five American cities, including Boston, New Haven, Wilmington, Baltimore, and Washington.

17 The Stamp Act of 1765 was the first internal tax levied against the American colonies by the British Parliament. It required that many American documents had to have a certain stamp or imprint in order to be legal documents. Franklin and his followers were staunchly against the Stamp Act, mainly because colonists saw it as an added tax.

18 Ibid.

19 Benjamin Franklin was on a committee to form the Declaration of Independence in June of 1776. After writing the Declaration by the committee, it was passed on July 2, 1776, and ratified on July 4, 1776, when Benjamin Franklin signed it.

20 The Treaty of Paris was signed on September 3, 1783, by representatives

from the United States and Canada, as well as asking George II of Great Britain. Among other things, it officially ended the American Revolutionary War. It also established other treaties between Great Britain and France, Spain, and the Dutch Republic, which still had interests in North America.

21 Benjamin Franklin's anti-slavery treatise of 1789 was first formulated on November 9, 1789, ratified by the Senate on February 3, 1790, and signed by the statesman on that day. It was Franklin's last public act, even though Franklin owned two male slaves named George and King for many years. Earlier in his life, Benjamin Franklin was one of the founders of the Pennsylvania Abolition Society, so his stand against slavery was long held by the first great American statesman.

22 Benjamin Franklin's parents, as well as his wife, Deborah, are buried in the Christ Church Burial Ground in Philadelphia. The graves of Josiah and Abiah Franklin has a large obelisk.

23 The edition of the "Articles of Belief and Acts of Religion" used in this study was initially printed in 1728 and reprinted by New York State on the occasion of Franklin's 260th birthday in 1966.

24 Ibid.

25 Ibid.

26 Ibid.

27 Ibid.

28 Carl Van Doren, *Benjamin Franklin* (New York: Viking Press, 1938), 31.

29 Ibid.

30 Ibid., 34.

31 "Articles of Belief," 66.

32 Benjamin Franklin, *On the Providence of God in the Government of the World*, with illustrations by John DePol (Islamabad: Kitab Hola, 1967). This work contains Benjamin Franklin's version of the "Argument from Design," which he learned from British philosopher William Paley.

33 "Self-Denial is not the Essence of Virtue" was originally published by Franklin on February 18, 1735. It can now be found in the *Papers of Benjamin Franklin*, published by the Madison and Adams Press in 2017.

34 "Dialogue Between Two Presbyterians" was originally published in the *Pennsylvania Gazette* by Benjamin Franklin on April 10, 1735. It was one of two works that he wrote in the defense of Rev. Hemphill.

35 Franklin called his autobiography a "memoir" on its title page of the first edition initially published in 1791. Interestingly enough, the first edition was in French and not in English.

36 Franklin, *Autobiography*, 59.
37 Ibid., 62.
38 Ibid., Part Three, 111.
39 Franklin, *Autobiography*, 121.
40 Ibid.
41 Ibid, Part One, 27.
42 John Bunyan, *Pilgrim's Progress* (New York: Dover Books, 2003).
43 Franklin, *Autobiography*, 1:69.
44 Ibid., 72–73.
45 Benjamin Franklin, "A Dissertation on Liberty and Necessity" in *Complete Works of Benjamin Franklin*, 499. Franklin was very much in favor of the idea of human free will, while at the same time against the idea of determinism.
46 Franklin, *Autobiography*, 1:70–71.
47 For more on the Argument from Design, see T. Ryan Gregory, "The Argument from Design: A Guided Tour of William Paley's *Natural Theology* (1802)" in *Evolution: Education and Outreach* 2 (2009): 602–611.
48 The Argument from Design was also one of Thomas Aquinas' *Quinque Viae*, or "Five Ways" for God's existence, in his *Summa Theologica* in the first part, question 2, where it is the fifth of Thomas' five arguments. The Argument can also be found even earlier among the Greeks in Aristotle's *Metaphysics*, for example, at VIII, 4 to 6.
49 The group of Presbyterian ministers bent on destroying the career of the Rev. Samuel Hemphill was led by one Rev. Jedediah Andrews (1674–1747). The Rev. Andrews was the first minister of the First Congregationalist Church in Philadelphia. The Philadelphia Presbyterian Synod, during the Rev. Hemphill affair, had six members. Franklin's essay was written originally as a letter addressed to the synod.
50 Benjamin Franklin, "A Defence of the Reverend Hemphill's Observations," October 30, 1735. This essay was significant for several reasons. One of those was that the case showed a great example of religious intolerance on the part of the Philadelphia Presbyterian Synod. Secondly, it allowed the statesman to show his knowledge and use of the Bible. He quoted scripture in the essay eight separate times. And thirdly, it allowed Franklin to get a handle on the nature of his own religious beliefs when the statesman was only twenty-nine years old.
51 Thomas Kidd, *Benjamin Franklin: The Religious Life of a Founding Father* (New Haven: Yale University Press, 2017), 2–3.

52 Phillis Wheatly (1753–1784) was born in the Gambia in northwest Africa and brought to Boston in 1761 on a slave ship. She was enslaved in Boston and became the first known African American female poet in America.
53 The Cedar Meeting House was the first location for the congregation of the Old South Church. It was also on the corner of Milk Street and Washington Street.
54 In general, both the Congregationalists of Franklin's mother and the Presbyterians of his father were Calvinists in their theologies.
55 Kidd, 6–7.
56 For more on the Calvinist acronym T-U-L-I-P, see Rev. Barry Gritten, "Tulip, Or the Five Points of Calvinism," https://bit.ly/3ovIDbR.
57 Philip Doddridge, *The Rise and Progress of Religion in the Soul* (New York: Palala Press, 2015).
58 Kidd, 27–28.
59 Isaac Newton, *Principia Mathematica* (Los Angeles: University of California Press, 2016), 900–963.
60 William Paley, *Natural Theology* (New York: Independent Press, 2019).
61 The Baron d'Holbach (1723–1789) was a French-German philosopher and encyclopedist during the Enlightenment.
62 Francois-Marie Arouet, better known as Voltaire (1694–1778), French writer, philosopher and friend of Benjamin Franklin, is best known for his 1758 novel *Candide*. Franklin and Voltaire met only once, in April of 1778. There is a letter in the Franklin papers from Voltaire dated February 21, 1778, two months before the two actually met.
63 Franklin, *Autobiography*, 1:37.
64 Benjamin Franklin, "Articles of Belief" (New York: New York State Printing Office, 1966). This edition was in honor of the 260th birthday of Benjamin Franklin.
65 Ibid., 31.
66 Franklin, *Autobiography*, 1:42.
67 Benjamin Franklin, "Doctrine to be Preached," https://bit.ly/3D3O7jL.
68 Franklin, *On the Providence of God in the Government of the World*.
69 Joseph Butler (1692–1752) was an English-Irish Bishop, philosopher, Christian apologist and theologian.
70 Franklin had several French lady admirers, including Madame Brillon, Madame Helvétius, the Countess d'Houdetot, and the Duchess de la Rochefoucauld. Some of these "friendships" made it difficult at times for Benjamin Franklin to keep his vow of temperance in his quest for "moral

perfection," as we shall see in Chapter Six of this study. Franklin's great fondness for beer was another impediment to the same virtue.

71 Fyodor Dostoevsky (1821–1881) made this observation in his 1880 novel *The Brothers Karamazov*.
72 Franklin to Jane Mecom, December 28, 1757.
73 Franklin, *Autobiography*, 1:44.
74 Kidd, 49.
75 Franklin, *Autobiography*, 53–55.
76 Ibid.
77 Ibid.
78 This view that the moral views of Jesus and the Church had somehow been corrupted was a common one among many of the Founding Fathers besides Franklin and Thomas Jefferson.
79 Benjamin Franklin to Polly Stevenson Henson, August 20, 1757. Franklin also discussed Jesus with Polly in a letter to her on September 8, 1776.
80 Ibid., September 8, 1776.
81 Ibid.
82 Kidd, 166–167.
83 Ibid.
84 Kidd, 25.
85 Franklin to Ezra Stiles, March 9, 1790.
86 Christ Church in Philadelphia remains an Episcopal congregation to this day.
87 John Bunyan, *Pilgrim's Progress* (New York: Dover Books, 2003). It was originally published in 1678 and originally entitled *The Pilgrim's Progress from the World*.
88 See Notes 70, 71, and 72.
89 J. H. to Benjamin Franklin, December 2, 1757. Benjamin Franklin to J. H., December 13, 1757.
90 George Whitefield (1714–1770) was an Anglican clergyman and preacher and was friends with Benjamin Franklin for many years. Franklin gave a stellar review of Whitefield in an article from 1739, but later they had a more contentious relationship; one might even say combative at points.
91 See Note 79.
92 Ibid. Franklin and Hewson also had many conversations about God, Jesus and the devil over the years, going all the way back to 1757.
93 Franklin speaks of this comment about "for Christ's sake" in the 1739 article that the statesman wrote about the preacher. It is also discussed in Franklin's autobiography, Part Two, 99–101. The National Humanities Center also

published a version of the Franklin essay on Whitefield. When Franklin saw Whitefield for the first time, the statesman remarked, "It seems the whole world has grown religious."

94 Thomas Aquinas made the distinction between Natural Truth and Revealed Truth in his *Summa Theologica*, Part One, questions 2 to 27. For more on the distinction, see James Brent's article on "Natural Theology," published in the *Internet Encyclopedia of Philosophy*, https://iep.utm.edu/theo-nat/. This same distinction between Natural and Revealed Truths has persisted from the time of Thomas Aquinas until the present day in thinkers like Norman Plantinga.

95 Aquinas, *Summa Theologica*, Part One, questions 6 and 7.

96 Franklin, *Autobiography*, 1:26.

97 Franklin began the Pennsylvania Hospital in 1751 along with Dr. Thomas Bond. It was established to "care for the sick, poor, and the insane who were wandering the streets of Philadelphia." Today, it is a 660-bed teaching hospital.

98 Benjamin Franklin mentions the "Rules for Good Living," developed by the Philadelphia Presbyterian Church in his autobiography in vol. 1, p. 39. There were five of these rules: 1. Keep holy the Sabbath Day, 2. Be diligent in reading the Holy Scriptures, 3. Attend daily Public Worship, 4. Partake in the Sacrament, and 5. Pay due Respect to God's Ministers. Franklin added the following comment after listing these rules of the Presbyterians, "These might all be good things, but as they were not the kind of good things that I expected from the Text, I despaired of ever meeting with them from any other, was disgusted, and attended his preaching no more." Thus, Franklin explained some of his reasoning for eschewing organized religious services.

99 Ibid., 40.

100 Ibid.

101 "Franklin and Jefferson on the National Seal," discussed in Jonathan Mullinix, "Rejected Designs for the Great Seal of the United States," https://bit.ly/3D48ldb.

102 Ibid.

103 Ibid., letter number 9.

104 Mullinix, 11.

105 Ibid.

106 Ibid.

107 Ibid.

108 Benjamin Franklin, *New Version of the Bible* (1782), Book of Job 1:6–11. Although Franklin called this a "New" version of the Bible, he only selected a

few passages to be rewritten in a more "modern" style.
109 Ibid.
110 Ibid.
111 Ibid.
112 Ibid.
113 Ibid.
114 Ibid.
115 Deuteronomy 27:23 (RSV).
116 Benjamin Franklin and Francis Dashwood, *New Version of the Anglican Book of Common Prayer*, p. 9. The original version of the Book of Common Prayer was distributed in 1549 during the reign of King Edward VI in the English Reformation after their split with the Roman Church.
117 Prudence Steiner, "Benjamin Franklin's Biblical Hoaxes," *Journal of the American Philosophical Society* 131, no. 2 (June 1987): 183–196.
118 Ibid., 188–190.
119 Ibid., 191.
120 Pennsylvania Constitutional Convention, September 28, 1776.
121 Ibid.
122 Ibid.
123 Ibid.
124 George Whitefield, *A Travelogue of the Voyages of George Whitefield* (Philadelphia: Franklin Press, 1740).
125 *The New Testament* (Philadelphia: Franklin Press, 1740). This is a reprint of a text published in London by the T. Baskett Company in 1729.
126 Benjamin Franklin, *An Inventory of Books in Stock*, (Philadelphia: Benjamin Franklin Printing Company). His printing company was on Market Street.
127 Benjamin Franklin, *Poor Richard's Improved* (Philadelphia: Franklin Printing Company, 1766).
128 Hezekiah 6:1 was another apocryphal Bible passage constructed by Benjamin Franklin. The text of Hezekiah 6:1 is, "God helps those who help themselves."
129 This version of Franklin's Genesis 51 comes from the *Ortago Wirness* from December 2, 1887, which is related to a website called *Papers Passed*, maintained by the National Library of New Zealand.
130 Ibid.
131 Ibid.
132 Ibid.
133 See Note 129.

134 Ibid. Another Bible hoax can be found in Franklin's autobiography. It involved a man who wanted to purchase an axe from a smithy whom he told he wanted the axe to be bright at the edge. The blacksmith agreed to give him a bright axe if the man would turn the grinding wheel. He agreed, and after a while, he wanted to examine the axe, but it was not quite as bright as he wanted. So he kept turning the wheel, and again, after a while, he told the smithy that he would take it the way it was. But the blacksmith said no, "We should press on, as it is now we only have a speckled axe." But the man said, "I think I like the speckled axe best." In this episode in his autobiography, on page 41 of Part One, Franklin discusses his quest to achieve "Moral Perfection," which we will discuss in Chapter Six. Franklin likens the color of the axe to morel character and the owner's quest to achieve "brightness." After a while, however, the man gives up the idea of finding perfection in the same way that Franklin speaks of falling short many times in his quest to be morally perfect. We say more about the "Speckled Axe" in Chapter Six of this study.

135 *The Holy Bible* (Cambridge: Cambridge University Press, 1763).

136 Baskerville was the name of the London publisher of the Franklin family Bible.

137 Sarah Franklin Bache (1743–1808) was the daughter of Benjamin and Deborah Franklin. She was active in relief work during the Revolutionary War and later in the women's suffrage movement.

138 Deborah Franklin Bache (1781–1863) was the daughter of Richard and Sarah Bache. She, too, was involved in war relief work, as well as suffrage work, for most of her life.

139 Franklin, *Autobiography*, 3:119.

140 Psalm 8:3 to 5 (RSV).

141 Kidd, 160.

142 Psalm 94:8 (NIV).

143 Psalm 106:34 to 36, quoted by Franklin in his *Autobiography*, 3:121–122.

144 Psalm 127:1 (NIV).

145 Deuteronomy 15:7 and 8 (NIV).

146 Psalm 82:3 and 4 (NIV).

147 Proverbs 14:21 (NIV).

148 Proverbs 22:22 and 23 (NIV).

149 *Euripides Unveiled* in *Grief Lessons: Four Plays by Euripides* (New York: Peter Laing, 2008).

150 The Holy Qur'an 13:11 (author's translation). *Poor Richard's Almanack*,

February 19, 1736.
151 Book of Judges 5:27.
152 Franklin to John Adams, March 17, 1776.
153 Gospel of John 10:34 (NIV).
154 Franklin, *Autobiography*, 3:29.
155 Ibid., 32.
156 Ibid., 40–42.
157 Franklin, "A Defence of the Reverend Hemphill's Observations," 7.
158 Ibid.
159 Titus 1:13 (NIV).
160 First Timothy 1:4 (NIV).
161 Franklin, "A Defence of the Reverend Hemphill's Observations," 8.
162 Ibid.
163 Ibid.
164 Benjamin Franklin, *The Autobiography of Benjamin Franklin: with Related Documents* (Boston: Bedford Books, 1993), 45.
165 Herbert of Cherbury's *De Veritate* was originally published in 1633. In 2010, EEBO Editions re-released the work.
166 John Locke's *Essay Concerning Human Understanding* was originally published in London in 1690. Penguin books published a recent version in New York in 1998.
167 Anthony, the Earl of Shaftesbury, (1671–1713), was an English politician and philosophical thinker.
168 Pierre Viret, *The Christian and the Magistrate* (London: Psalm 78 Ministries, 2015). This is the title that Viret's book is now known by.
169 This scene is described by Pamela Hernandez Chavez in her essay, "Benjamin Franklin: deist or Not?" https://bit.ly/3MJrl77.
170 Matthew Tindal, *Christianity as Old as Creation* (London: Forgotten Books, 2012).
171 David Hume, *Natural History of Religion* (New York: Create Space 2015).
172 David Hume, *The Dialogues Concerning Natural Religion* (New York: Hackett Books, 1998).
173 Ibid., 19.
174 See Notes 175 and 176.
175 Pierre Bayle (1647–1700); Swiss-born Jean-Jacques Rousseau (1712–1778); Charles Montesquieu (1689–1755); and Maximilian Robespierre (1758–1794), the great leader of the French Revolution.
176 Thomas Paine, *The Religion of deism Compared With the Christian Religion*

177 David Hume, "Of Miracles," in *An Inquiry Concerning Human Understanding* (New York: Hackett Books, 1993).
178 Franklin, *Autobiography*, 1:27–28.
179 Franklin, "Articles of Belief," 20.
180 Franklin, "On the Providence of God in the Government of the World," https://bit.ly/3JQlewT.
181 Ibid.
182 See, for example, *Poor Richard's Almanack*, June 19, 1759, where Franklin still seems to be leaning in the direction of deistic beliefs.
183 The Greek expression *Deus Absconditis* or the "Hidden God" was used by many Christian theologians, particularly in the Reformation Period, including Nicolaus of Cusa, Blaise Pascal, John Calvin, and Martin Luther, who treats the idea extensively in his Latin work *De Servo Arbitrio*, published in 1525.
184 Ezra Stiles to Benjamin Franklin, February 29, 1790, and Benjamin Franklin to Ezra Stiles, March 9, 1790.
185 Isaac Newton, *Principia Mathematica* (Los Angeles: University of California Press, 2016), particularly 900–963, where he discusses the watch analogy.
186 Jean Jacques Rousseau, *The Social Contract* (New York: Hackett Books, 2019).
187 In the eighteenth century, European philosophy was divided between the Rationalists and the Empiricists. The former were mostly in France and Germany with thinkers like Descartes and Leibniz, while the Empiricists were generally British, like figures like John Locke and David Hume. The biggest difference between the two groups was that the Rationalists thought that all knowledge comes from the use of the mind, and the Empiricists believed knowledge comes from the application of the senses.
188 The Leather Apron Club was also called the Junto Club. It was established by twelve Philadelphia businessmen in 1727 when Benjamin Franklin was only twenty-one years old.
189 Classical republicanism is also sometimes known as civic republicanism. The idea was originally developed by Aristotle and Cicero, revived in the Renaissance, and then again in the eighteenth century with the French and American Revolutions.
190 Franklin, *Autobiography*, 2:59–65.
191 James Madison on the Constitutional Convention. In the "James Madison Papers," several pieces concern the Federal Constitutional Convention of 1787. One piece from the summer of 1787 documents Madison's participation

in the convention and his recommendation about the Constitution and its content.

192 Edmund Burke (1729–1782) was an Anglo-Irish statesman and philosopher. He served as a member of Parliament from 1766 until 1772.

193 George Buchanan (1506–1582) was a Scottish historian and humanist, and one of the leaders, along with John Knox, of the Scottish Revolution.

194 Franklin met David Hume in the spring of 1775. Later, after touring Edinburgh with the philosopher, Hume sent him a letter telling him that "America has sent us many things… but none more valuable than you."

195 John Locke's *A Letter Concerning Toleration* was originally published in Latin in London in 1689. Some say that Locke was concerned about Catholicism taking over England in the wake of the discovery of the Rye House Plot and King Charles II's persecutions of the Whig Party. E. G. Rudberg as the physicist, quoted in this account about Franklin as a scientist.

196 E. G. Rudberg, physicist, quoted in this account about Franklin as a scientist.

197 The Academy of Pennsylvania started in 1743 after Benjamin Franklin had just retired from business. The statesman was only thirty-six years old at the time. Later, the Academy, of course, would become the University of Pennsylvania.

198 Christine Leigh Heyman, "What is the First Great Awakening?" https://bit.ly/3OP5Qo3.

199 Ibid.

200 Diane Severance, "What was the Great Awakening?" https://bit.ly/3OT62CS.

201 Ibid.

202 Franklin, *Autobiography*, 3:200.

203 Ibid.

204 The George Whitefield statue is located in the dormitory quadrangle standing in front of the Morris and Bodine wings of the Ware College House. The bronze statue was created by R. Tait McKenzie and was unveiled in 1919.

205 Franklin's Philadelphia print company published Whitefield's *Travelogue* in 1740 and his *Sermons* in 1746.

206 The *Benjamin Franklin Papers* contains the lengthy correspondence between Benjamin Franklin and Rev. George Whitefield. The correspondence reveals that the two great men were not always on good terms with each other.

207 See the article in the *Pennsylvania Gazette* from November 8, 1739.

208 Ibid.

209 In many London papers in the 1730s and early 1740s, the Rev. Whitefield advertised his services, offering lectures, sermons and "enlightening

theological musings."
210 Arnold Dallimore, *The Biography of George Whitefield* (New York: Crossway Publishers, 2010), 177.
211 *Autobiography*, 3:301–302.
212 Ibid., Part One, 33.
213 Ibid.
214 Ibid.
215 Ibid.
216 Cotton Mather, *Essays to Do Good* (London: Forgotten Books, 2018).
217 See the Bibliography for these citations.
218 Cotton Mather is still considered one of the greatest churchmen to ever preach in America, along with Jonathan Edwards and George Whitefield from Benjamin Franklin's generation.
219 *Bonifacius* was the original Latin title of Mather's *Essays to Do Good*.
220 Franklin, *Autobiography*, 3:57–59.
221 See Note 166.
222 Samuel Sewall, *The Selling of Joseph* (Jerusalem: Gehenna Press, 1966).
223 Samuel Sewall (1757–1814) was an American lawyer, judge and congressman. In 1814, Fort Sewall in Marblehead, Massachusetts, was renamed after him.
224 Judge Sewall was also active in the Massachusetts Abolition Society, particularly while he was the chief judge of the Massachusetts Supreme Court.
225 Addison's play first premiered in London on April 14, 1713, in what was then called the Globe Theatre.
226 "Give me liberty or give me death" can be found in the first act, scene one, of Addison's drama.
227 Kidd, 23–24.
228 John Trenchard and Thomas Gordon, *Cato's Letters*, ed. Ronald Hamory (Washington: Liberty Fund, 1995).
229 Ibid., 113.
230 Ibid., 191.
231 Ibid., 191–192.
232 These statistics come from an article entitled "The Growth of the Colonies," https://bit.ly/3N94bbt.
233 Ibid.
234 Ibid.
235 Benjamin Franklin proposed that a prayer be said by a local clergyman to

begin the Continental Congress on June 28, 1787. The proposal was soundly defeated the following day after being tabled on June 27.

236   James Madison, "Comments on the Continental Congress in the *James Madison Papers*, which are held by the Library of Congress.

237   The Congregation Mikveh Israel traces its beginnings to 1740 when Franklin and many others donated money to its being built. The synagogue still exists in the Old City Historic District adjacent to Independence Hall in Philadelphia. It is among the oldest synagogues in America.

238   In different places in the American colonies during the seventeenth and eighteenth centuries, many suggestions were made to bar both Jews and Catholics from American citizenship. This phenomenon continued in Franklin's day, and the issue of "religious tests" sometimes came to the fore. We say more about religious tests in Chapter Nine of this study.

239   Franklin left a note among his *Papers* regarding his funeral arrangements. The note said simply, "The bearers of my coffin shall be religious leaders of all the sects of Philadelphia."

240   "A Witch Trial at Mount Holly" was published in the *Pennsylvania Gazette* on October 22, 1730. Franklin parodies the Massachusetts Bay Colony witch trials in the piece by putting the so-called witches on a scale with the Great Bible on the other side to see which was heavier. Franklin's parody also has the witches bound and thrown in a river to see if they float. If not, they were witches. Similarly, if the Bible weighed more than the suspected witch, then she was fine. If not, she was to be punished, perhaps with her life.

241   Ibid.

242   Ibid.

243   This incident occurred in Lancaster, Pennsylvania, in December of 1763, when a group of frontiersmen murdered twenty Conestoga Native Americans. Days later, the same group killed six adults and eight more Native American children. The settlers became known as the "Paxton Boys." Benjamin Franklin was appalled by their behavior. Franklin's account of this episode was called "A Narrative of the Late Massacres," *Pennsylvania Gazette*, January 30, 1764.

244   Ibid.

245   Ibid.

246   Ibid.

247   Ibid.

248   Ibid.

249   Ibid.

250 Ibid.
251 We have taken this quote by Adams about Franklin being too chummy with the Catholics from the anonymous article called "The Founder's Toleration," https://bit.ly/3qnm39J.
252 Stacy Schiff, *A Great Improvisation: Franklin, France, and the Birth of America* (New York: Holt, 2006), 171.
253 Ibid.
254 Ibid.
255 Most of these men were either Congregationalist or Presbyterian ministers with whom Franklin was familiar.
256 Alexander Craighead (1705–1760) was an Irish-born preacher from Donegal County. He emigrated with his father to North America and served Presbyterian churches, mostly in North Carolina. For more on Roger Williams and religious tolerations, see John M. Barry's essay, "God, Government and Roger Williams' Big Idea," *Smithsonian*, January 2012.
257 Roger Williams, "The Bloudy Tenent of Persecution for the Cause of Conscience or A Plea for Religious Liberty" on Ending Enforced Uniformity of Religion, http://bit.ly/3Q2ucLI.
258 The term "Freedom of Conscience" was used by the Founding Fathers in the final decades of the eighteenth century. For more on the use of the phrase, see Thomas Kidd, "The American Founding: Understanding the Connection Between Religious and Civil Liberties," *Religious Freedom Institute*, June 14, 2016.
259 The First Amendment to the US Constitution.
260 Reynolds v. United States (1878).
261 This is the normal Supreme Court interpretation of the "Right to Practice."
262 The question of contraceptives, within the context of the Affordable Care Act, became an issue in the Trump Administration when in January 2019, the Trump Administration filed a petition asking the Supreme Court to review an ongoing legal tussle over the Affordable Care Act contraception coverage requirement.
263 James Madison, "Religious Toleration," *Madison Papers*, 7:131, Library of Congress.
264 John Locke, *Letter on Toleration* (New York: Penguin Books, 1998).
265 Voltaire preferred the term "Intolerance" with respect to questions about expressing religious rights, see his *Toleration and Other Essays* (New York: Create Space, 2017).
266 Ron Chernow, *Washington: A Life* (New York: Penguin Books, 2011). 132.

267 Kenneth G. Davis, "America's True History of Religious Tolerance," *Smithsonian*, October 2010.

268 For George Mason's views on religious liberties, see *The Papers of George Mason*, Robert A. Rutland, ed. (Chapel Hill: UNC Press, 1970), 3:1071 and 1119.

269 Ibid., 1071.

270 For more on Patrick Henry's views on religious liberties, see Mark David Hall and Emily-Lynn Warren, "The Fiery Patrick Henry," in *Law & Liberty*, August 23, 2017, https://lawliberty.org/the-fiery-patrick-henry/.

271 This expression comes from William Penn, the founder of the Pennsylvania Colony. See "Holy Experiment" quoted in *Befriend the Past*, January 25, 2020.

272 Franklin, *Autobiography*, 3:66.

273 Benjamin Franklin, "Religious Tolerance in Old and New England," *The London Packet*, June 3, 1772.

274 Ibid.

275 Ibid.

276 Ibid.

277 Ibid.

278 Ibid.

279 Franklin, *Autobiography*, 1:100–101.

280 Ibid., 101.

281 Franklin, *Autobiography*, 1:49.

282 Ibid.

283 See article by Billy G. Smith in Bibliography.

284 Franklin, *Autobiography*, 1:49.

285 Ibid., 50.

286 Immanuel Kant, *Lectures on Ethics* (New York: Hackett Books, 1980). Kant calls his moral theory the "Categorical Imperative," that is, "act only according to that maxim through which you can at the same time will that it become a universal law."

287 In the history of philosophy, Divine Command Theory was first discussed by Plato in his dialogue called "The Euthyphro." The view was held by Augustine of Hippo, Thomas Aquinas, and, it appears, Benjamin Franklin, as well, at times in his life.

288 Aristotle, *Nicomachean Ethics* (New York: Create Space, 2016).

289 Franklin, *Autobiography*, 1:64.

290 Ibid.

291 Ibid.
292 Ibid.
293 Ibid., 53–54.
294 Thomas S. Kidd, *Benjamin Franklin: The Religious Life of a Founding Father* (New Haven: Yale University Press, 2017), 19–20.
295 Although Franklin only mentions Chapter Three of Proverbs as a source of his view of virtue, there are many other passages in the book as well where the writer of Proverbs mentions "Virtue," such as 8:18, 11:3, and 19:1, for example. Other New Testament passages that also speak of virtue include Philippians 4:8 and 2Peter 1:3.
296 Cicero, *Tusculan Disputations* (London: Kessinger Books, 2010).
297 Joseph Addison, *Cato: A Tragedy* (Washington: Liberty Fund, 2004).
298 Franklin, "Articles of Belief," 22.
299 Ibid., 23.
300 Ibid., 23–24.
301 Kidd, 39.
302 Aristotle, 17.
303 Franklin, *Autobiography*, 1:31.
304 Aristotle, 53.
305 Ibid., 49.
306 Ibid., 9.
307 Franklin, "Articles of Belief," 25.
308 Franklin, *Autobiography*, 1:33–34.
309 Addison, Act I, scene 1.
310 Ibid., Act I, scene 2.
311 Ibid., Act III, scene 5.
312 Ibid., Act II, scene 2.
313 Ibid., Act III, scene 6.
314 Aristotle, 63.
315 Franklin, *Autobiography*, 1:34–35.
316 Ibid., 35.
317 Ibid.
318 Ibid., 36.
319 D. H. Lawrence, "Studies in Classic American Literature," ch. 2, https://bit.ly/3Y4iX7i.
320 Ibid. Max Weber (1864–1920) was another critic of Franklin's views on moral perfection, although Weber believed that Franklin was the "Personification" of his "Spirit of Capitalism."

321 Franklin, *Autobiography*, 1:36.
322 Ibid.
323 Ibid., 36–37.
324 Ibid., 37.
325 We mean here the 1781 and 1790 letters to Madame Brillon and President Ezra Stiles of what was then called Yale College.
326 Mrs. Silence Dogood, Letter 14.
327 Franklin, *Autobiography*, 1:40–41.
328 Ibid., 41.
329 Ibid.
330 These are all taken from all three volumes of the *Autobiography*.
331 Benjamin Franklin died at his home in Philadelphia on April 17, 1790. His physician and servants were present. Deborah had died several years before, in 1774.
332 Franklin, "A Defence of the Reverend Hemphill's Observations," 12.
333 Franklin, *Autobiography*.
334 Ibid. Franklin made this very prescient comment about himself at the end of Part Three of the *Autobiography*.
335 Ibid., 1:43.
336 Ibid., 44.
337 Ibid., 45.
338 Ibid., 47.
339 Ibid., 48.
340 Ibid.
341 Ibid., 50.
342 Ibid.
343 Ibid., 3:29.
344 Ibid., 1:55.
345 Ibid.
346 Franklin discussed this idea of Moral Perfection in his autobiography, 2:131–132.
347 Mendel Leflin, *Cheshbon ha-Nefesh* (New York: Feldheim Publishers, 1996).
348 Shai Afsai, "Benjamin Franklin's Influence on Mussar," *Review of Rabbinic Judaism* 20.2 (September 2019): 228–276.
349 Shai Afsai, *Franklin and the Art of Virtue* (New York: Acorn Publishing, 1996).
350 Gordon S. Wood, *The Americanization of Benjamin Franklin* (New York: Penguin, 2005), 39.

351　Norman Fiering, *Jonathan Edwards' Moral Thought and Its British Context* (Chapel Hill: University of North Carolina Press, 1981), 100.
352　Wood, 42.
353　Leflin, 43.
354　Ibid.
355　Ibid., 44.
356　Nancy Sinkoff, "Benjamin Franklin in Jewish Eastern Europe: Cultural Appropriation in the Age of the Enlightenment," https://bit.ly/3Yi0LHp.
357　Ibid.
358　Ibid.
359　Franklin contributed to the Mikveh Israel building fund in 1740 and again in 1788 when the synagogue congregation "was floundering."
360　Manuel Josephson (1729–1796) was one of the most scholarly of the Mikveh Israel Congregation. He had the best collection of rabbinic texts in all of Philadelphia.
361　John Adams, *The Papers of John Adams*, 6:141, Massachusetts Historical Society, Boston.
362　Franklin, *Autobiography*, 1:193–194.
363　Ibid., 194.
364　Ibid.
365　Ibid.
366　The Quebec Act of 1774 formally provided for religious freedom in the Province of Quebec, Canada.
367　Harvard was founded by Puritans, Yale by Congregationalists, the College of New Jersey (Princeton) by Presbyterians, and William & Mary by the Anglican Church.
368　James Campbell, *Recovering Benjamin Franklin* (New York: Open Court Press, 1999), 55–56.
369　Ibid., 56.
370　Benjamin Franklin met Father John Carroll in the spring of 1776 when the two traveled to Quebec for diplomatic purposes.
371　John Carrol finally became the Bishop of Baltimore and the Dean of the American Catholic Church in 1789. He served as bishop and archbishop until his death in 1815.
372　John Gilmary Shea, *The Life and Times of Bishop John Carroll* (Washington: Franklin Press, 2018), 313.
373　Ibid.
374　Ibid.

375 Elizabeth Seton established the first Catholic girl's school in America in Emmitsburg, Maryland, in 1809. It is now called the Mother Elizabeth Seton School.
376 Church of Saint Anselm and Saint Cecilia still exists in London, next to the Holborn Tube Station. It began in 1727.
377 Thomas Kidd, *Benjamin Franklin: The Religious Life of a Founding Father* (New Haven: Yale University Press, 2019), 47–48.
378 Ibid., 48.
379 Ibid.
380 Ibid.
381 Franklin, *Autobiography*, 3:111–112.
382 Ibid., 112.
383 Benjamin Franklin to Polly Hewson, March 8, 1762.
384 See, for example, 1:27–28, 2:147–150, and 3: 229–235 of Franklin's autobiography.
385 For more on Sambo Anderson, see Stephen J. Vicchio, *Muslim Slaves in the Chesapeake, 1634 to 1865* (Minneapolis: Calumet Editions), 387–391.
386 Ibid., 6–7.
387 Ibid., 296–302.
388 Ibid., 297.
389 Ibid., 298.
390 Ibid.
391 Ibid.
392 Ibid., 42–43.
393 Ibid., 19–25.
394 Ibid., 42–43.
395 Ibid., 31–32.
396 Ibid., 284–285.
397 Franklin, *Autobiography*, 2:111–112. Whitefield arrived in Philadelphia for the first time on June 17, 1739.
398 For more on Jefferson and Adams' versions of Al-Qur'an, see Stephen Vicchio, *Jefferson's Religion* (Eugene: Wipf and Stock, 2007).
399 Ellison was sworn in on Jefferson's Qur'an on January 5, 2007.
400 Cotton Mather quoted in "Muslim Americans Find Their Voice Amid The Shouts," *National Public Radio*, September 5, 2010.
401 Ibid.
402 Michael Gomez, *Black Crescent* (Cambridge: Cambridge University Press, 2005).

403 Ludovico Marracci, *Latin Translation of Al-Qur'an* (Berlin: Harrassowitz Verlag, 2016).
404 James Lyon, *The True Nature of Imposture Fully Displayed in the Life of Mohamet*. John Adams to Thomas Jefferson, September 24, 1821.
405 Robert Allison, *The Crescent Observed* (Chicago: University of Chicago Press, 2000), 53.
406 In Classical Arabic, *Iftar* is the meal in which Muslims end their daily fast during Ramadan.
407 Voltaire, *Mahomet* (London: Wilder Publications, 2018).
408 Edward Gibbon, *The Decline and Fall of the Roman Empire* (New York: Penguin Books, 2001).
409 Charles-Louis Montesquieu, *The Spirit of Laws* (New York: Prometheus Books, 2002).
410 Benjamin Franklin, "A Narrative on a Great Massacres," January 30, 1764.
411 Ibid.
412 Benjamin Franklin to Polly Hewson, March 8, 1762.
413 Benjamin Franklin to Peter Collinson, May 9, 1753.
414 Ibid.
415 Henry Muhlenberg (1711–1787), born in Germany, became the father of the American Lutheran Church.
416 Muhlenberg quoted by Franklin in "Observations Concerning the Increase of Mankind, Peopling of Countries, etc."
417 Pennsylvania Assembly Bill to "Forbid the Importation of Convicts" (1749).
418 Benjamin Franklin, "Convicts and Rattlesnakes," *Pennsylvania Gazette*, May 9, 1751.
419 John Jay said, "A wall of brass around the Country to protect from Alien invaders," presumably referring to Roman Catholics.
420 The Alien Act of 1798, passed during the John Adams Administration, was one of four acts that were collectively known as the Alien and Sedition Acts designed to "curtail the excesses of the unrestricted press."
421 The Anti-Coolie Act was passed by the United States on February 9, 1862, to respond to the increase in Chinese immigration to the United States.
422 The Burlingame-Seward Treaty of 1868 was an extension of the Tianjin Treaty of 1858 between China and the US regarding Chinese immigration to the US. The Burlingame-Seward Treaty set quotas for the number of Chinese coming to the US.
423 The Asiatic Barred Zone Act of 1917 continued the quotas on Chinese immigrants and also required an English literacy test.

424 The American Ku Klux Klan was formed in America in 1865. By 1870, there were members of the KKK in every southern state.
425 One of the provisions of the Alien and Sedition Acts was to extend the residency requirement for aliens from five years to fourteen years.
426 *The Papers of Alexander Hamilton*, 4:212, Library of Congress, Washington, DC.
427 Ibid., 213–214.
428 Thomas Jefferson quoted in Madison Brown, "Thomas Jefferson and Things German," https://bit.ly/3Ykm4YY.
429 Ibid.
430 Ibid.
431 This execution of four Quakers occurred in Boston on October 27, 1659. The leader was a woman named Mary Dyer.
432 These arrests in Virginia of Baptists began in the spring of 1699 when the first Baptists came to the Virginia Colony.
433 See the Rhode Island Constitution of 1787. This was later replaced in 1842.
434 These Papist inspectors were appointed in the Georgia Colony beginning in 1732.
435 Antoinette Sutto, *Loyal Protestants and Dangerous Papists* (Charlottesville: University of Virginia Press, 2016), 200.
436 Stephen J. Vicchio and Sister Virgina Geiger, "The Origins and Development of Anti-Catholicism in America, *Perspectives on the American Catholic Church* (Westminster: Christian Classics, 1989), 84–103.
437 Ibid., 88.
438 Ibid.
439 Ibid., 87.
440 Ibid.
441 Ibid.
442 Ibid., 89.
443 Ibid., 92.
444 Ibid., 93.
445 Ibid., 90–92.
446 Ibid., 90.
447 Franklin, *Autobiography*, 2:73.
448 Takao Ozawa v. United States (1922); Takuji Yamashita v. Hinkle (1922).
449 Thind v. United States (1923).
450 For more on Mexican repatriation, see "America's Forgotten History of Mexican-American Repatriation," *National Public Radio*, September 10,

2015.
451 Balderrama quoted in Ibid.
452 For more on the Japanese internment camps, see Richard Reeves, *Infamy: The Shocking Story of Japanese-American Internment in World War II* (New York: Picador Press, 2016).
453 Ibid., 13.
454 *Gallop Poll on Attitudes Toward Immigration*, 1965 to 2016.
455 Ibid.
456 Ibid.
457 Several other German cities and towns followed in Pennsylvania in the first half of the eighteenth century.
458 For more on immigration statistics of Philadelphia in the eighteenth century, see Billy G. Smith's "Death and Life in a Colonial Immigrant City: A Demographic Analysis of Philadelphia," *The Journal of Economic History* 37, no. 4 (December 1977).
459 Franklin, "Observations."
460 Michael Welfare is discussed in John Frantz, "Franklin and the Pennsylvania Germans," *Pennsylvania History* 65, no 1 (Winter 19987): 21–34.
461 Gilbert Tennent, *The Doctrine of Christianity as Held by the People Called Quakers* (New York: Gale Sabin American, 2012).
462 Members of the Moravian Brethren fled Saxony in 1722 and several members came at that time to Philadelphia, where Franklin published the *Moravian Catechism*. For more on Franklin and the Moravians, see "Benjamin Franklin and the Moravians," in *This Month in Moravian History* (May 2006).
463 John Knox (1514–1572) was a Scottish minister, theologian, writer and leader of the Scottish Reformation. He was also the founder of the Presbyterian Church of Scotland. After attending St. Andrews University, he worked as a notary. He was later influenced by early church reformers such as George Wishart. In 1546, John Knox first embraced the Protestant Reformation after returning from exile in France.
464 For the Scottish Test Act of 1681, see: Hugh Chisholm, "Test acts," in *Encyclopedia Britannica* (Cambridge: Cambridge University Press, 1911), vol. 26, 665–666.
465 Ibid.
466 Ibid., 665.
467 Ibid.
468 Ibid., 666.

469 Ibid.
470 "Test and Corporation Act of 1661," Spartacus Educational, https://spartacus-educational.com/Ltest.htm.
471 Ibid.
472 Ibid.
473 Chisholm, 666.
474 The "Five Popish Lords" were five Jesuits: Thomas Whitebread, William Barrow, John Fenwick, John Gavan and Anthony Turner. They were tried for conspiracy, found guilty and executed in 1679. See J. P. Kenyon, *The Popish Plot* (Phoenix: Phoenix Press, 2000), 158.
475 Ibid.
476 The Exclusion Crisis of 1679 to 1681 sought to exclude the king's brother, a Catholic, from serving on the throne of England. See Kenyon, 2–3.
477 Ibid.
478 Vicchio and Geiger, 84–103.
479 This wording comes from comments made by the Massachusetts Delegation at the Continental Convention in 1787.
480 "The Debate Over Religious Tests," Center for the Study of the American Constitution, https://bit.ly/47tkzvx.
481 James Madison to Edmund Pendelton, October 28, 1787.
482 "The Debate Over Religious Tests."
483 For Adams' view, see *Massachusetts Centinel*, November 10, 1787.
484 "The Debate Over Religious Tests."
485 John Jay, quoted in Jonathan Den Hartog, "Religion, the Federalists, and American Nationalism," https://bit.ly/45rs8B5.
486 "Benjamin Franklin: In His Own Words," Library of Congress, https://bit.ly/3sb67lI.
487 Ibid.
488 Roger Sherman (1721–1793) represented the state of Connecticut at the Continental Congress in 1787. For more on Sherman, see "Roger Sherman Statue," Architect of the Capitol, https://bit.ly/3DU3XzJ.
489 This outline has been adapted from Benjamin Franklin, *The Autobiography of Benjamin Franklin* (New York: Dover Books, 1990).
490 The edition of the Silence Dogood letters used for this chapter is Carl Van Doren, *Benjamin Franklin* (New York: Penguin Books, 1938).
491 This edition of Franklin's *Articles of Belief* was originally printed in 1728 and reprinted by New York State on the occasion of Franklin's 260th birthday in 1966.

492 "Self-Denial is not the Essence of Virtue" was originally published on February 18, 1735. It can now be found in the *Papers of Benjamin Franklin*, published by the Madison and Adams Press in 2017. This is the *Complete Works of Benjamin Franklin*.

493 Benjamin Franklin, "Dialogue Between Two Presbyterians," *Complete Works of Benjamin Franklin*, 277–273.

494 Franklin's letters to Madame Brillon are located at the University of Pennsylvania, *Benjamin Franklin's Papers*, Manuscript Collection 900.

495 Ibid.

496 Franklin, "A Defence of the Reverend Hemphill's Observations," *Papers of Benjamin Franklin* 1:432.

497 Jane Franklin Mecom (1712–1794) was the youngest of Benjamin Franklin's sisters and siblings and one of his most trusted confidants, particularly about religious matters. Jane Mecom, if alive today, would be called an "Evangelical."

498 John Bunyan, *Pilgrim's Progress* (New York: Dover Books, 2003); Philip Doddridge, *The Rise and Progress of the Religion of the Soul* (New York: Palala Press, 2015).

499 Isaac Newton, *Principia Mathematica* (Los Angeles: University of California Press, 2016), 900–963.

500 William Paley, *Natural Theology* (New York: Independent Press, 2019).

501 See Note 495.

502 The letter to Franklin's atheist friend, T. H., was written on December 13, 1757. It is in the *Complete Works of Benjamin Franklin*, 353.

503 Michael W. Austin, "Divine Command Theory," *Internet Encyclopedia of Philosophy*, https://iep.utm.edu/divine-command-theory/.

504 Franklin, *Autobiography*, 119–122.

505 Benjamin Franklin to Polly Hewson, January 27, 1783.

506 This quotation about a Bible in every home was taken from the *Congressional Record* 48, no. 95, July 15, 2001.

507 See the Bibliography for these citations.

508 Van Doren, 43.

509 In two of his letters, Benjamin Franklin quoted the Book of Daniel 4:27 regarding the poor.

510 Benjamin Franklin, "On the Prices of Corn and the Management of the Poor," *Writings* (New York: Library of America, 1987), 387–388.

511 The citations are all in the notes of the *Defense*.

512 Herbert of Cherbury (1583–1648) was a seventeenth-century deist. His views

can be seen in his *De religione gentilium*. Pierre Viret (1511–1571) was a Swiss Reform theologian and later a deist.

513   Thomas Paine, "Of the Religion of Deism," is in the first part of *Age of Reason*, published in 1794. An edition was published in Detroit by Michigan Legal Publishing Ltd. in 2014.

514   For more on the Franklin-Whitefield relationship, see Randy Peterson, *The Printer and the Preacher* (Nashville: Thomas Nelson, 2015).

515   Franklin, *Autobiography*, 45–47.

516   Ibid., 46.

517   These citations are all in the Bibliography.

518   These statistics were taken from www.lumenlearning.com.

519   Franklin gave three pounds to the building fund of the Mikveh Israel Synagogue in Philadelphia on April 30, 1788, two years before the statesman's death.

520   The Christ Church burial grounds in Philadelphia, where the Franklin family members are buried, is on 5th and Arch Streets. The cemetery was established in 1719. There are now 4,000 church members interred there.

521   For more on the Establishment Clause, see Michael McConnel and Marci Hamilton, "The Establishment Clause," https://bit.ly/3OVBorR.

522   Jefferson's "Virginia Bill to Establish Religious Freedom" was first proposed in the Virginia Legislature on January 16, 1786.

523   Benjamin Franklin, "Religious Tolerance in Old and New England," *The London Packet*, June 3, 1772. It can also be found in the *Collected Works* 1:668.

524   For more on Franklin and religious tests, see the interview with Professor John DiIulio with the Pew Research Center, on May 23, 2005. The discussion was moderated by Michael Cromartie and was responded to by William Rasberry, a columnist for the *Washington Post*.

525   At certain times of his life, Benjamin Franklin believed that if God did not exist, then there would be no standard for moral goodness.

526   Joseph Addison, *Cato: A Tragedy* (Washington: Liberty Fund, 2004).

527   We have in mind here Franklin's response to the massacre of Native Americans by colonists and the exchange between the Swiss missionary and Native Americans in the Delaware Colony discussed earlier in this study.

528   See Note 524.

529   Franklin, "A Defence of the Reverend Hemphill's Observations," 11.

530   The Classical Greek term *Eudaimonia* was first used by Aristotle to designate "human flourishing." In more recent times, it has meant "human happiness,"

the sum total of the moral virtues for the Greek philosopher.
531   Benjamin Franklin, "On True Happiness," in *On True Happiness and Other Essays* (Philadelphia: Typophiles monographs, 1958).
532   Aristotle, *Nicomachean Ethics*, trans. Robert Bartlett and Susan D. Collins (Chicago: University of Chicago Press, 2012), bk. 1, sec. 1–7.
533   Franklin, *On True Happiness*, 7–9.
534   Augustine of Hippo, "The City of God," vol. 2, bk. 11, chap. 9, in *Nicene and Post-Nicene Fathers*, ed. Philip Schaff. The idea of evil as a privation of the good can also be seen in the first of Plotinus' *The Enneads* and the works of thirteenth-century Italian philosopher Thomas Aquinas.
535   Utilitarianism is the nineteenth-century theory of ethics championed by Jeremy Bentham and John Stuart Mill that says the moral good is "producing the most pleasure or happiness for the most number of people."
536   Franklin, "On True Happiness," 10–11.
537   Plato's metaphor of the chariot and two horses can be found in his *The Republic*, bk. 4, sec. 1–4.
538   Sigmund Freud, *Introductory Lectures in Psychoanalysis*, ed. James Strachey (London: Liveright, 1989), particularly lectures 18–27.
539   Franklin, "On True Happiness," 21–23.
540   Aristotle, *Nicomachean Ethics*, bk. 3, *Ethics with Aristotle*, ed. S. Brodie (Oxford: Oxford University Press, 1991).
541   Franklin, *Autobiography* (New York: Digireads, 2016).
542   Ibid., 71.
543   Ibid., 72–73.
544   Ibid., 73.
545   This line from the *Declaration of Independence* was written by Thomas Jefferson and then circulated in a committee of the Continental Congress, of which Franklin was a member.
546   Thomas Kidd, "The Complicated Religious Life of Ben Franklin," *Baylor Magazine*, Fall 2017. Professor Kidd (1971-) of Baylor University is an expert on American colonial history. See his classic *American Colonial History* (New Haven: Yale University Press, 2023).
547   For more on Anne Louise Brillon de Jouy (1744–1824), who was a lady friend of Franklin, as well as a musician and composer, see Christine de Pas, *Madame Brillon de Jouy et son salon: Une musicienne des Lumieres, intime de Benjamin Franklin* (Paris: Editions du Petit Page, 2014); and Rebecca Cypress, *Women and Musical Salons in the Enlightenment* (Chicago and London: University of Chicago Press, 2022). Madame Brillon is also featured

as a character in the 1939 children's book *Ben and Me* by Robert Lawson about Franklin's time in Paris. She does not appear, however, in the Disney 1953 Academy Award-nominated animated short film adapted from the book.

548 The two main sources for the information in this appendix are the anonymous article entitled "Fact Sheet: Benjamin Franklin's Inventions," Visit Philadelphia, https://bit.ly/3OYLjNw; and Benjamin Franklin, *The Autobiography of Benjamin Franklin*, ed. J. A. Leo Lemay (New York: Library of America, 2005).

549 Ibid., https://bit.ly/3OYLjNw.

550 Franklin, *Autobiography*, 225.

551 Ibid.

552 Ibid., 226.

553 Ibid., 227.

554 Ibid., 228.

555 Rich Goyetter, "Historic Glass Armonica," MFA Collection, https://bit.ly/45bDU36.

556 Visit Philadelphia, https://bit.ly/3OYLjNw.

557 Jacqueline Ruttimann, "Better Bifocals on the Horizon," *Nature*, April 3, 2006.

558 James Ferguson, "Three-Wheeled Clock," The Friends of Franklin, https://bit.ly/45sjKSF.

559 Visit Philadelphia, https://bit.ly/3OYLjNw.

560 Ibid and Franklin, *Autobiography*, 53.

561 Visit Philadelphia, https://bit.ly/3OYLjNw.

562 Ibid.

563 Ibid.

564 Franklin, *Autobiography*, 250–251.

565 For more on the Boston smallpox outbreak of 1721, see Benjamin Colman, *A narrative of the method and success of inoculation*, Houghton Library, Harvard University.

566 Franklin, *Autobiography*, 390–392.

567 Visit Philadelphia, https://bit.ly/3OYLjNw.

568 Ibid.

569 For more on Franklin and barometric pressure, see "Barometric Pressure Protocol," In *Globe* (2014), 1–6. https://bit.ly/45gDisW.

570 Eddie Hyatt, *The Faith and Vision of Benjamin Franklin* (Hyatt Press, 2016), 44.

571 Ibid, 40.

572 Paul makes this distinction at 2 Corinthians 3:6. In the process, he also quotes Psalm 119:97.
573 Benjamin Franklin, "A Proposal Relating to the Education of Youth in Pennsylvania," October 10, 1749. The proposal appeared in a letter to Whitefield on the same day.
574 Benjamin Franklin, *The Autobiography of Benjamin Franklin* (New York: Henry Holt, 1916), 78–80.
575 Sir Isaac Newton, *The Principia* (Los Angeles: University of California Press, 2016).
576 The expression *Deus Absconditis* (latin for "hidden God"), refers to the Christian theological concept of the fundamental unknowability of the essence of God. The source of the expression is usually attributed to the prophet Isaiah 45:15 that reveals, "Truly, you are a God who hides himself, O God of Israel, the Savior."
577 Lord Edward Herbert of Cherbury's (1583–1648) *De Veritate*, or "On Truth," was published in Paris in 1624. He later expanded the text in his *De Causis Errorum*, or "The Causes of Errors," published in 1645.
578 Ibid., 19.
579 David Holmes, *The Faiths of the Founding Fathers* (Oxford: Oxford University Press, 2006), 11–13.
580 Ibid.
581 Ethan Allen, *Reason, The Only Oracle of Man* (New York: Kindle Editions, 2011).
582 See, for example, Frank Edward Manel, "Deism," *Encyclopedia Britannica* (May 23, 2023).
583 Thomas Paine, *The Age of Reason* (Detroit: Michigan Legal Publishing, 2014).
584 Ibid., 140–145.
585 Ibid., 140.
586 Ibid., 141–142.
587 Ibid., 142.
588 Ibid., 143.
589 Ibid., 145.
590 Ibid.
591 James V. Schall, "The God of the Founding Fathers: Nature's God," *Crisis* 19, no. 3, March 2001, 34.
592 Thomas Jefferson to William Short, October 31, 1819. Also see Stephen Vicchio, *Jefferson's Religion* (Eugene: Wipf and Stock Publishing, 2007), 130

and 134–135.
593   Vicchio, 134–135.
594   Thomas Jefferson, *Notes on the State of Virginia* (Gale Ecco Books, 2018).
595   Vicchio, *Jefferson's Religion*, 97–115.
596   What Thomas Jefferson pasted back together can be found in Vicchio, 121–144.
597   Franklin, *Autobiography*. See Vicchio, 55–65.
598   Benjamin Franklin quoted at the Constitutional Congress on September 17, 1787. See "Closing Speech at the Constitutional Convention," *National Constitution Center*, Philadelphia, Pennsylvania.
599   As we have shown, in both the correspondence written back to madame Brillon and President Ezra Stiles of Yale, the first great American statesman provided a catalog of his religious beliefs late in life that, perhaps ironically, look very much like his mother's Congregationalist beliefs and his father's Presbyterianism. In this sense, his theology went full circle from traditional monotheism, through deism for a time, and then finally settling back on his original beliefs about God, the Church, immortality and other fundamental Christian beliefs.
600   *The Papers of Benjamin Franklin* (New Haven: Yale University Press), 21:363, 408, and 437, www.yale.edu/franklinpapers.
601   "Treaty of Alliance with France," *National Archives* (February 6, 1778).
602   *The Papers of Benjamin Franklin*, 29:750ff.
603   Ibid., 18:7.
604   Ibid., 7:206.
605   Ibid., 21:550.
606   Ibid., 552.
607   Ibid., 27:lxv.
608   Harvey Sicherman, "Benjamin Franklin and the Tradition of American Diplomacy," *Orbis* 55, no. 3 (2011): 399.
609   Ibid., 400.
610   Ibid., 402–403.
611   Ibid., 406.
612   Keith Lohnes, "Battle of Saratoga," *Encyclopedia Britannica*.
613   Walter Isaacson, *Benjamin Franklin: An American Life* (New York: Simon and Schuster, 2004), 316.
614   Ibid.
615   John McCrary, "Chess and Benjamin Franklin," https://bit.ly/3YKVjgl.
616   Isaacson, 317–318.

617 Ibid., 318.
618 Ibid.
619 McCrary.
620 Isaacson, 319.
621 Ibid.
622 Ibid., 320.
623 Ibid.
624 Anonymous, "Franklin's Gambit," *American History Magazine*, June 2022.
625 Everson v. Board of Education, 330 US 1 (1947). The Supreme Court ruled as constitutional a New Jersey law allocating taxpayer money for children bused to religious school because it did not breach the "wall of separation."
626 Engel v. Vitale, 370 US 421 (1962). The Supreme Court ruled that it is unconstitutional for state officials to compose an official school prayer and encourage its recitation in public schools due to violating the First Amendment.
627 Judd W. Patton, "The Wall of Separation Between Church and State," Fee, November 1, 1995, https://bit.ly/44oXDuG.
628 Ibid.
629 Austin Cline, "Why Religions Should Support Themselves," Learn Religions, May 24, 2018, https://bit.ly/3KUGcvf.
630 "Student Bible Clubs & Religious Uses of School Facilities," *American Center for Law and Justice*, ACLJ commenting on *Westside Board of Education v. Mergens* 496 US 266 (1990), https://bit.ly/45EAg1h.
631 Ibid.
632 "Gorsuch and Kavanaugh Seem Ready to Send 'Lemon Test' to History's Dustbin," Law (April 25, 2022), https://bit.ly/3QPveea.
633 Kennedy v. Bremerton School District, 597 U.S. ___ (2022) reversed.
634 Rebecca R. Bibbs, "Founders spoke out on church/state," *The Herald Bulletin*, July 22, 2017, https://bit.ly/45sZgcs.
635 Ibid.
636 Ibid.
637 Ibid.
638 Karl Marx, *Critique of 'Hegel's Philosophy of Right'* (Cambridge: Cambridge University Press, 1977), 199–200.
639 Irving Brant, "Madison on the Separation of Church and State," *The William and Mary Quarterly* 8, no. 1 (January 1951), 3–24.
640 Roger Williams, quoted in Alan J. Reinach, "The Two Tables of Law," in *Liberty* (May/June 2005).

641 Benjamin Franklin, "Church and State," *Poor Richard's Almanac* (New York: Barnes and Noble, 2004), 108.
642 Steve Straub, "Benjamin Franklin, Best Way of Doing Good to the Poor is not Making Them Easy in Poverty," July 3, 2012, https://bit.ly/45K0WOr.
643 Ibid.
644 Ibid.
645 Franklin, *Autobiography*, 333.
646 Ibid., 191.
647 Ibid.
648 *The Oxford Edition of Blackstone's Commentaries on the Laws of England*, six volumes (Oxford: Oxford University Press, 2016).
649 Ibid., 1:247–248.
650 Ibid., 248.
651 Samuel Buell, "Criminal Abortion Revisited," *New York University Law Review* 66, no 6, 1774–1831.
652 Ibid., 1775–1776.
653 Dobbs v. Jackson Women's Health Organization, No. 19-1392, 597 U.S. ___ (2022).
654 James Wilson quoted in Nur Ibrahim, "Did Ben Franklin Publish a Recipe in a Math Textbook on How to Induce Abortion?" Snopes, May 16, 2022, https://bit.ly/3L44l2F.
655 Ibid.
656 Ibid.
657 Ibid.
658 Ibid., Martha Careful letter, January 24, 1778.
659 Ibid., Celia Shortface letter, November 27, 1778.
660 Ibid.
661 John Tennant, *The Poor Planter's Physician*, quoted in ibid.
662 Quoted in ibid. Also see Kelly Macquire, "Abortion in the Ancient World," *World History Encyclopedia*, September 27, 2022, https://bit.ly/3PgSCAi.
663 Ibrahim, "Did Ben Franklin Publish a Recipe in a Math Textbook on How to Induce Abortion?"
664 Emily Feng, "Ben Franklin Put an Abortion Recipe in His Math Textbook," Slate, May 18, 2022, https://bit.ly/3Pi8r9P.
665 Quoted in Ibrahim article, Walter Isaacson, *Benjamin Franklin: An American Life*.

Index

A

Adams, John 4, 66, 100, 141, 146, 152–154, 157–158, 163, 165, 178, 187, 189–190, 197, 217, 273, 280
Adams, Samuel 30
Addison, Joseph
   Cato: A Tragedy 88, 90, 93
Aesop
   Fables 65
Afsai, Shai 141–142
Ali, Yusuf ben 151
Allen, Ethan 260, 263–264
   Reason: The Only Oracle of Man 260
Allison, Robert 154
   The Crescent Observed 154
Anderson, Sambo 151
Andrews, Rev. Jedediah 22
Anglican 10, 20, 58, 82, 90–91, 100, 108, 146, 166, 183, 196, 206, 216–217
Aquinas, Thomas 52, 75, 237
   Summa Theologica 52, 237, 296, 301, 310, 313
   Truths of Reason 52, 75
   Truths of Revelation 52, 75
Argument from Design or Teleological Argument for God's existence 22, 24–25, 35, 75, 77, 204–205, 207
Aristotle 117, 119–120, 122–124, 126, 130, 136, 204, 219–220, 227–228, 230, 237
   Nicomachean Ethics 117, 124, 228, 237
Arnold, Benedict 107
atheism 33, 40–41, 47–48, 107, 119, 207

B

Bache, Deborah Franklin 62, 116
Balderrama, Francisco 169
Baptists 20, 31, 84, 166, 175, 277–278
Bartram, John 11
Battle of Saratoga 271
Bayle, Pierre 33, 76
Beall, Samuel, Jr. 152
Beethoven 72, 243
Behuukkotai, Behar 65
   A Little Black Mark 65
Bible 1, 49, 51–56, 58–63, 59, 66, 69–70, 75, 82, 98, 152, 202, 208–210, 212, 236–237, 251, 254, 258, 263
   New Testament 2, 35, 42, 44, 52, 54, 60, 66–70, 119, 186, 209–212, 254, 261–262
   Old Testament 1, 18, 51, 56, 58, 61–65, 69, 119, 194–195, 197, 209–210, 212, 224, 236–237, 251, 254–255
Bick, Jacob Samuel 143
Biden, Joe 176–177, 285, 287
Blackstone, Sir William 285–286
   Commentaries on the Laws of England 285
Blair, Samuel Jacob 101
Blount, Charles 261

Bond, Dr. Thomas 12, 24
Boston, Massachusettes 1, 8–10, 12, 20–21, 24, 26, 30–32, 47, 89, 108, 110, 113, 119, 131, 147, 166–167, 171, 201, 205–206, 247, 253, 264
  17 Milk Street 8, 30
  Cedar Meeting House 31
  First Church 30–31
  Old South Church, aka Third Church 21, 30–32, 47, 119, 201, 205–206
  Schismatics 30
Boyle, Robert 78
Brethren of the Saint John's Masons Lodge 11
Brillon, Madame 14, 16–17, 26, 36–37, 47–48, 78, 203–204, 206–207, 233, 264
British Crown / British Empire 17, 76, 147, 273
Buchanan, George 81
Bunyan, John 20, 47, 206
  The Pilgrim's Progress 20, 47, 206
Burgoyne, General John 271
Burke, Edmund 80–81, 81
Butler, Joseph 35

C

Calvinist 7, 18, 21–22, 32, 39, 82, 85, 89, 96, 119, 136, 202, 205, 261
Calvinist Congregationalism 32, 96
Calvinist Presbyterianism 18, 22, 24, 96
Calvin, John 21, 31–32, 74, 85
  Instruction Chretienne 74
Cambridge University 62, 243
Campbell, James 147–148
  Recovering Benjamin Franklin 147
Carroll, Charles 148–149
Carroll, Rev. John 148–149, 166
Catholic Church 75, 76, 145, 146, 148–149, 157, 221
Catholics 10, 100, 102, 113, 137, 145–146, 148, 150, 157, 163, 166–168, 182–183, 186, 191, 197, 217, 219, 221

Charles II, King 183–184, 269
Cherbury, Lord Herbert of 74, 91, 213, 236, 238, 258–259
  De Veritate 74, 258
Chernow, Ron 107
  Washington: A Life 107
Christianity 19, 23, 34, 36, 44–45, 74–75, 77, 99–100, 127, 131–132, 146, 154–155, 203, 253, 255, 258–259, 262, 282–283
Chubb, Thomas 74
Church of England 14, 21, 85, 100, 110, 113, 146, 148, 181, 183, 217, 281
Civil War, American 151–152, 167
Clarke, Samuel 35
Clement XIV, Pope 148
College of New Jersey 147
College of William & Mary 82, 147, 255, 288
Collinson, Peter 3, 171, 173–174, 178, 223
Congregationalism 2, 18, 20–21, 23, 25, 31–32, 84, 100, 113, 141, 146, 205, 217, 260, 264
Connecticut 3, 167, 185, 193, 197, 223, 232, 252, 278
conservatism 79–81
Constitutional Convention 3, 13, 80, 95, 188, 198, 278
Continental Army 80, 151–152, 157, 222
Continental Congress 13, 25, 35, 55, 97, 148, 185, 189, 191–193, 197, 263, 267, 270, 273
cosmopolitanism 79, 92, 213
Craighead, Rev. Alexander 101
  Covenant 101
  Solemn League 101
  The Renewal of the Scottish National Covenant 101
Cyran, Saint 75
Czartoryski, Adam Kazimierz 144

D

Darrell, Ed

Blog of Ed Darrell 51
Dashwood, Francis 58–59
Davies, Samuel 101
Deane, Silas 271
Declaration of Independence, The 13, 25, 96, 101, 108, 148, 154, 192, 226–227, 231, 257
deism 2, 30, 32–34, 36, 47, 51, 63, 68, 71, 73–79, 91, 204–207, 213, 216, 257–264
Delaval, Edmund 243
Denham, Thomas 269
Deontological Theory 118, 122, 136, 219
de'Ricci, Scippione 167
Descartes, René 92
devil 31, 49, 195, 208
d'Holbach, Baron 33
Diallo, Job 151
Diderot, Denis 33
Divine Command Theory 118
Doddridge, Philip 32, 47
   The Rise and Progress of Religion in the Soul 32, 47, 206
Dostoevsky, Fyodor 41
Douglass, Frederick 151
Dryden, John 117
Duane, William 62
Duan, Zhang
   "Benjamin Franklin's Religious Views" 29
Dudley, Rev. Paul 166, 178
Dutch 33, 153, 172–174, 269

E

Edinburgh, Scotland 33, 81
Edwards, Jonathan 84–85, 92, 214
Ellis, Clare Duane 62
Ellison, Keith 152
Ellsworth, Oliver 187, 189, 197
empiricism 79, 92, 213
England 3, 12, 14–15, 21, 31, 38, 60–61, 75, 84–85, 100–101, 109–111, 113–114, 133, 138, 146, 148, 168, 173, 181, 183–185, 192, 194, 196, 198, 213, 217–218, 221–224, 243, 248, 252–253, 260–261, 269–270, 281, 285–286
English Test Acts 182
Enlightenment 2, 21–22, 24–26, 32, 35, 46, 53, 73, 77–84, 91, 106, 141–143, 154, 157, 213–214, 260, 280
Episcopal Church, Philadelphia 39
Erskine, Ralph 101
Euripides 65, 236
   Hippolytus Veiled 65, 236
Europe 25, 33, 72, 78, 83, 101–102, 118, 138, 144, 147, 153, 157, 164, 168, 171, 178, 221, 259, 261, 274

F

Fea, John
   "Religion and Early Politics" 29
federal government 3, 104, 114, 164, 167, 176, 185, 191, 193, 218
Ferguson, James 244
   "The Three Wheel Clock" 244
Fiering, Norman 143
Filleau, Jean 75
Finger, Stanley 241
   "Benjamin Franklin's Risk Factors for Gout and Stones" 241
Finley, Samuel 101
First Great Awakening 2, 83–85, 92, 175, 192, 214
First Presbyterian Church of Philadelphia 22
Founding documents 2, 101, 104, 113, 216–217
Founding Fathers 2, 4, 41, 43, 64, 76, 96, 105–108, 112–113, 133, 146, 151, 154, 157, 168, 182, 187–188, 196–197, 216–217, 222, 224, 245, 257, 259–260, 262, 277, 279–280, 285, 287
France 13, 17, 30, 35, 47, 66, 74–76, 94, 133, 147, 154–155, 184, 192, 213,

222, 245, 253, 267–268, 270–273
Franklin, Abiah Folger 8, 14, 20, 23, 30, 42
Franklin, Benjamin
  "A Defence of the Reverend Hemphill's Observations" 22–23, 45, 67, 70, 111, 131, 137, 205, 212
  "A Dissertation on Liberty and Necessity" 21, 77
  ambassador 13, 17, 148, 270, 273–274
  "A Narrative of the Late Massacres" 100, 112, 155, 217
  "A Proposal Relating to the Education of Youth in Pennsylvania" 255
  "Article of Faith" 47, 206
  "Articles of Belief and Acts of Religion" 14–15, 21, 34, 77, 121–122, 124, 129, 203–204
  Autobiography of Benjamin Franklin, The 9, 14, 17–21, 26, 34, 43–44, 46, 51–53, 62, 64–65, 73, 76, 85, 87–89, 92, 119–120, 122–123, 125, 129, 131, 142, 150, 203, 214, 230–231, 237, 263, 273, 286, 288
  "A Witch Trial at Mount Holly" 98, 112, 217
  catheter 12, 81, 241, 246, 247, 306
  "Dialogue Between Two Presbyterians" 14, 16, 22, 25, 129–130, 203–205
  diplomat 1, 82, 244, 267, 273–274
  "Doctrine to be Preached" 14–16, 35, 203
  electricity 12, 18, 81, 83, 134, 245–248, 253
  fire department 12, 24, 80, 131, 248
  George Brownell's English School 8
  hoaxes 59–61, 69, 210, 274
  inventions 1, 12, 81–82, 201–202, 241–242, 244, 246, 281
    bifocals 12
    catheter 12, 81, 241, 246–247
    celebrity 242, 245
    Franklin stove 12, 81, 134, 242, 244–245
    glass armonica 12, 72, 81, 134, 242–243
    lightning rod 12, 81, 201, 246–248
    long-arm device 242–244
    odometer 242–243
    political cartooning 242, 245
    swim fins 12, 81, 242, 245
    three-wheel clock 242, 244
    vocabulary 242, 245
  Junto Club/Leather Apron Club 10, 17, 24, 82
  Leather Apron Club 10, 80
  Library Company of Philadelphia 11–12, 17, 24
  Market Street bookshop 60
  Masonry 11, 143
  medical discoveries 246
  Milk Street, Boston 1, 8, 30
  "Observations Concerning the Increase of Mankind" 171–172, 178, 223
  "On Slavery" 245–246
  "On the Price of Corn and Management of the Poor" 45
  "On the Providence of God in the Government of the World" 14, 16, 19, 22, 30, 35, 47, 77, 129, 203–204, 206–207
  "On True Happiness" 228–229
  Philadelphia Contribution for Insurance Against Loss of Fire 12
  Philosophical Society/American Philosophical Society 11–12, 24, 82, 88, 171
  Poor Richard Improved 60
  Poor Richard's Almanack 7, 17, 26, 51, 60, 65, 78, 134
  printing 1, 9–10, 12, 17, 24, 41, 67, 86, 88, 144, 179, 202–203, 268–269, 288–290
  "Proposals Relating to the Education of the Youth of Pennsylvania" 11
  publisher 1, 22, 41, 58, 60, 179, 253, 263

scientific discoveries 78, 81, 201, 242, 246–247, 247
scientist 1, 32, 81–82, 192, 198, 214, 241
"Self-Denial is Not the Essence of Virtue" 14, 16, 203–204
Silence Dogood 9, 14–15, 55, 69, 88, 96, 112, 129, 203, 210, 216
South Grammar School/Boston Latin School 8
The American Instructor or Young Man's Best Companion 289
"The Morals of Chess" 268, 272
Treaty of Peace 36
vegetarian 9
Franklin, Benjamin (Benjamin, the Elder) 20, 30–31, 47, 202
Franklin, Deborah 9–10, 13–14, 24, 62, 180, 195
Franklin, Francis Folger 247
Franklin, James 9, 24
The New England Courant 9
Franklin, Jane White 20
Franklin, Josiah 2, 8, 10, 14, 20–21, 23, 30, 42, 74, 87–88, 92, 110, 214
Franklin, Sarah 62
Franklin, William 10, 17, 150
governor of New Jersey 12, 17
Freemasonry 141–143
French 13, 16–17, 19, 33, 35–36, 38, 48, 58, 74–76, 78, 94, 107, 161, 163, 168, 173, 175, 193, 204, 207, 213, 233, 235, 237, 240, 245, 263, 267–274
Freud, Sigmund 229
Introductory Lectures in Psychoanalysis 229

G

Galileo 78, 258
Gavin, Anthony 167
George III, King 101, 168, 193
George II, King 93, 147, 215
Georgia Colony 252

Germans 3, 118, 134, 161–162, 165, 172–176, 178–179, 223, 235, 237, 281
Gibbon, Edward 154–155, 158, 222
Gordon, Thomas 88, 90–91, 93, 143
"Cato's Letters" 88
Great Awakening 2, 60, 73, 83–86, 92, 175, 192, 205, 213–214, 255
Great Britain 3, 179, 182, 193, 196, 223, 274
Great Depression 169, 178
Great Seal of the United States 18, 25, 41, 54–56, 69, 210, 271
Greeks 164, 175, 178, 223, 291

H

Halevi, Rabbi Meir 144
Haley, Alex 151
Hall, David 290
Hamilton, Alexander 4, 165, 178, 188, 197, 259, 280–281
Harvard Divinity School 8, 82, 89, 166
Harvard University 147
Hemphill, Samuel 22–23, 25, 45, 49, 53–54, 66–68, 70–71, 78, 102, 111, 114, 131, 137–138, 205, 208, 211–212, 218, 221, 232
Henry, Patrick 2, 90, 101, 108, 113, 162, 184, 218, 259
Hewson, Polly Stevenson 45, 49, 150, 157
Heyman, Christine Leigh
"The First Great Awakening" 83–84
Hobbes, Thomas 80, 92
Holmes, David 257, 259–260
The Faiths of the Founding Fathers 257, 259
Holy Scriptures 16, 23, 34, 46, 49, 51–55, 58, 62, 69, 186, 209
Hooke, Robert 258
Howe, Admiral Lord Richard 266–267, 273
Howe, General William 273
Howe, Lady Caroline 266–267, 273

Hubbard, Elizabeth 232
Hume, David 33, 35, 75–76, 81, 91
  An Enquiry Concerning Human Understanding
  "Of Miracles" 76
  Natural History of Religion 75–76
  The Dialogues Concerning Natural Religion 76
Huth, E. J. 241
  "Benjamin Franklin's place in the history of medicine" 241

I

immigration 3, 156, 162–165, 167–168, 170–171, 173–178, 202, 222–223
Independence Hall 11, 24
Iredell, James 187–188, 197
Isaacson, Walter 88, 172, 267, 274, 291
  Benjamin Franklin: An American Life 267, 291
  "Citizen Ben's Seven Great Virtues" 88
Islam 2, 136, 138, 141, 150–158, 221–222, 258, 259
Israel 18, 41, 56, 98, 145, 156, 195, 222, 236

J

James II, King 267
James I, King 183–184, 196
Jansen, Cornelius 75
Jay, John 163–164, 167, 178, 188, 191–192, 197, 259
Jayne, Allen 257
  Jefferson's Declaration of Independence 257
Jefferson, Thomas 2, 4, 13, 23, 42–44, 48, 53–56, 58, 76, 80, 89, 96, 103, 106–108, 113, 133, 152–154, 158, 165–166, 178, 187, 189–190, 197, 218, 227, 257, 260, 262–264, 267, 277–278, 280, 282–283
  Notes on the State of Virginia 262
  The Life and Morals of Jesus of Nazareth 263
Jesus 1, 19, 21, 23–24, 26, 29, 31–32, 38–46, 48–49, 52, 55, 58, 66, 70, 88, 99, 119–120, 122, 125, 131–133, 147–148, 185, 202, 205–209, 211, 231, 255, 259, 261–263
J. H. 33, 40–41, 48, 207
Josephson, Manuel 145
Judaism 2, 10, 19, 34, 41, 56, 59, 64–65, 95, 98, 100, 107, 131, 136–138, 141–145, 150, 156–157, 167–168, 178, 186, 190, 203, 218, 221–222, 254, 258–259, 261, 281

K

Kavanaugh, Justice Brett 279
Keimer, Samuel 9, 288–289, 291
Keith, Sir William 10, 268
Kennedy, John F. 170, 178, 279
Kidd, Thomas 43, 45, 63, 120, 122, 201, 231
  Benjamin Franklin: The Religious Life of a Founding Father 43, 120
  "The Complicated Religious Life of Ben Franklin" 231
Kierkegaard, Soren 161
Kinte, Kunta 151
Klu Klux Klan 164
Knox, John 31, 81, 182
Krochmal, Rabbi Nahman 144

L

Lawrence. D. H. 127, 137, 220
Lee, Arthur 271
Leflin, Rabbi Mendel 142–145, 156–157
  The Book of Spiritual Accounting 142, 145
Leland, John 103
liberalism 79–81
Lincoln, Abraham 2, 8
Locke, John 46, 74, 80–81, 88–90, 92–93, 102, 106–107, 215, 261, 281
  A Letter Concerning Toleration 81, 88–89, 92, 102, 215

An Essay Concerning Human Understanding 46, 74, 89
London, England 13, 24–25, 54, 60, 62, 74, 86, 89–90, 109, 114, 149, 157, 218, 252–253, 267–270, 273, 289, 290
Lutheran 100
Lyon, James 154, 158
The True Nature of the Imposture Fully Displayed in the Life of Mahomet 154

M

Madison, James 2, 80, 96–97, 103, 106–107, 113, 187–191, 197, 218, 280–281, 288
Manout, Yarrow 152
Marracci, Ludovico 153–155, 158, 222
Marx, Karl 281
  Critique of Hegel's Philosophy of Right 281
Maryland Colony 98, 166
Mason, George 2, 11, 107–108, 113, 143–144, 188, 191, 197, 218
Massachusettes Bay Colony 8, 30, 43, 98, 106, 166
Massachusetts Assembly 9
Mather, Cotton 20, 88–89, 92–93, 153–154, 158, 215, 222, 235
  Bonifacius, or Essays to do Good 20, 88–89, 92, 215, 235
Mecom, Jane Franklin 26, 42–43, 205, 229–231
Mennonites 10
Meredith, Hugh 10, 24
Meslier, Jean 75
Mikveh Israel Synagogue 98, 145, 156, 222, 236
Milton, John 15, 281
  Paradise Lost 15
monotheism 1, 16, 25, 33, 36, 63, 75, 204–206
Montesquieu, Charles-Louis 76, 154–155, 158, 222

Mozart 72, 243
Muhamed, Bampett 151
Muhlenberg, Rev. Henry 162
Muslim 65, 151–154, 157–158, 222

N

New-England Courant, The 9, 15, 55, 60, 96
New Testament 2, 35, 42–45, 52, 54, 60, 66–70, 119, 186, 209–212, 254, 261–262
Newton, Sir Isaac 22, 32–33, 35, 47, 78, 81–82, 206, 237, 258
  Principia Mathematica 22, 32, 206, 237, 258
New World 10, 64, 109, 153, 168, 259
New York City 9, 271

O

Oates, Titus 184, 197, 223
Ohno, Kate
  "Ben Franklin on Toleration" 95
Old Testament 1, 18, 51, 56, 58–65, 69, 119, 194–195, 197, 209–210, 212, 224, 236–237, 251, 254–255
O'Malley, Martin 7
Ozawa, Takao 169

P

Paine, Thomas 43, 73, 76–77, 91, 96, 142, 213, 256, 260–264, 280–281
  Common Sense 96, 281
  Of the Religion of Deism Compared with the Christian Religion 73, 76, 91, 213
  The Age of Reason 261
Paley, William 33–35, 47, 75, 207
  Natural Theology: Or, Evidences of the Existence and Attributes of the Deity 33
Palmer, Samuel 268
pantheist 33
Parliament 13, 147, 162, 182–183,

196–197, 269–270
Patot, Simon Tyssot de 75
Penn family 12, 24, 100, 163, 269
Pennsylvania Assembly 59, 162, 173, 269–270
Pennsylvania Colony 10, 24, 59, 61, 98, 108, 148, 163, 168, 173, 177, 269
Pennsylvania Constitution 55, 59, 69, 186, 194, 198, 210
Pennsylvania Convention 59
Pennsylvania Gazette, The 8, 10, 22, 24, 43, 60, 134, 163, 202, 228, 245, 253, 288
Pennsylvania Hospital 11, 24, 53, 160
Pennsylvania Society for the Abolition of Slavery 131
Penn, William 12, 24, 100, 103, 163, 269
Philadelphia 1, 3, 8–14, 17, 22, 24, 28, 35, 39, 46–47, 49–50, 53, 58, 60, 62, 67, 70, 80–83, 85–86, 88, 98, 100, 102, 108, 110–112, 114, 116, 131, 135, 143, 145–146, 154, 156, 160, 171–175, 179–180, 185, 192–193, 202–203, 205–206, 209–210, 212, 216–218, 221–223, 236–237, 243–244, 251–253, 255, 263, 268–270, 282, 288
  Christ Church 14, 39, 47, 206, 216
  Independence Hall 11, 24
Philidor, Francois Andre 273–274
Phillips Museum of Art 243
Pilgrims 30
Pinckney, Charles 3–4, 185–188, 191–194, 196–198, 223–224
Pius VI, Pope 149
Plato 228–229, 232, 236
Plutarch
  Life of Pericles 88–89
Pocosin, Black Mingo 152
polytheism 15, 25, 30, 34, 36, 47, 63, 75, 203–206
Popish Plot 184, 197, 223
Presbyterianism 2, 14, 16, 18, 20, 21–22, 24–25, 31–32, 43, 67, 82, 84, 100, 113, 129–130, 141, 146, 148, 182,
203–205, 217, 260, 264
Price, Richard 192, 194–195, 198, 224
Priestly, Joseph 192, 194, 198
Princeton Theological Seminary 84
Princeton University 82
progressivism 79, 92, 213
Protestant Christians 96, 112, 216
Puritanism 20, 30, 42–43, 84, 96, 110, 113, 119, 122, 131, 137, 166, 168, 218, 220
Puritan Reformers 30

Q

Quakers 10, 20, 22, 100, 109, 127, 129, 137, 146, 166, 217, 220
Qur'an, Al- 65, 152–155, 158, 236

R

Randolph, Edmund 188, 190–191, 197
rationalism 79, 92, 213
Read, Deborah 9–10, 180
Read, John 9
Reagan, Ronald 2
Reed, James 167, 253
Reform Christian 21, 96
religious tests 3–4, 158, 179, 181–182, 184–185, 187–198, 202, 223–224
Remsburg, John E.
  "Six Historic Americans" 95
republicanism 79–80
Revolutionary War 13, 64, 66, 85, 106–107, 112, 148–149, 168, 175, 193, 216, 270–271
Rhode Island Colony 102, 166, 281
Robespierre, Maximilien 76
Roman Catholicism 2, 79, 92, 141, 156–157, 213
Roosevelt, Franklin D. 170
Rousseau, Jean-Jacques 35, 75–76, 78, 80
  The Social Contract 78
Rush, Benjamin 288
  Medical Inquiries and Observations Upon Diseases of the Mind 288

S

Salim, Peter 151
Satan 21, 45, 49, 56–57, 195, 208
Schall, Rev. James V. 262, 335
    "The God of the Founding Fathers: Nature's God" 262
Schiff, Stacy 100
scientific progress 79
Scottish Parliament 182
Scottish Reformation 182
Scottish Test Act 182, 196
Scougal, Henry 101
Second Continental Congress 13, 270, 273
Seton, Elizabeth 149
Seven Years' War 147, 168
Severance, Diane
    "What was the Great Awakening?" 84
Sewall, Samuel 30, 88–89, 93, 215
    The Selling of Joseph 88–89, 93, 215
Shaftesbury, 3rd Earl of (Anthony Ashley Cooper) 74
Sherman, Roger 3, 185, 193, 197, 223
Short, William 262
Sinkoff, Nancy 144
Slater, Philip 201
slavery 2, 14, 25, 89, 93, 118, 131, 137, 151, 163, 215, 246, 281
smallpox 247
Smiles, Samuel
    Mrs. Isabella Beeton and Benjamin Franklin 73
Smith, Josiah 101, 104, 147
Smith, William 147
Society of Friends 100–101, 113, 217
South Carolina 3, 62, 167, 185, 193, 197
Spaniards 161, 173, 175
Spinoza, Baruch 33
Stiles, Ezra 37–40, 47–48, 78, 200, 204, 206–207, 264
Story, Joseph 181
Sumter, General Thomas 151
Supreme Executive Council of Pennsylvania 13
Synod of Philadelphia 22, 53, 70, 102, 111, 114, 212, 218, 221

T

Teleological Theory 22, 118, 122, 136, 219
Tennent, Gilbert 101, 175
    "The Danger of an Unconverted Ministry" 175
Tennent, John
    The Poor Planter's Physician 290
Tennent, the Rev. William 84, 175
Test Act of 1673 182–184, 196
Thayer, Rev. John 148
theism 33, 36
Thind, Bhagat Singh 169
Thompson, Mary V. 151
    "Islam at Mount Vernon" 151
Tilford, Gregory L. 291
    Edible and Medicinal Plants of the West 291
Tindal, Matthew 75, 91, 213
    Christianity as Old as the Creation 75
Toland, John
    Christianity Not Mysterious 74
toleration 2, 10, 18–19, 31, 39–40, 79, 81, 89, 91, 93, 95–96, 101–102, 104–108, 110–114, 145, 150, 153–154, 156, 167, 202, 215–219
Torah 64, 70, 211, 237
transubstantiation 52, 146–147, 147, 157, 182–183, 196
Treaty of Amity and Commerce 13, 268
Treaty of Paris 13, 25, 193, 270–271
Treaty of the Alliance 13, 272
Trenchard, John 88, 90–91, 93
    "Cato's Letters" 88
Trump Administration 105, 161, 176
Truths of Reason 52, 75
Truths of Revelation 52, 75
Tubman, Harriet 151
Tucker, St. George 288

U

University of Pennsylvania 11, 82, 86,

146, 152, 157, 160, 255
US Constitution 3, 55, 59–60, 69, 91, 97, 102–104, 106, 112–113, 145, 147, 163, 167, 181–182, 184–188, 190–198, 210, 216–217, 223–224, 277–278, 286–287
    Article VI, Clause 3 3, 145, 181, 184–187, 189, 192–194, 197–198, 223–224
    First Amendment 3, 91, 97, 102–103, 106, 112, 145, 147, 216, 277, 278
US Supreme Court 103–105, 113, 163, 169, 178, 188–189, 191, 217, 278–279, 287
Utilitarianism 118, 136, 219

V

Van Dyke, Tom
    "Ben Franklin and the Bible" 51
Vaughan, Benjamin 59
Viret, Pierre 74, 213, 237
Virtue Ethics 118–119, 122, 136, 219
Voltaire 26, 33, 47, 75–76, 107, 154–155, 158, 205, 207, 213, 222
von Kempelen, Wolfgang 274

W

Ward, Nathaniel 161
Washington, George 2, 8, 30–31, 80, 96, 107–108, 108, 113, 149, 151–153, 157, 218, 280
Watt, James 269
Watts, Isaac 60
Welfare, Michael 175
Wheatley, Phillis 30, 151
Whitefield, Rev. George 17, 26, 42–43, 46, 49, 60, 73, 85–87, 92, 101, 146–147, 152, 168, 192, 205, 208–209, 214, 250–255, 264
Williams, Roger 102–103, 106, 280–281, 283
Wilson, James 287–288
witchcraft 65
witch trials 89, 98, 217

Witherspoon, John 96
Wood, Gordon S. 143
Woolston, Thomas 74
World War II 170, 223
Wren, Christopher 258

Y

Yale College 37–38, 47–48, 82–84, 147, 200, 204, 207, 255, 264
Yamashita, Takuji 169
Young, Thomas 260, 289
    Reason: The Only Oracle of Man 260

Acknowledgments

This book has been the product of the labor of many people. Among these are the staff of Calumet Editions, the publisher of this volume. Steve Kent, who helped with much of the IT issues related to this study. I am indebted to the support of my cousin Peter Celli for his gracious support in my writing career. To my childhood friend, Joseph Cieslowski, for support. And finally, to my son John "Jack" Vicchio, my major intellectual companion these days so late in my life.

SJV
October 2023

About the Author

Stephen Vicchio was educated at the University of Maryland, Yale, Oxford, and Saint Andrews University in Fife, Scotland, where he received his Ph.D. He is the author of forty books that include works in drama, stories, essays, religion, philosophy, and books about the Bible. He retired from full-time teaching after having taught at several universities in the United States, Britain, Syria, Egypt, and Portugal, among other places.

www.ingramcontent.com/pod-product-compliance
Lightning Source LLC
Chambersburg PA
CBHW020219170426
43201CB00007B/262